A STOLEN LIFE
EFTIHIA'S STORY

VOULA ANTOINE

The dead cannot speak, so we must speak
for them. The horror of it—the deliberate
destruction, the despair, the savage violence left
an indelible mark that time cannot erase.
Do not let them tell you it was not as bad as
we say. It was worse.

DEDICATION

For my grandmother, Eftihia, my great-grandmother, Mariegó and the members of my family whose lives were lost, whose faces I never had the chance to know. Your voices, your strength, and your memory live on through these pages.

And for the family members who live today, may you carry our story with you, as a reminder of where we come from, and of the strength that flows in our blood.

A NOTE FROM THE AUTHOR

This memoir has been lovingly created from the memories and stories shared with me by my late grandmother, Eftihia. It is her story but also that of my great-grandmother Mariegó. For me, writing this has been more than a work of memory; it has been an act of love, of honour, and of healing. Their courage and suffering shaped the generations that followed, and I would not be who I am today without their strength. By sharing their journey, I hope their story lingers in your heart as it does in mine, a reminder of resilience, sacrifice, and the importance of never forgetting.

In writing her story, I have sought to remain true to her voice and the experiences she lived, striving to preserve the essence of her life as she recounted it to me. I have done my best to be accurate in the details, but any errors, omissions, or deviations from historical fact are my own. My hope is that, through the telling of her story, you may come to know her—her courage, her spirit, and the moments that shaped her life, and that her story, now lives on in the pages of this book.

My thanks to my aunt Maria Mikromanolis, my cousin Georgia Kourtesis, and other members of my family for their help in filling in the missing pieces of the story.

PROLOGUE

THE FIRE AND THE SILENCE

You asked me, *agapi mou*, to tell you what happened. To tell you what I saw, what I lived through. Some have called it the first genocide of the 20th century. You know the truth, though it is a truth the world has tried to forget. But I have not forgotten. I cannot.

I was there.

Smyrna—Smyrni, as we knew it—had been tense for weeks. News from the front line carried disturbing news. The truth could no longer be denied. The Greek army had been decimated and was now retreating, pushing back toward Smyrni for evacuation. Fear began to spread quickly. We knew what this meant for us.

When the Turkish army entered the city on September 9th, 1922, they did so as conquerors, not as liberators. On the fringes of the city, so too did the irregular fighters, the *Tsetes*. The looting and killing began almost immediately. They showed no mercy. They took what they wanted and destroyed the rest. They did not distinguish between homes, businesses, or places of worship.

The Greek army had already fled, abandoning us like lambs to the slaughter. And a slaughter it was.

We believed that our Allies — the Europeans and Americans, your so-called civilised world, with their embassies, their diplomats, their great warships sitting in the bay, would protect us. And yet they did nothing. No one came to help us. Mercy and salvation arrived far too late.

Alexandra, history will argue over the details, over who gave the order and who merely stood by, but for those of us who lived through it, there is no doubt about what happened. The fire, the massacres, the suffering, they were no accident, nor was the chaos of war. They were a deliberate act of extermination by the Turks.

Nureddin Paşa, Smyrni's military governor, was known for his hatred of us. His thirst for revenge was no secret. In March 1919, the Metropolitan of Smyrni, Chrysostomos, had publicly denounced him to the British, accusing him of atrocities committed during the Armenian genocide. 'This man ought to be shot for his crimes,' he had said. Perhaps if the British had listened and then acted, the course of events that followed might have been different.

To us, Nureddin was the vengeful face of Turkish nationalism. The murder of Chrysostomos was not just a war crime; it was a calculated act of revenge, orchestrated by Nureddin himself. In that single act, the legacies of both men were sealed—one as a martyr, the other as a man accused of unspeakable atrocities.

It was Nureddin who gave the order to set Smyrni ablaze. Some say that if not for him, the destruction might have been avoided. But it was not. It was vengeance. The ultimate act of destruction.

And Mustafa Kemal was there.

He stood watching as the city burned, as thousands of people screamed for help, as bodies floated in the harbour. And while watching, he reportedly declared that the flames were a sign, that Turkey had purged itself of traitors, of Christians, of foreigners—that Turkey was for the Turks.

"Let it burn, let it crash down," he reportedly said.

Perhaps he did not strike the match, nor give the order himself. But he watched, and he did nothing to stop it. The fire raged for four days. Smyrni, that great city, the jewel of the Aegean, was turned to ash.

The world did nothing. Twenty warships sat idle in the harbour, their crews watching as thousands perished. Diplomats, politicians, the so-called protectors of civilisation, none intervened.

They came down the streets, the soldiers, the *Tsetes*, rifles slung over their shoulders, their knives ready, eyes gleaming with hatred and hunger. The Armenians suffered first. They always suffered first. They dragged men from their shops, from their homes, tied their hands, and shot them in the streets.

The women—oh, the women. Do you understand what it is to hear a woman scream for mercy and know there will be none? To hear her wail for her children even as they tear her from them? Their cries echoed through the city, unforgettable. They dragged them to the cemetery of Agia Foteini—a place once sacred, became a place of torment. What happened there defied all humanity. When they were done, they butchered them — mothers and daughters together. When the screams stopped, only silence remained.

There was no order. No law. Soldiers, irregular fighters, even civilians, all joined in. Each acted as if cruelty itself had been sanctioned.

We hid at first, in our cousin Konstantinos' house, praying to God that we would be spared. The soldiers came and banged on our door. Hard, loud, demanding. We held our breath as they shouted outside. For a moment, I was sure they would break down the door, that they would find us and drag us away like so many others. But by some miracle, they moved on.

The days that followed were worse. We stayed locked inside. We heard gunshots, cries, and the desperate wailing of those being ripped from this life in agony. Then, on September 13th, the fire began.

Do not let them lie to you and say the Armenians set it. The Turkish soldiers started the fire. They went into the Armenian quarter with torches, doused buildings with kerosene, and set them ablaze. The flames spread like a living thing, roaring through the streets, swallowing homes, shops, churches, everything in its path. Only the Turkish and Jewish neighbourhoods stood untouched, and the foreign consulates remained pristine, as if mocking our destruction. It was no accident. The fire's purpose was to erase us. The wind carried the fire towards us.

The Turks made sure of that.

Day turned into night as the smoke choked the sky. People ran screaming through the streets, clutching their children, the old, the sick. There was nowhere to go. Behind us, the fire. In front of us, the sea. And the world watched. French, Italian, British, and American warships sat in the harbour, close enough that we could see the men on their decks. Close enough that they could hear our desperate pleas.

And yet they did nothing.

They watched as men leapt into the water, trying to swim to safety, only to drown. They watched as mothers threw their babies into the sea rather than let them be taken by the Turks. Heard the screams of women and girls being dragged into alleyways, and gunshots as men were executed, one by one.

And still they did nothing.

I remember the smell of the fire, the thick acrid smoke, as the city burned, the ashes raining down on us, how they clung to our clothes, to our hair, to our skin. How impossible it was to breathe, each breath catching in our throats and burning our lungs until we coughed and gasped, eyes stinging with tears we could not wipe away. But most of all, I remember the stench of burning flesh — a sickening, unforgettable scent that settled into the very marrow of my bones. Even now, the memory of those thick plumes of smoke rising over Smyrni haunts me, a black pall that blotted out the sky and smothered hope itself.

We reached the Quay — my mother, Stamatis, Persephone, and I, together with Konstantinos and his family. We stood there among the thousands, packed so tightly we could barely move. The suffocating heat of the fire and the smoke made the air thick and unbreathable, while ahead, the dark waters of the harbour offered no salvation. The foreign ships sat there, indifferent, their crews unmoved. Despair drove some to leap into the sea. They swam towards the boats, but the sailors struck them back with poles, scalded them with boiling water. I could not comprehend such cruelty. No one would help us. No one.

We watched in disbelief as the Levantines—the foreign merchants, diplomats, and families of mixed European and local descent were evacuated. Many held foreign passports, proof of protection that allowed them safe passage onto waiting ships. Meanwhile, we, the Greeks and Armenians, remained trapped, our pleas unheard, our fates bound to the chaos surrounding us. There was no mercy, no negotiation. Only fear, pressing in from every side, and the bitter knowledge that our lives held no value in the eyes of those who could have saved us.

By luck, fate, or God's final mercy, we found a boat. We left behind everything. And our Smyrni was left to burn. By the time the fire burned itself out, the heart of Smyrni was gone. The Armenians and the Greeks were gone. Only the Turks remained to gloat over the ashes of our city.

The world pretended not to see. The newspapers buried the truth within their pages. Governments turned their backs. And the Turks? They celebrated.

What followed for those left behind was slaughter and despair. Men between the ages of eighteen and forty-five were seized and sent into the depths of the interior. They called them *'Working Battalions'*. But we knew them for what they were. *'Death Marches'*. Few ever returned. They perished from hunger, exhaustion, and cruelty, their bodies lost in the barren lands. Entire families vanished before they could even reach Greece.

In the land once called Ionia, the Greeks had built lives, traditions, and memories over millennia. We were not newcomers; we were the heirs of a civilization older than most, the descendants of those who had shaped cities. And yet, our people, who had lived on that soil for over three thousand years, were uprooted in a matter of weeks. The Turkish forces marched in with ruthless intent, seeking to extinguish that presence entirely. Our history, our culture, and our very existence became their target.

The Turks called our city "Giaur Izmir"—Smyrna of the unbelievers. To them, we were less than human.

You ask me why I tell you this? Because you must know. Because it must not be forgotten. History reveals that hundreds of thousands of lives were lost in that catastrophe, and close to one and a half million people were driven from their homes. The dead cannot speak, so we must speak for them. The horror of it, the deliberate destruction, the despair, the brutal violence left an indelible mark that time cannot erase.

Do not let them tell you it was not as bad as we say.

It was worse.

CHAPTER ONE

My beloved granddaughter, you were born many decades later, in a time and place far removed from those lands. The story I share with you is not just a lesson in history; it is our story — one of resilience, love, and heartache. I tell it so you may know where you come from and understand the strength that flows through your veins. My mother, your great-grandmother Maria, or Mariegó, as she was called, was a woman who endured more than anyone should ever have to bear.

As you carry our family's story forward, remember her courage, her resilience, and the love that shaped us. Know that she is with you, as am I, in the stories we pass on and in the love that never fades.

The story begins with your great-grandmother Mariegó. She was the only daughter of Dimitri and Dafnoula Kourtesis from the village of Ano Vathy in Samos. But life often has different plans for us, as you will see. Her journey took her from the shelter of an affluent household, to one of love, loss, unimaginable grief, and hardship.

I want you to close your eyes, Alexandra, and picture Sokia, our home in the early 1900s. When I think of it, I remember the warm, rich soil and acres of cotton stretching out like an endless carpet of white bolls at harvest time, under a bright blue sky and cooled by the breeze from the Meander River. Sokia, as it was known then (the Turks later changed it to Söke), was nestled in the fertile plains of *Mikrá Asía* (Asia Minor), where the land was as rich as the culture that thrived there. It was also a time when the air was filled with the sounds of trade and the rhythm of agriculture, and society was a blend of wealth and deep-rooted customs.

Among the influential families, the Kourtesis name held particular prominence. Their land was more than a symbol of their wealth. It was at the very heart of our family's influence. In Sokia, land was everything. It was power, it was sustenance, it was respect, and they were looked upon as pillars of the community, not just for their wealth, but for their integrity and their commitment to the people.

How did a family from Samos come to own land in Sokia? Alexandra, you come from a line of people who knew how to recognise good fertile land. The Greeks of Samos, our people, had been traders, shipbuilders, and farmers for generations. The Ottoman Empire granted Samos its own special status. This gave the Samian Greeks a certain amount of freedom and allowed them to build considerable wealth and engage in trade with nearby Anatolia.

When landownership in Turkey changed, and the Ottoman rulers allowed foreigners to buy land, our people took advantage of that. Those Samian men and their families crossed over and began buying large acreages of land. They were drawn to Sokia's rich, fertile plains, with soil as black as ink, and they knew how to work it. They planted cotton—white fields that soon became gold. With demand so great, every harvest carried the promise of a better life.

When they invested in Sokia, it did not just benefit them. The local economy grew, and many Turks found steady work, which created a strong sense of mutual reliance. The Greeks and Turks lived in harmony, working side by side. With good fertile land and skilled agricultural practices, Sokia grew into a thriving agricultural town, bringing prosperity to both communities.

Our family's land stretched so far that the fields seemed endless. To hold so much meant to carry a certain weight of responsibility, and my grandparents understood that well. The family's reputation attracted seasonal labourers from across the region, especially from the neighbouring islands of Samos and Chios. Every harvest season, young men came to Sokia, eager for the steady work and fair wages that my grandparents offered. These labourers would live on the family's estate, and were provided with food and accommodation, becoming a part of the rhythm of the land. My mother grew up watching this annual migration, the comings and goings of the workers, and the complex interplay of trust and respect between her father and those who worked his land.

My grandmother, Dafnoula, understood what it meant to care for those who were not so fortunate and to honour our family's name. She taught my mother about kindness, generosity, and strength, values that would become her foundation and carry her in times of loss and hardship.

One season, as the cotton fields lay waiting to be picked, a young man named Stamatis Kourtesis arrived from Samos, seeking work for the harvest. The moment they heard his surname, they were surprised but also curious to discover if they were related, for to share a surname was no small matter. In the end, it was only coincidence, yet both the name and the man himself would prove to have their place in our story.

Stamatis quickly stood out. He was strong, dependable, and had a quiet confidence that my grandparents respected. Stamatis quickly proved himself to be reliable and dedicated, with a strong work ethic that caught the eye of my grandfather. He was an excellent judge of character, my grandfather, and he saw something special in Stamatis, something worthy of trust.

Where other men might grow weary from the long hours under the sun, Stamatis worked with a quiet pride, a commitment to excellence that set him apart. He was lean and tall, with dark hair and dark chocolate eyes and with a quiet humility, a man who seemed to belong not just to his work but to the land itself. It wasn't long before my grandparents trusted him with greater responsibilities. At first, he was given the smaller tasks, helping with irrigation, overseeing daily routines, making sure the cotton was handled with care. But in time, my grandfather came to rely on him for more important matters. He was becoming like a son to him. Stamatis became an integral part of the family's operations, not just as a worker but as someone he valued and trusted.

My mother saw all of this, of course, and for her, his presence brought a new warmth into her life. She was no stranger to the young men who came to work on the land, but there was something different about him, something that drew her in. And in that time, as he grew closer to the family, they exchanged small amounts of conversation, coveted looks, a simple greeting here, a shared glance there. Then, something even more special blossomed. My mother fell in love with him.

I tried to imagine that type of love, one born in a world where emotions were rarely spoken about, where looks spoke more than words could ever say. My grandparents saw it, too, and in time, they gave their blessing for my mother and Stamatis to marry. And so they did. For a time, it was a joyful union. It was as though all the world's goodness had gathered around them, promising them a future filled with happiness and children.

But happiness can be fleeting, Alexandra. Life can be cruel at times.

Only a few months after their wedding, Stamatis died unexpectedly. My mother was widowed, left to mourn a future that vanished in an instant. She was shattered, plunged into shock and grief.

During those darkest days, she discovered she was pregnant—a bittersweet revelation. A moment that should have brought joy became a complicated blend of sorrow and anticipation. Yet through this child, she would carry a part of Stamatis into the future.

She gave birth to a boy and named him Dimitri, after his grandfather, a strong name for a child who would grow up without the man who had given him life. He was not only her son, but a piece of Stamatis, the husband taken from her before he could ever hold him. She often said Dimitri was her salvation amidst her grief for the father who would never hear his first cry, never feel his weight in his arms, never watch him take his first steps. In his small cries, his laughter, and his wide-eyed innocence, she clung to a reason to go on.

My mother carried her widowhood with quiet dignity, and she devoted herself to raising her son. Though Stamatis was gone, the family and the estate continued. She also found solace in her work, her routines, and in the responsibility of helping her parents with the day-to-day activities on the land. With my grandparents' help, she could give her son a life filled with love and stability.

And then, as if out of nowhere, came Emmanouil Ndaousani, my father. He was another landowner in Sokia, and a man who was highly regarded. He came to see my grandparents and spoke openly about his desire to marry my mother.

In those days, Alexandra, a man of standing rarely married a widow with a child. Yet my father did not see a woman marked by tragedy. He saw someone who had known love, endured loss, and still carried herself with quiet dignity. She was striking—dark hair framing a face alive with expression, eyes the warm brown of melted chocolate, filled with tenderness and resolve. But it was not beauty that held him. He admired her strength, her grace in hardship, the quiet courage with which she met life's cruelties and refused to break.

How shocked she must have been. I imagined her sitting there, staring at this man, wondering why he would want to take on not only her, but her young son as well. Yet he did just that. When my mother spoke about this period of her life, she would say that my father brought the light back into her life. She never expected to find love again and had even closed her heart to the idea. But life often surprises us. And so, when Emmanouil Ndaousani came into her life, it was as unexpected as it was significant. His proposal was a blessing my mother had not dared to hope for. A second chance at love.

He raised Dimitri or Mitsos, as we called him, as his own, treating him with the same care and affection he would later show to me and my siblings. Never once did he speak of Dimitri as anything other than 'his son,' and he guarded him fiercely, ensuring that no one in Sokia questioned Dimitri's place in our family. It was one of the many reasons my mother loved him so deeply. That kind of acceptance, *agapi mou*, is not something you see every day, and I hope you understand how rare and precious it was. Together, they created a new family, and in time, I became their firstborn and was named after my paternal grandmother.

*　　*　　*

Alexandra, let me tell you about my father—your great-grandfather, Emmanouil. He was a remarkable man. He came from a family much like my mother's, a family of wealth built up by hard work. They too understood the importance of landownership and the power it could wield. Having made their way from Greece to Turkey, they quickly established themselves, buying rich fertile land in Sokia, where they cultivated both cotton and tobacco.

He had a mind that thirsted for knowledge, and his parents saw this early on. His father had higher aspirations for his only son, wanting more for him than the life of an estate manager and merchant. His education was of the utmost importance to him. He believed education could elevate a man, and Smyrni's Evangelical School offered exactly that — an education that opened doors across the Ottoman empire and beyond.

The school was Smyrni's most important Greek institution. Wealthy local merchants and notable families traditionally sent their sons there. I grew up hearing him speak of it—the great library, the teachers who demanded discipline, the sense that within those walls a boy could be shaped into a man of learning and stature. To study there was an honour, a mark of distinction. The school was known for producing men who went on to prestigious careers, lawyers, judges, even officials within the Ottoman administration. They learned not only Greek but also the languages of power: Ottoman Turkish and French. With their strong foundation in ethics, logic, and language, they were well-prepared to navigate the complexities of the Ottoman legal system.

That education stayed with my father all his life. He valued discipline, order, the weight that words could bear, the way they could shape a life, and he carried himself with a dignity that seemed to come from those years. Even when he returned to the land, there was a refinement about him that set him apart.

Some of his classmates became merchants, leading trade networks or managing large import-export businesses. Smyrni was a hub of commerce, and for many, their education gave them the skills to thrive in the bustling world of trade and diplomacy, bringing prosperity to their families and the wider community.

A few, like my father, returned to manage the family estates. Though he had the intellect and skill to pursue a high-profile career in law or commerce, he felt bound to the land. He knew our family's wealth lay in the cotton and tobacco fields of Sokia. My paternal grandfather had built that wealth, overseeing the cultivation and export of these crops, and he felt a duty to continue the legacy.

Working alongside his father, he came to know the land intimately, learning everything from planting to harvesting to export. He studied methods to improve productivity, combining his formal education with practical knowledge. He used his European language skills to communicate directly with merchants and buyers abroad, strengthening our trade connections and opening new markets. Over time, he became not only a skilled businessman but a respected figure within the Greek community in Sokia, valued for his culture, intellect, and compassion.

Eventually, when it came time for him to marry, my father built himself a home, a magnificent, two-storey house in the neighbourhood called Patriarhis Iyoakimis. This was the neighbourhood where affluent cotton merchants and other wealthy residents, who played a significant role in the local economy, lived. A house like that, in such a central position, was a sign of success and respectability. It was beautiful, a place that showed not just wealth but elegance.

Our house, like so many built by the Greeks of Sokia, rose above a cool basement. From the street, a few stone steps led to the front door, set back within a niche—a shallow recess in the wall that sheltered the entrance from sun and rain. Its glass inserts, framed in iron lace, allowed the afternoon light to filter through in shifting patterns across the floor. The windows were tall, their wooden shutters opening to the hum of the street, while behind the house, the courtyard stretched wide and was bathed in sunlight.

On the ground floor stood the grand lounge and dining room, where my father would host friends, family, and business acquaintances. The polished wooden furniture gleamed beneath chandeliers that shimmered in the evenings, and at the long dining table, our laughter and conversation often lingered long after our meal had ended. My parent's bedroom was also on this level. Upstairs were the children's bedrooms, and Persephone, our housekeeper's room, where each room was filled with natural light. There were also a set of French doors, which led to a balcony trimmed with intricate ironwork, which looked over the street.

It was in this house that my parents began their new life together. I know my mother felt a deep sense of respect for him. It must have felt like a new beginning for her, the start of a different life in a beautiful home — one filled with both comfort and stability, something that she could share with Dimitri and, eventually, with me and my other siblings.

I came into this world on the 17th of July 1903, much to the delight of my parents and grandparents. In the years that followed, they welcomed another daughter, Polyxeni and then a son, Stamatis.

*　　　*　　　*

Growing up in Sokia was like living in a world filled with tradition and a sense of belonging that I realise, even now, was a true gift. I remember the wooden bridge that once joined the two worlds of Sokia. It rose gently from the Turkish quarter and crossed into the Greek neighbourhood, where our lives unfolded.

At the beginning of the road that led from the bridge to our neighbourhood stood Doctor Aleko Perikli's pharmacy, with his office just above it. Beside it was a toy shop that still glimmers in my memory, its windows filled with colour and wonder for us children whenever we visited. A little further on, beneath the shade of a vast plane tree, was the café and the Zacharoplasteion.

The Greek-Orthodox Church of Saint Dimitrios had always been the heart of our community in Sokia. It stood on the road leading from the bridge over the stream. Not far from the church lived Father Michael, with his family. Their home was simple. Their lives moved with the rhythm of the parish — baptisms, weddings, feast days, the steady comfort of prayer.

Sokia itself had deep roots. Long before our time it was known as Anea, an ancient settlement that later became an ecclesiastical centre. Our town served as the seat of the Diocese of Anea under the Ecumenical Patriarchate of Constantinople. By the early years of the twentieth century, Sokia held a strong Greek-Orthodox presence, our numbers nearly equal to those of the Muslim population in the district. We lived side by side, each community woven through the daily life of the town. For us, though, the church was our anchor — the place where we gathered, celebrated, mourned, and found strength.

Ours was a family that was both close-knit, and guided by my parents' values and the love they gave us. I was lucky enough to spend the first nineteen years of my life in a home where every day was filled with the familiar, in a world that seemed as though it would never change. Those years were special. Our lives were charmed, and looking back, I see how deeply Sokia, and my family, shaped the person I became.

Even now I can still picture our family home vividly, a beautiful house with a large rear garden, with an assortment of trees and flowers and fragrant with herbs my mother grew. I loved the mornings most of all. I would wake up, open the shutters to allow the sunlight to stream into my room, the birds singing their morning melody outside, and the faint sounds of breakfast being prepared in the kitchen signalling that a new day had begun. Our home felt like our own little world, a place that offered us not just shelter but a deep sense of security.

And at the heart of our home was Persephone, our housekeeper. She had come to us from Aidíni. Orphaned at a young age, she had been raised by her grandparents, who passed away not long after she married. At twenty-five, she also lost her husband. With no family left and no desire to remarry, she left Aidíni and settled in Sokia, hoping to begin anew.

There she met my mother, newly married to my father and searching for a housekeeper. Fate seemed to have guided their meeting. Both had known the grief of widowhood too young, and in that shared sorrow, they found a quiet understanding. From then on, Persephone became part of our household—loyal, discreet, and devoted, as if she had always belonged with us. To the world, she might have been a servant, but to us, she was a valued member of our family, a gentle soul who infused each day with her warmth, patience, and quiet wisdom. She had been with the family since before I was born, and my siblings and I developed a close bond with her.

I loved to watch her work in the kitchen. Polyxeni and I would stand beside her as she worked. She would laugh as she looked down at us to see our expectant faces, knowing how eager we were to learn her secrets. For Persephone, cooking was not just a skill but a tradition, a craft honed over years, passed down through generations.

Our family's prominence in Sokia meant that Polyxeni and I would one day marry well, likely into families who expected grace and competence in a wife. In our culture, a well-run home was as much a sign of character as it was a practical necessity. She understood this, and she took her role as our guide seriously. She wasn't just teaching us to cook; she was teaching us how to manage a home, to nurture a family, to ensure that we could one day carry forward the traditions expected of us.

Persephone's lessons were never rushed. She would stand at the kitchen table showing us the technique for rolling out the phyllo dough she would use for spanakopita and her delicious baklava.

'Ένα πιάτο που το κάνεις με υπομονή, είναι ένα πιάτο που το κάνεις με αγάπη, κορίτσια μου. A dish made with patience, is a dish made with love, my girls!" she would say, calling us 'girls' with affection.

I can still remember the way she would slowly drizzle the syrup over a tray of baklava, letting each layer absorb the golden sweetness until the entire kitchen smelled of honey and golden pastry. Her recipes had been handed down from her grandmother. Many of them had no written instructions, and she knew them by heart, each step committed to memory through years of repetition. These were recipes that carried with them the flavours of our culture, Greek tradition mingled with the influences of Turkish and Ottoman kitchens. Some dishes were shared across communities. Even when the names differed slightly, the essence of the food spoke of centuries of co-existence, and just like Smyrni, Sokia was alive with the scents and tastes of many people.

As I grew older, I came to understand that what Persephone gave us was much more than recipes or techniques. We learned that hospitality should be done with grace and that the details mattered. Persephone never let us take shortcuts; she taught us to work with care, to respect the process, and to appreciate the quiet satisfaction that came with a job well done.

She would often say, "One day, you will make your husbands proud. You will make your family proud. But first, you must be proud of yourselves." Those words stayed with me, a reminder that genuine pride came from within, from knowing that we had done our best.

That is a valuable lesson, *agapi mou*, one that I know I urged you to carry throughout your life.

*   *   *

Sokia was a tapestry of languages, where Greek and Turkish intertwined in daily life. My grandparents were native Greek speakers but moved effortlessly between both, reflecting our bilingual community. The Greek we spoke was Smyrneika, a dialect shaped by centuries of co-existence under the Ottoman Empire, blending Greek with Turkish, Italian, and French influences. Language was more than words; it reflected intertwined lives, a living testament to the vibrant, multicultural community I remember so vividly.

We often went to the market with Persephone, Polyxeni and I, more for the gossip that would take place between the servants of other households than for the shopping itself. My sister and I would sit at a small table, eating our sweet or ice cream, listening as they exchanged the latest news. The market was alive, where Smyrneika and Turkish blended together, with vendors shouting out their wares, women bargaining, and children laughing as servants ran after their charges.

It was there we often met Giasemina, who worked in the home of one of the town's prominent families. She would embrace Polyxeni and I and shower us with kisses on both cheeks. Sometimes she would slip a sweet into our hands—a piece of *loukoúmi* dusted in sugar, or a handful of roasted chickpeas she claimed were 'magic' and would make us grow into beautiful young women.

On one occasion, Giasemina came up to us, her brown eyes bright, as she settled next to Persephone. She was young, beautiful, with dark hair that caught the sunlight, and a confidence that drew attention wherever she went. Like Persephone, she and her elder brother had been orphaned and raised by their grandparents, but where Persephone was quiet and steady, Giasemina was lively, unabashed, and mischievous. She often caught the eye of the surrounding men, offering smiles and glances that were daring and deliberate. It was impossible not to notice her, and impossible, too, not to feel that she revelled in the attention, a shameless flirt in the best possible way.

Polyxeni and I loved the stories she told us, especially about her current *yvouklou tis*, her sweetheart. We couldn't help but laugh shyly as she regaled us with her latest exploits. She always smelt nice too, and we knew the reason why.

"*Évala tis Kiras tin akriví kolónia!* I put on the lady's expensive perfume."

On this occasion, Persephone was not impressed by what she had heard about Giasemina's latest exploits and the rumours as to who she was secretly seeing. "*Kséro me pión daraverízis. Bás ke káti maghirévis m' aftón ton Leonída?* I know who you're seeing. Are you cooking something up with that Leonidas?"

"*Óhi, Persefóni mou! Dhen ine tipota. Dhen thélo na bo se beládes.* No, Persephone! It's nothing. I don't want to get into trouble," she said, her expression suddenly serious. Then, with a mischievous glint, she added, "*Án ke pósi théne na me kortárisoune!* Many want to court me!"

Persephone let out a long-suffering sigh. "*Áera éhoun pári ta mialá sou, mou fénete. Án blextís me aftón ton ahairéfto Leonída, alímonó sou. Ólo gíro gíro edó sto mahallá mas seryanái.* The wind has carried off your senses, it seems. If you get mixed up with that wretched Leonidas, heaven help you. He's always wandering about our neighbourhood!"

Leonidas had accused her of flirting with another man. Then, for effect, Giasmina mimicked him exactly. "*Morí, tha me vghális ap' ta roúha mou ke tha ghíni kaná makelió sto mahallá!* You'll make me furious, and there will be chaos in the neighbourhood!"

Persephone was not impressed. She thought Christoforos, the man Leonidas had accused her of flirting with, was a much better prospect. She fixed Giasemina with that look—part admonishment, part amusement. "*Ma páli s' to ksanaléo, áse pia ta polá ta soúrta–férta m' aftón ton Leonída. O Christóforos éhi kalá fersímata. Oréo pedhí ine, tímios, dhouleftáras, ke se glikokitázi káthe forá pou tha se dī. Kaká hoúya dhen éhi — bekrís, hasistzís dhen íne. Ti thélis álo!* I tell you again, leave off all the fuss with that Leonidas. Christoforos has good manners. He's good-looking, honest, hardworking, and he looks at you sweetly every time he sees you. No bad habits—no drunkenness, no hashish. What more do you want?"

Giasemina looked downhearted. "*Ftohó korítsi íme, Persefóni, kai óli píso ap' tin príka tréhoune.* I'm a poor girl, Persephone, and they are all chasing a dowry."

Persephone tutted and placed a comforting hand on her arm. Polyxeni and I exchanged a look and ate our ice cream. "*Óso gia tin príka, na 'rhi i kalí óra ke tha se frodísi o Kýrios. Tha taktopiísi to théma. Íne kalópsihos.* As for the dowry, when the time is right, the master will see to it. He will sort things out. He is good-hearted."

She would roll her eyes when the women teased her about Christoforos. Yet when he appeared—tall, broad-shouldered, and strikingly handsome—her cheeks flushed a delicate pink. Her laughter softened, her voice gentled. The way her smile lingered when he passed. How his eyes always searched for hers. She might have tried to hide her feelings, but we knew her heart had already given itself to him.

The teasing and coveted looks soon turned into preparations. Christoforos and his father visited the master of the house where Giasemina worked, and soon all the servants could talk about was the news of their engagement. It was more than any of them had expected. A servant girl with no dowry, no land, promised to a man as steady and well-respected as Christoforos.

The master of the house approved, pleased to have been asked formally for Giasemina's hand in marriage. The other girls whispered that fortune had smiled on her. Yet Giasemina stayed humble. She spoke of him softly, as though afraid that saying too much might break the spell. Still, whenever Christoforos looked at her, everyone could see it. She had captured his heart as surely as he had captured hers.

On the morning of the wedding, Giasemina was the most beautiful bride my young eyes had ever seen. I remember how the sunlight caught in her dark hair, braided with tiny white blossoms, and how her gown of fine silk and delicate lace seemed to shimmer when she walked. Her eyes shone with a mixture of excitement and gentle trepidation, her cheeks softly flushed. I can still remember the quiet awe Polyxeni and I shared, whispering to each other that we wanted to be just like her when our own wedding day came. She had captured the heart of the best young man, and she knew it. And when Christoforos took her hand, together they stepped into the life she had always hoped was waiting for her. Even now, many years later, the image of her grace and beauty still lingers in my memory, together with the sweetness of that morning in Sokia.

*　　*　　*

Religious festivals were a part of our culture. Easter was by far the most cherished and significant, a time when the Greek community came alive with spiritual fervour and celebration. We lived side by side with our Turkish neighbours, and there was a quiet harmony between us. Each of us respected the other's traditions—our festivals, their feasts, the rhythms of daily life, and mostly, we carried on peacefully, observing our customs without interference or ill will.

It began with the solemnity of Lent and culminated in the radiant joy of Pascha, or Easter Sunday. The period of Lent was a time of fasting, and a test of our discipline for us as children. It was a time of spiritual cleansing for the holy days ahead. Polyxeni and I would help Persephone in the kitchen as she prepared simple, meatless dishes.

As Holy Week approached, the atmosphere became charged with anticipation. I remember the scent of incense that filled the church during the services, the flickering candlelight, and the hauntingly beautiful hymns. Each day of Holy Week held a unique meaning and ritual, which culminated on Good Friday, when the Greek community gathered to mourn the crucifixion with a solemn procession through the streets. We would follow the *Epitaphios*, the decorated icon of Christ covered in flowers, holding our candles as we paid our respects.

On Holy Saturday, we waited in anticipation for the midnight service. My mother would help us put on our best clothes, and then we would join other families gathered in the church near our home, each person holding an unlit candle in preparation to receive the flame. As midnight approached, the priest's voice rang out, announcing, *'Christos Anesti!'*—'Christ is risen!' We would respond with *'Alithos Anesti!'*—'Truly, He is risen!' In that moment, the church would burst into light as everyone lit their candles, the darkness banished by a sea of flickering flames. The bells rang joyously, and we would greet each other with kisses and embraces, feeling the pure joy of Easter.

Easter Sunday was a day of feasting. Tables overflowed with traditional foods like lamb, baked breads, and eggs dyed the deepest red, symbolising Christ's resurrection, and *Koulourakia* Easter cookies and the *tsoureki*, the sweet brioche-like bread. Our family would gather to celebrate and to appreciate the blessing of being together. These were the moments I cherished most, seeing the happiness in the faces of my family. Looking back, I realise Easter was the foundation of my faith. It reminded us of renewal, of hope, and of the enduring bonds that held us together as a family.

Christmas in our home was always special, made even more meaningful because it was also my father's name day, a celebration our family cherished. On that day, our family gathered together to share a meal. Our home was alive with the sounds of music, laughter and the aromas of a feast being lovingly prepared by Persephone, and the female members of our household. We spent days preparing for the occasion, filling the table with beautifully roasted meats, traditional Greek dishes, delicate pastries, and breads spiced with cinnamon and cloves. My father, Emmanouil, sat proudly at the head of the table, surrounded by the people who loved him the most.

Each year, we would host an elaborate party in the evening to celebrate his name day. As dusk approached, the house took on an even livelier atmosphere as family, friends, neighbours, and members of the community began to arrive.

He was well known and respected in Sokia, admired for his wisdom, generosity, and steadfast character. It was a Greek tradition to honour a man's name day, and on this day, people came not only to pay their respects but to show their appreciation for the man he was.

My father greeted each guest warmly, his strong presence softened by a modest smile as he accepted the congratulations and well-wishes. I could see how much it meant to him, the pride he took in being part of this community and in knowing he had earned its respect. For hours, the house was filled with conversation, toasts, and blessings. As the evening wore on, I would look around at the crowded room, feeling grateful for the love that surrounded us and for my father, whom I loved deeply. I still hold his memory close to my heart.

*   *   *

In the Sokia of my childhood, I remember the cotton season best. My father, Emmanouil, was among the cotton landowners of the Sokia plain, where the soil was deep and black, enriched each year by the flooding of the Maiandros River. Our cotton fields lay just beyond the town, and from late spring through to the harvest, his days were spent more in the fields than in town. He was not the kind of man to sit behind a desk, nor one who sent others to walk the fields for him.

Each morning he left on horseback, visiting the irrigation ditches, speaking with the men in the fields, and inspecting the growth of the plants. His hands knew the weight of the soil, the feel of a ripe cotton boll, the ache of long days beneath the Aegean sun. When he returned home, his fingernails were always rimmed with earth, his shirts sweat-darkened at the collar and back.

Near the river, narrow irrigation ditches had been opened the night before — the clay-lined channels that carried life to the furrows. My father would lift a wooden flap in a gate, to peer down and make sure the water flowed. Satisfied, he signalled the men further upstream to release the gates. The cotton needed steady moisture. Too little and the fibre would grow coarse; too much and rot could set in. When harvest time came, the rows looked like scattered snow beneath the sun.

Cotton governed the rhythm of our lives. Sowing began in March, once the earth had warmed and the water from the river could be safely drawn through the channels. The men broke the clods with wooden ploughs and oxen, then cast the seed by hand. Through the long, hot months that followed, they kept the ditches clear and weeded the rows. By late August, the bolls opened, and that signalled the arrival of the seasonal workers.

My father greeted every worker by name, men from the town, seasonal labourers who came each year from neighbouring islands or villages. They brought their own bedding and rolled-up mattresses, slung over their shoulders. He made sure there was enough food and shaded courtyards where they could rest in the heat of the midday blaze. Their quarters lay apart from our house — modest but solid, built of stone and timber — and he never treated them as disposable hands. He listened when they spoke, paid fair wages, and even sometimes more when the crop was exceptional. In return, they trusted him. Even when the rains came too late, or the market eased, or pests ruined part of the yield, they came back the next season. People called him generous. But I know he believed in something simpler, that for the land to give a good return, one must take care of those who worked it.

At harvest he was everywhere: overseeing the picking, supervising the weighing of the seed-cotton, inspecting the bundles. We had no machines then. Everything was done by hand, pulling the fibre gently from the husk and filling their sacks. When full, the sacks were carried to the shade, where the men emptied them into heaps. There were no ginning machines in Sokia then. The separation of seed from fibre was done entirely by hand — slow, careful work. The women used wooden combs or small rollers, teasing the seeds out. The seeds were pulled from the lint by the women my father trusted most, who had worked the same fields for him and for his father before him. I remember sitting beside them as they showed me how to tease the seeds from the lint.

Once cleaned, the cotton was spread out onto wide sheets to dry in the afternoon sun. It was then packed by hand into thick canvas and burlap bags and pressed down into tight bundles that would survive the journey, then tied with heavy rope. My father supervised the weighing and marking of each bale himself. He refused to send a single bale that had not been checked twice; his sharp eyes searched each one for dampness or looseness and to ensure that the cotton was free of stains. Each of our bales was stamped with our mark, an olive branch intertwined with the letters E. N. and Sokia. A bale labelled 'Sokia' that met the standard could fetch a higher price.

My father supervised the loading of cotton bales onto mule and ox carts bound for the Aidíni railway station. The men stacked the pressed bales onto the wagons, securing them with rope before setting off across the plain. At the station, porters weighed and marked each one before it was transferred to the freight wagons for Smyrni. Smaller buyers in Aidíni often purchased directly from the growers, sold to brokers, or sent the fibre to ginning houses near the larger towns. Yet the best prices were always in Smyrni, where the great export firms — Greek, Armenian, and foreign — traded cotton for the markets of Marseille, Trieste, and Manchester.

Most landowners sold their crops in Aidíni. It was closer, convenient, with the railway and buyers waiting, ledgers open. My father preferred Smyrni. He had an arrangement with a Levantine trading house connected to Marseille, a major Mediterranean port for cotton. He followed the Smyrni Exchange closely, read the reports merchants brought, and spoke often with his partners there. Cotton was white gold, he said, the wealth of the valley. In good years, it brought prosperity to all who depended on it, from landowners to merchants and labourers alike.

When the loading was done, he would sit among the workers, sipping bitter coffee, laughing, and speaking in Turkish or Greek depending on who sat beside him. Later, back at the house, he and Osman, the overseer, opened the ledgers. They recorded hours worked, the cost of seed and fertiliser, yields from each plot, and the expense of transporting the bales to Smyrni for export.

Afterward, he would change from his work clothes into his other face — clean-shaven, wearing a fine linen shirt, dark waistcoat, and tailored trousers. The table was set, and we gathered for the evening meal, my mother, my brother, Dimitri, Persephone, and I. Conversation turned to family matters, a letter from my uncle in Smyrni, news of my mother's cousins in Samos, our lessons at school. My father listened with that steady look of his, his eyes bright with pride when Dimitri or I spoke of our marks or the praise we had received from our teachers. Sometimes he would rest a hand on my brother's shoulder, saying little, yet the gesture said enough. I remember the soft glow of the lamp on his face, the cadence of our voices, and the peace that seemed to settle over the house when he was home.

After our meal, my father settled into his quiet space, penknife in hand, opening letters laid aside during the day. There might be a dispatch for Smyrni, sent by courier or cart, or a brief telegram dictated at the post office. By then, the telegraph connected Sokia to the main line running through Aidíni to Smyrni. He wrote to brokers and cotton merchants, noting the yield, bale weights, and the state of the crop.

Sometimes he went out to the café in the square to meet with friends, merchants, notables, and other landowners, where conversation flowed easily between them. They spoke of rain and river levels, of prices in the Smyrna Exchange, of ships leaving for Marseille or Trieste. Cups of bitter coffee cooled beside them, or they indulged in glasses of raki, the smell of tobacco thick in the air.

In 1922, I was nineteen years of age. That year, everyone expected the harvest to surpass all others. The cotton bolls were full, the plants heavy, the sky generous with sun. When I think of that year, I can still see my father standing at the edge of the field, his hat in his hands, his eyes fixed on the rows that promised an abundant harvest. The air was unnaturally still, the kind that pressed against us. And though we did not yet know it, that quiet was the first sign of the impending disaster that would sweep through our lives. That harvest would never be gathered. The fields would lie untended, the cotton would brown on the stems, and the carts would never leave for the station. And my father too would be swallowed up in that silence.

*   *   *

In Sokia, fever season came from the lowland areas of the fertile Maiandros, Büyük Menderes (Meander) River valley and would peak in the hottest months from June to August, where standing water and marshes were ideal for mosquitoes. We dreaded the nights most of all when the mosquitoes buzzed at the edges of sleep. Mosquito nets were hung over our beds, and my mother would light small charcoal braziers, *kapnistiri* we called them, and sprinkled them with dried *faskómilo* (sage) and *thymári* (thyme). Sometimes they added *aplokivania* (wild rue), the sharp peel of bitter oranges, or even *liváni* (frankincense).

The smoke curled through the rooms, its scent both bitter and comforting. It was meant to keep the mosquitoes at bay, those small, humming messengers of fever we all dreaded. I remember lying awake, breathing in that heavy, acrid smoke, hoping it would be enough to keep the sickness from finding us. Even later in life, the smell of burning sage and thyme would carry me back to those restless summer nights in Sokia, when we placed our faith in that smoke.

Even the strong men who worked the fields would fall ill again and again, sometimes leaving them too weak to work the fields when the harvest came.

In truth, disease was a part of daily life. We lived carefully, trusting in the remedies we knew. In Greek Orthodox families, mothers pinned small protective amulets called a *filachto,* inside our clothing to protect us from sickness, the evil eye *(to kako mati),* and bad luck. These tiny cloth pouches, contained items that varied by family and local tradition, dried flowers from the Holy week Epitaphios, small scraps of paper with prayers written by a priest, a few grains of liváni, and herbs like *daphni* (bay leaf), *faskómilo* (sage), or *aplokivania* (wild rue). Prepared by priests, grandmothers, or mothers themselves, they were renewed or re-blessed if the child fell ill.

I was nine years of age when sickness came for my mother's parents. My grandfather fell ill first. I remember the hush that settled over the house, as my grandmother, my mother and the household staff kept vigil by his bedside.

Doctor Periklis, our family doctor, came each day with bottles of quinine, the bitter draught we hoped would ease the fever. But we did not rely on medicine alone. My grandmother and mother brewed infusions of wormwood and chamomile to soothe the trembling, and placed cloths soaked in lemon and vinegar on his forehead to draw the heat away. In the evenings, they burned rosemary and bay leaves in the sickroom, the sharp scent curling through the air in the hope it might cleanse it. Clove and cinnamon tea was brought to strengthen the heart. Even the windows were left slightly open behind gauze, so the night breeze might carry the fever out. Yet despite every remedy we could offer — the doctor's medicine and the old ways that we hoped would calm the fever, the shaking and sweats only worsened. One morning, before the sun had risen, he slipped away.

Not long after, my grandmother too was taken by the same fever. I can still see her lying there quietly beneath the white linen, her skin damp with perspiration, eyes half-open as though she were already looking elsewhere. The doctor could do little more than offer the same bitter draughts, while we continued with the local remedies we knew best.

However, even those with means could not always hold illness at bay. Malaria cared nothing for land, titles, or coin, and soon we lost my grandmother as well.

As I tried to make sense of the emptiness left by my maternal grandparents, my thoughts inevitably turned to my father's family in Smyrni. Their world was different — bustling streets, grand homes, and the weight of social expectation — yet it too would leave its mark on me.

I was twelve when I lost my paternal grandparents. They had long retired to Smyrni, to the neighbourhood of Fanari, where the air carried the scent of the sea. My grandfather's health had never fully recovered from the bouts of malaria that had weakened him years earlier. Still, life in the city suited them. They were comfortable, with servants to tend to the house, and my uncle and his family, not far away in Bournabat.

In the early months of 1914, sickness spread once more through Smyrni. It was said that a fever had come in with the ships from Alexandria, typhoid, some called it, though others spoke of a flux that took the old first. The narrow streets of Fanari grew quiet as doors were shut. Priests made the rounds, offering prayers and blessings to the afflicted, while doctors moved from house to house with little to offer.

My grandparents' house, once lively with visitors and music, fell silent. My grandfather was the first to take to his bed; his strength quickly faded, and my grandmother refused to leave his side. Despite every effort, the doctor's visits, the prayers, the bitter medicine that promised relief, the fever took him within a week. My grandmother followed soon after. They said her heart simply failed from grief.

Their passing cast a dark pall over our family. My father spoke little in those days, and together with my uncle, they arranged their funerals. It was another cruel loss, coming only three years after we had buried my maternal grandparents.

When we returned to Sokia, my mother placed a photograph of them both in the *eikonostátis*, our little home shrine. She then lit the *kandili*, for the next forty days. Its light spilled softly across the room, the flame flickering as if it held our grief within its small heart. Our house fell quiet and heavy with sadness. My mother explained that the forty days after death were a sacred time. The soul of the departed, she said, journeyed in ways we could not see, and the prayers we offered, the light we kept burning, helped to guide them along the way. In our home, that photograph placed among the icons was more than a memory. It was a bridge between the world we could see and the world we could not, a way to hold on to those we had lost while trusting they were not truly gone.

CHAPTER TWO

Smyrni, on the coast of western *Mikrá Asía*, Asia Minor, was a city of breathtaking beauty. It was a haven where Greeks, Armenians, Italians, Levantines, Jews, and Turks lived side by side, the beating heart of the East, the bridge between continents. It was a city of trade, culture, and dreams. Ships came and went daily, bringing goods from America, Europe, and across the Middle East. Everything that moved between continents seemed to pass through the port.

As ships sailed into its harbour, they entered a near-perfect half-moon bay, lined with long piers where vessels from every nation docked. Each European power and major trading company had its own wharf. From the deck of a steamer, a visitor arriving at the port would have realised immediately that they had arrived in a place of prosperity and commerce. Along the impressive two-mile-long seafront stood two, three and four-storey buildings designed by European architects. These housed banks, insurance companies, consulates, hotels, private clubs, cafés and restaurants, as well as the houses of wealthy merchants. Smyrni was a city of diversity and brilliance, vibrant in every sense.

Beyond the seafront lay the true heart of the city. Smyrni was not only European and modern, it was also deeply Ottoman. Like all great cities of the Empire, it was divided into quarters. To the south stretched the narrow, winding streets of the Turkish quarter. Pressed between Turkish and Armenian homes lay the smaller Jewish quarter, quiet and modest. Beyond that rose the Armenian Quarter, elegant and prosperous. And finally, dominating the northern slopes of Pagos, stood the Greek quarter. From this prominent hill, one could see the harbour, the Quay, and much of the city's bustling trade. Its streets and gardens gave it a quieter, residential feel compared with the commercial waterfront, a place both vibrant and commanding in its presence.

The Greeks and Turks were the city's backbone, its largest peoples, bound together in trade and proximity. Yet for all its differences, Smyrni had found a rhythm of co-existence, a fragile balance that seemed, at the time, unbreakable.

During the year, our family would travel periodically to visit our relatives in Smyrni. These trips to me felt like we were making a journey to another world. Smyrni was bustling, cosmopolitan, and alive with a vibrancy that was both intimidating and fascinating. For me, Smyrni was pure magic. Our visits were always filled with excitement and a sense of awe, a journey into a world of grace and sophistication. My paternal grandparents lived in the heart of the Greek Quarter, known as Fanari or Frangomahalas. It was a place of elegance and charm.

The streets were lined with neoclassical homes, with their tall windows, intricate ironwork balconies, whose design spoke of refinement. It was a place where wealth and culture were celebrated and displayed, yet there was a quiet dignity about it that made it even more beautiful. At the heart of the neighbourhood stood Agia Foteini, the Greek Orthodox church with its distinctive bell tower and its elegant dome and marble facade, which made it a landmark for Greek families who gathered there for baptisms, weddings, and Sunday services. I remember the way the church bells would echo through the streets, a reminder of the faith that tied us all together.

Our favourite part was the Kordon waterfront, the wide seaside promenade or *prokymaia* that ran along the Aegean, within walking distance from Fanari. As dusk settled over the city, our family would walk to Smyrni's famed waterfront promenade. This wide, elegant stretch along the sea was where people met and mingled for their evening walk, against the backdrop of the Aegean's cool waters. Greek families strolled arm in arm, the men in fine tailored suits, and the women dressed exquisitely in flowing skirts, fitted jackets, and wide-brimmed hats that added a touch of glamour to the evening. Smyrni was famous for its fashion, and here, the women's beauty and sophistication were on full display.

Smyrni was renowned for its energy after dark, its streets alive with people from all backgrounds, Greeks, Turks, Armenians, and foreigners, all sharing in the city's vibrant spirit. Fine cafés, restaurants, and even an opera house offered entertainment to those seeking elegance and culture. At night, Smyrni's opera house drew well-dressed crowds; its performances were a point of pride for the city. Those who weren't attending the opera could be found in local cafés and nightclubs, where lively music and conversation filled the air.

As we walked, the air was filled with music from nearby cafés and tavernas. The sounds of Greek rebetiko and Turkish folk songs were woven together, blending in a harmony that reflected Smyrni's mixed identity. I often heard other foreign languages, which reflected Smyrni's melting pot of cultures. Even as night fell, the city came alive in a different way, as if Smyrni's energy and beauty could not be contained by the setting sun.

We would also visit our uncle Evangelos, my grandfather's brother, in Bournabat (now Bornova) a neighbourhood that was originally a village on Smyrni's outskirts. It differed from Fanari's urban bustle with its spacious estates, lush gardens, and the quiet elegance of its countryside homes. Many prominent Greek and foreign families lived there, drawn to the beauty of its grand homes and the calm atmosphere that offered a retreat from the city's faster pace. Walking through Bournabat was like stepping into a different world, where tall trees shaded the paths, and beautiful gardens stretched out behind high fences. The air was fresher, and the calm was almost tangible.

Our trips to Smyrni always carried an air of excitement. Part of that thrill came from the rituals we kept whenever we visited. Of course, it would not be complete without a visit to one of the European-style department stores along the Rue Franque and Kordelio which catered to the European tastes of Smyrni's elite, selling fashion and luxury goods both local and imported, often from Paris or other fashionable European cities.

Along the bustling Kordon of Smyrni, the Alhambra Café stood as a jewel of the waterfront, its façade a graceful mix of neoclassical lines and Levantine flair. Tall windows welcomed sunlight that danced across marble floors and delicate wrought-iron balconies. Inside, small round tables bore the weight of animated conversations in Greek, Turkish, and European accents, while the aroma of strong coffee and sweet pastries lingered in the air. Patrons—artists, merchants, theatre folk—mingled freely, the café pulsing with the city itself, cultured, cosmopolitan, alive. Each year, on the 6th of January, the Epiphany ceremony spilled onto its waterfront, after the service at the church of Agia Foteini. Here the faithful gathered to watch the cross-diving ritual, adding a layer of sacred celebration to the café's vibrant life.

The Hermes Café offered a different charm. Modest from the outside, inside it radiated warmth. Dark polished wood, brass fittings, and deep velvet upholstery gave it a cosy, intimate air. Here, the lyric theatre community gathered, their chatter and laughter mingling with the soft clink of cups. Light filtered through narrow windows, casting patterns on mosaic-tiled floors, while the scent of roasted coffee beans hung in the air. Known as 'the most Greek café on the waterfront,' Hermes was a haven for art, conversation, and the heartbeat of Smyrni's Greek community.

Both cafés, each in its own style, embodied the cosmopolitan spirit of Smyrni. But for us, after visiting the shops, we would end our outings at Café de Paris or, occasionally, the Kordelio Café. Both places offered a welcome respite, but Café de Paris had a particular charm. My grandmother would lead the way, and when we arrived, she would guide us up the marble steps to the terrace, where tables looked out onto the Aegean. There was an elegance to the café with its high windows, which opened onto the sea and its polished wooden floors. The scent of strong coffee and warm pastries would greet us as we settled into our seats, to await the delights we knew so well.

My sister and I would watch the servers move gracefully between tables, with their silver trays balanced effortlessly on their fingertips. A delicious assortment of pastries was arranged in glass cases, some made of puff pastry and cream dusted with powdered sugar, others topped with glazed fruits and of course the traditional offerings of baklava, *kadaifi* and *sekerloukomia*.

My mother and grandmother would always order coffee, which was served in delicate porcelain cups arriving with small silver trays of sweets. For me, the highlight was always the *mille-feuille*, with its crisp, golden layers of pastry and soft vanilla cream filling. I loved how the pastry crumbled and the vanilla cream melted on my tongue with such blissful sweetness. My sister often chose *éclairs* or tiny *petit fours*, each more perfect than the last.

From where we sat, we could peruse Smyrni's wealthy matrons moving gracefully through the cafe, dressed finely and catch the fragrance of their perfume, and the way the sunlight caught their jewellery. Their laughter rang out with ease, their conversation fluent in French, Greek, or Levantine dialects. My mother and grandmother would exchange conversation, but my sister and I often just listened, eyes wide with wonder at the life unfolding around us.

Coming from Sokia, our family was considered well-off, but our manners and dress bore the simpler elegance of a provincial upbringing. Even in our best clothes, we carried a modesty that marked us as outsiders, the sort who admired from the edges rather than moved confidently through the centre. I noticed the subtle differences: the way Smyrni's women walked without effort, their voices carrying authority, the way they spoke of travel, art, and society as though it were the air they breathed. We were invited into their world, yes, but only just watched, measured, and found polite enough, yet undeniably provincial. Even so, I loved every moment of observing them.

Smyrni was so different from our life in Sokia. It was a city that worked hard, traded hard, and celebrated life with equal passion. There was music in the air, laughter in the cafés, and the sound of church bells mingling with the call to prayer. It was said that nowhere in the East could one live so well. Smyrni was wealth, refinement, and pleasure, all glittering beneath the Aegean sun. There was an excitement to it all, a sense of being at the centre of something grand and worldly.

But there were days when we craved something quieter, and on those afternoons, we took the ferry across the bay to the Kordelio Café. The journey itself felt like part of the ritual, with the ferry cutting through the waves, the breeze carrying the salty scent of the sea. In Kordelio, time moved slower. The café's charm was more understated, and the tables on the terrace offered views of Smyrni from a distance.

The offerings reflected Smyrni's unique blend of cultures. There were trays of syrup-soaked baklava, crisp *kadayif*, and soft, sweet *şekerpare*, alongside French confections like buttery tarts and chocolate *gateaux*. Sometimes, we shared a savory plate of warm Borek, its flaky layers filled with cheese or spinach, before finishing with a sweet treat.

Yet, for all its charm and elegance, Smyrni could be overwhelming. We felt quiet relief in knowing that we would soon return to Sokia. There, life was simpler. Our days followed the slow, steady rhythm of the seasons, offering a peace that was comforting. Smyrni dazzled us, but Sokia was where we could breathe, where we belonged.

*   *   *

The Greek Nationalist movement was on the rise in Greece, and many dreamed of the *Megáli Idéa*, the Great Idea, the vision of uniting all Greek lands, including Smyrni, with its rich Greek heritage. Venizelos, our Prime Minister, was the man who gave voice to it, and had pushed at the Paris Peace Conference for Greece to occupy Smyrni and the surrounding lands. The British supported him, not out of love for Greece, or so my father told us, but because they feared the Italians would side with the Turks. To them, we were a convenient army to fight their battles in Anatolia.

We were fighting for a dream, a vision of a Greater Greece. The voices of the Venizelists echoed through the streets of Athens, calling for union with the land that was once ours, the land we believed we could reclaim. These nationalist aspirations were buoyed by the successes of the Greek army against the Ottoman Empire and had begun to expand its reach to reclaim all the Greek-populated regions under Ottoman rule.

I was only sixteen years of age when the *Megáli Idéa* took hold. I remember the passion with which people spoke of it, the vision of a restored Greece, a nation that stretched across the Aegean and into the heart of Anatolia. For so long, we clung to the hope that the land of our ancestors, the land of Ionia, would once again be ours. It wasn't just a political dream; it was a piece of our identity, a promise of something greater, something that could lift us from the ashes of the past.

But it was never simple.

The Turks had their own vision, one that was strong, unyielding, and led by Mustafa Kemal, which stirred the fierce nationalism that burned through the hearts of those who wanted to rid their land of foreign influence. It wasn't just the Ottomans anymore; it was about building something new, something independent, something entirely their own. They looked at us, the Greeks, and saw a threat, and we looked at them in the same way, but neither side understood the cost of such dreams.

In May 1919, news reached Sokia that the Greek army had landed in Smyrni. Commanded by High Commissioner Aristides Sterghiades, the Greek force quickly secured Smyrni and the surrounding areas. For days, the town buzzed with the news. Smyrni, a city that held such cultural and historical importance to us, was now at the centre of something monumental. For many Greek families, this was the moment they had been waiting for. The Greeks in Sokia spoke of the liberation of Smyrni as a victory ordained by God Himself. After centuries under Ottoman rule, they believed the ancient glory of Hellenism might be restored. For many, this was a moment of vindication.

I felt this too — a surge of pride that rippled through our community, a belief that perhaps a new era was dawning.

But there was another side to the news. When the Greek soldiers entered Smyrni, we rejoiced and called them liberators. Yet for the Turks it was different. For them, our joy was a threat. They looked on with fear and revulsion. Many believed the Greeks intended to exterminate them or drive them out of Western Anatolia. Those first days planted deep anger in their hearts, and it gave strength to the emerging Turkish Nationalist movement under Mustafa Kemal.

That day, Smyrni's waterfront was alive with pride and joy. The Greek population lined the *Prokymaea* (Quay), waving flags to welcome the troops, their voices rising in triumphant chants as they greeted the soldiers. Yet, amid the cheering crowds and jubilation, unexpected shots rang out. To this day, no one knows who fired them. Some said a Turkish soldier, others a frightened local Greek, but the spark they ignited was unmistakable.

Violence erupted almost immediately, as tensions that had simmered beneath the surface flared into open hostility. Greek soldiers, caught off guard by the sudden turn of events, returned fire toward the nearby government buildings and barracks. The jubilant celebration quickly gave way to confusion and fear. Scores of Greeks were killed or wounded, and many Turks lost their lives in the chaos. This unexpected outbreak of violence was a troubling omen of what might come.

My father saw it too, but he also saw something deeper, a reality the rest of us were not yet ready to confront, and his reservations tempered my youthful excitement. A man of education and experience, I had learned to trust his instincts. He knew Smyrni well, a place where different communities had lived side by side for generations. He understood that the consequences of disturbing that fragile peace could be more terrible than any victory.

'Smyrni is a delicate place,' he said to us one evening. 'It is made of many different threads, Greek, Turkish, Armenian and Levantines. One wrong move could unravel it all,' he told us, his voice calm but firm. 'There is much to be proud of in our heritage, but we must be cautious. The excitement we feel may not be shared by those who see us as intruders, not liberators. Remember," he continued, "our strength as a community has always come from our ability to live peacefully with others. If we let pride turn into arrogance, we may lose more than we gain."

At first, the initial occupation was limited to Smyrni. It became the heart of the Greek occupation, its harbour crowded with ships unloading soldiers, supplies and reinforcements bound for the interior. By the end of the month they had marched east, seizing Aidíni. For the Greek army advancing inland from Smyrni, taking Aidíni was strategically important, as its capture helped secure the surrounding region.

The town lay northwest of Sokia, close enough that news of military movements or approaching forces could reach us quickly. The proximity also meant that should the Turks regain Aidíni, Sokia's safety was in immediate danger.

Buoyed by Allied support, primarily from the British, the Greek army pushed outward from Smyrni, seizing towns such as Usak, Panoromos, Prusa, and Adrianople by the end of July. From the start, the struggle was uneven, unpredictable, and brutal. It wasn't only the Turkish army they faced; everywhere, irregular fighters launched raids and ambushes. Both Turks and Greeks suffered in a war that seemed endless. The harsher the Greek occupation, the fiercer the resistance became.

For the Greeks in Sokia, one figure stood out among the Turks: Cafer Efe. A Zeybek — an irregular militia fighter — born in Crete, he carried a dark and violent past. People said he had killed a Greek man named Acaritsis, a deed that forced him into exile. When he arrived in Sokia, his name already inspired dread among us.

In Sokia and the nearby villages — Ortaklar, Aziziye, Germencik — he gathered a band of fighters. We called them *Zevbekides*. They followed him fiercely, seeing in him a defender of their land and a force against the Greek occupation. His methods were harsh, uncompromising. Raids, ambushes, sudden attacks along the roads, each one deepened our fear and uncertainty.

To the Turks, he was a leader worthy of respect. To us, he was a figure of fear, a constant reminder of how precarious our lives had become.

On July 19, 1919, in Germencik, Cafer Efe met his end. In the heat of battle, he was shot and killed. Those who followed him mourned his death, hailing him as a martyr to their cause. Yet, for many of us Greeks, who still remembered the terror and bloodshed that marked his rise, his death brought a grim sense of relief.

Even without him, the struggle he was part of continued. The Kuva-yi Milliye, irregular forces inspired by the *Zevbekides* like Cafer Efe, kept the fight alive. They pressed forward, unpredictable, and relentless, determined to reclaim their land.

*   *   *

In early 1921, the Conference of London drew the attention of every discussion my father and his associates engaged in. The Allies tried to force a compromise between the Greeks and the Turks. Neither side would yield. The Greeks had invested too much, and the Turks fought as if the very survival of their people was at stake. Over a year after the first landings, the weak hand of Sultan Mehmed VI was finally forced to sign the Treaty of Sèvres.

The Treaty promised Greece control over Smyrni and parts of Western Anatolia. Armenia was to become an independent state, while the Ottoman Arab provinces were to be divided under French and British supervision. The Straits of the Bosporus and Dardanelles—the narrow passage connecting the Aegean to the Sea of Marmara—were to be internationalised, and the Ottoman army and navy strictly limited. Minority populations were to receive guarantees of protection and autonomy.

For the Greek families of Anatolia, the treaty offered a fragile hope—a promise that perhaps justice and safety would finally prevail. Yet that hope was quickly undermined. The Turkish nationalist forces under Mustafa Kemal rejected its terms, and the Allied powers, politically divided and hesitant, failed to enforce them. Their inaction left our fate hanging in the balance. Our lives were still being gambled upon, and by allowing the Turks to defy the treaty, the Allies condemned us to uncertainty and danger once more.

Yet, to the supporters of Venizelos, it felt like a dream come true. The idea of a 'Greater Greece,' stretching across Europe and Asia, touching five seas, seemed within reach. They spoke excitedly of the Greece that might be, as if the war could bring nothing but glory.

But reality turned cruel. Two months later, King Alexander died. The Greek elections that followed in November tore the country apart. Venizelos, the man who had envisioned this Greater Greece, was soundly defeated, unable to hold even his own seat in parliament. Even those who had backed him were shaken by the result. It was a bitter reminder that the Greek people themselves had grown weary of endless conflict. The royalists took over, and despite their earlier criticism of the war effort, they had no intention of leaving Anatolia. Instead, they launched a renewed offensive in January 1921. Yet even then, word was reaching us that Mustafa Kemal and his nationalist forces were gathering strength in the heart of Anatolia. From then on, the fighting only grew more widespread, more savage, more relentless, and we all began to fear of what might follow, of the reprisals that could come if the Turks regained control.

*   *   *

Life in Sokia, once so steady and secure, was beginning to feel different. I was older now, and I could sense the currents of change stirring beneath the surface of our town, and within our own home. While we still celebrated traditions and gathered with family, there was an undercurrent of worry, a tension that was becoming more difficult to ignore especially in the growing tension between us Greeks and our Turkish neighbours, that cast a shadow over our sense of security. Our town was changing, and, as I would come to understand later, these changes were far more profound than I could have ever imagined.

I often overheard conversations between my father and his closest friends and business associates, their low, tense voices drifting from behind closed doors, even though he tried to shield us from such discussions. Some spoke of support for the Greek resurgence, eager to reclaim lands lost over centuries and honour our heritage. He, however, viewed it as a precarious shift that could unsettle the delicate balance we had long known. A proud Greek, devoted to our traditions, he was also wary of the repercussions of political fervour, sensing the turmoil it could bring.

I remember watching him then, seated in silence, a shadow darkening his usually calm expression. 'Pride and passion have their place," he once told me, 'but they can be dangerous when they turn into fuel for division. "

As the Greek army advanced further into the interior, my father's words echoed in my mind. In Sokia, the mood grew tense, guarded. A heaviness settled over the town as questions of loyalty and identity stirred unease. Once, Greek, and Turkish neighbours had shared the rhythm of life, celebrating each other's festivals, respecting each other's customs. Now, that balance was beginning to unravel. The tensions from Smyrni and the army's advance had begun to seep into our streets, and what had once been a peaceful co-existence was becoming strained.

Even my mother began voicing her fears.

The sense of worry was unmistakable. It was woven into the discussions between my parents and in the silent glances they exchanged when they thought we weren't watching. My father remained composed, but I could see the weight of his concerns in the set of his jaw, the way he would sit in thought, lost in quiet contemplation. I knew he was trying to shield us from his fears, but I was old enough now to recognise that his heart was heavy with the changes he saw around us and what the eventual repercussions would be to us as a family.

As tensions grew, the conversations at home turned towards questions of loyalty, of survival, and of what our future in Sokia might hold. Every day brought a new challenge to the peace we had taken for granted. Even the visits of friends and relatives brought conversations filled with words of caution and words of fear. I would listen intently, feeling both drawn to their discussions and frightened by what they implied. We were standing on the brink of something that could change our lives forever, and it was only a matter of time before we would be swept up in its tide.

Amid all this, my thoughts turned to my future, one that had always felt secure but now seemed full of uncertainty. For years, I had dreamt of marrying and starting a family of my own. But now, those dreams felt overshadowed by an anxiety I could not ignore. This terrible sense of foreboding remained. It was as if the very fabric of our lives was being stretched thin, as if it might tear under the weight of forces beyond our control. The confidence I once felt about my future was fading, replaced by questions I wasn't sure how to answer.

*   *   *

The first reports of the Greek army advancing inland were met with pride. Towns such as Philadelphia, Ousakeion, and Akroinos fell quickly, and it seemed as if the dream of a greater Greece, was within reach. But my father remained uneasy.

'Smyrni is one thing,' he explained one evening as we walked back to our home after an evening out visiting some friends. 'It is a city with a strong Greek presence, but Anatolia is not ours. It belongs to the Turks, and they will not let us keep it without a fight. We are overstretching ourselves, and when the reckoning comes, it will be swift.'

In 1921, the tone of the news shifted. We heard there were small skirmishes, nothing to fear. The newspapers printed maps showing our forces deep in Anatolia and wrote words celebrating and praising our fearless and brave Greek army.

But my father was not so certain. He had a gnawing unease that those maps and the glowing praise of their words, hid the truth. The front was stretched thin, the supply lines long and fragile, and the enemy was fighting for their homeland.

He listened when others in Sokia celebrated, but when he returned home, his shoulders sagged. I remember sitting beside him one evening as he reached for my hand and said, 'Hope is a fine thing, Eftihia,' he told me, 'but it must be tempered with caution. Wars are not won by dreams.'

He had lived long enough to understand the currents of history, what started with triumph often ended in tragedy. The Allies, who had promised to support us, were fickle, each nation pursuing its own interest, he would say. The British, the French, the Italians—they had supported Greece's territorial claims only because it suited their designs after the Great War.

He often reminded us that their support was rooted in their own ambitions. "They use us as pawns," he said. "And when the game changes, we will be left to fend for ourselves."

What would happen when we no longer served their purpose? These thoughts kept him awake at night, though he said little to my mother and to us children. A father must appear strong, even when his heart is heavy.

As victories turned to stalemates and defeats, stories emerged, stories that were deeply troubling. Villages burned, civilians slaughtered, their homes looted by our soldiers. The atrocities were not one-sided; the Turks retaliated with equal savagery, but knowing that our army, the army of my nation, was complicit in such acts gnawed at my conscience and deeply shamed my father.

"This is not how a just war should be fought," he would say, shaking his head.

What troubled him the most was the brutality of it all. At first, it was dismissed as a wartime necessity, 'collateral damage,' the men of influence in our town called it. But my father was not one to look away from the truth.

'Liberators should not leave ashes in their wake," he told us quietly.

He worried these actions would harden Turkish resistance and stain the honour of our people and also spoke of the army's weaknesses, though not in public. He was too cautious a man to voice such things openly during those fervent days. At home, however, he shared his fears with my mother, my elder brother and sometimes with me, as I quietly stitched beside them. Many of the officers were inexperienced, appointed not for their merit but for their loyalty to King Constantine.

"Their hearts may be strong," he said, "but courage alone cannot sustain them. They are far from home, fighting in lands that do not belong to us." He paused, his hands gripping the edge of the table. 'If they lose, Mariegó, the Turks will not spare us."

I had never seen him look so grave. His fear was not just for the soldiers or the war but for us, his family, and the Greeks of Anatolia. Though we were not in the direct path of the fighting, my father knew the tides of war did not respect distance. If the Turkish forces regained control, they would surely seek vengeance for the atrocities committed by our army.

News from the front was slow to arrive, but when it did, it painted a troubling picture. The Greeks had initially captured the towns of Philadelphia (Alaşehir) and Ousakeion (Uşak) with ease, but resistance stiffened. In places like Akroinos (Afyonkarahisar) and Eskisehir, Turkish forces regrouped under Mustafa Kemal, who had galvanised his men into a formidable force.

Our army was brave but ill-prepared. Morale dwindled as the months dragged on. The further they advanced, the more overextended their supply lines became. By August 1921, they stood on the banks of the Sakarya River. They came frighteningly close to Ankara—only eighty kilometres—but could go no further. It was there that the advance faltered. Word came that the battle raged for weeks, the Turks throwing everything they had into stopping them. After holding on through the month of September, the Greeks were compelled to withdraw. It was Kemal's leadership, his determination, and the impossible stretch of the Greek lines that saved the nationalists at Sakarya.

That defeat was the beginning of the end, though many refused to see it. Father followed the news obsessively, piecing together scraps of information from travellers and letters. When the truth reached us, his face was grave. From then on, the news no longer spoke of steady conquests but of Turkish forces regaining ground. My father listened with a heavy heart; he had known from the beginning that such rapid gains could not last, and now the reckoning had come.

In October 1921, news reached us that France had signed an agreement with Mustafa Kemal's government in Ankara, bringing an end to the Franco-Turkish War. The French would withdraw from Cilikia, the south-eastern part along the Mediterranean coast, giving up the cities of Adana, Mersíni, and Áintap. By January 1922, their troops were gone. In return, France received guarantees for the protection of Christian minorities and for its economic and cultural interests in the region.

Even the British grew colder toward the continued commitment to the Greek cause. By the end of 1921, we understood why the British had abandoned us. The Greek army had suffered terrible losses, especially at Sakarya in August, and their advance had ground to a halt. Inside Greece, the government had changed—Venizelos was gone, and King Constantine I was back, a man whose past sympathies with Germany made the British wary. They were now focused on keeping the Middle East stable and, more importantly, protecting their own interests. They sent no more arms, no more money.

Italy was next to turn away. It first adopted a neutral stance, then gradually began co-operating with Mustafa Kemal's nationalist government in Ankara. In the Italian-controlled zones, nationalist forces operated with relative freedom, and Italian authorities often turned a blind eye to arms and supplies moving north. Italian banks even extended loans to Ankara. In return, Italy, like France, secured protection for its commercial interests and influence in the region. An understanding was reached that brought an end to Italy's occupation of the southwestern coast, including Antalya, Kusandasi, and Marmarida. Their troops withdrew in the months that followed, and by early 1922 they were gone.

With each withdrawal of support and as the power of the Turkish nationalist movement grew and the Allied–Greek position weakened, we realised we had been abandoned, that the dream of holding onto Anatolia was slipping away. We were left to face whatever would come next.

My father had begun to worry in earnest. His warning returned to me with chilling clarity: the Allies will cast us aside the moment we cease to serve their purpose. He had spoken those words often, and now they proved true. The growing strength of the Turkish nationalists and the lack of commitment of the Great Powers, who had turned their backs on us, left the Greek army exposed and vulnerable to what was coming.

From then on, the news darkened. On August 26, 1922, Kemal launched his great offensive against the Greek lines at Doumploupinar, an assault that would decide the fate of us all. The Greek army, already weakened and demoralised, could not withstand the force of the Turkish assault. Within days, the front line collapsed, and the soldiers began a desperate retreat to escape encirclement and annihilation.

I can still hear the panic in the conversations being conducted when the news reached us. The Greek army had been decimated, suffering devastating losses. Soldiers who had once marched proudly into *Mikrá Asía* were now retreating in disarray. The word 'evacuation' was suddenly everywhere, as the Greek government scrambled to send ships to Smyrni, not for victory but to rescue its soldiers. However, when the army retreated, it was not in an orderly fashion but in chaos, leaving behind supplies, wounded soldiers and torching entire Turkish villages and engaging in frequent massacres.

The consequences for those of us left behind, the Greeks who lived in towns like Sokia, were becoming terrifyingly clear. Though our family home still stood firm, a sense of foreboding had seeped into its walls. At night, as the cicadas hummed outside our windows, I would sit quietly in the dining room, pretending to read while I listened to my parents speak in low, urgent tones. My mother, always the practical one, had urged my father to act.

"Emmanouil," she said one evening, her voice trembling, "we must leave. We have to go to Smyrni while there is still time. They are sending ships for the soldiers. Perhaps they will take us too. There will be safety in Smyrni, among our own people."

My father, however, was resolute in his belief that our family would be spared the violence sweeping through the region. He was a prominent member of our community, well-respected and well-connected. The cotton and tobacco fields he owned provided livelihoods for many of the town's inhabitants, Greeks, and Turks alike. He believed that his position would shield us.

"They will not harm us," he said with a quiet conviction that I wanted to trust but could not fully believe. "I have done nothing but good for this town. I employ their fathers, their sons, their brothers. I am not an enemy to them."

But my mother's eyes told a different story. "You think they will remember that? When the mob comes, when the violence begins, do you think they will care about the cotton or tobacco fields?"

I could see the conflict on my father's face, the tension between his pride and his growing awareness of the danger we faced. He had always been a man of reason, but even reason seemed powerless in the face of what was unfolding.

The news grew darker with each passing day. Messengers brought word of towns being systematically emptied of their Greek populations, of homes set ablaze, and of unspeakable violence enacted on those who resisted. Refugees from the interior passed along the outskirts of Sokia in ragged groups, making their way towards the coast, their belongings reduced to whatever they could carry. They spoke of the advancing Turkish forces, of looting and slaughter.

"It is not just the army they are driving out," they told us. "It is us, all of us."

For the first time in my life, I saw my father falter.

We could feel the shift in the air. Fear had spread through the very heart of our community. The fragile peace that had once bound us together was crumbling. It was no longer about pride or ideals. It was about survival. The fear was not just a passing thought; it was a constant presence. Would the Turks come for us next? Would they show mercy, or would they carry out the same terror they had visited upon the other Greek communities in the region?

It was not long before those fears became reality. The Turkish forces were now sweeping through towns, and the Greeks in Sokia gathered, speaking of escape, of where to go when the terror reached us. We already knew the fate of those left behind—violence without mercy. Fear hung heavy in the air, etched on every face I saw. We were no longer safe. The dream of reclaiming the land of our ancestors, the lands of Ionia, had vanished, leaving only a darker truth. Survival was all that remained.

I remember looking at my father, his face a mask of worry, his silence heavier than words could ever be. He had long feared the cost of the *Megáli Idéa*, but now a new dread had taken its place. What would follow? Would we be exposed to the vengeance of the Turks? In towns like Sokia, we could only wait, knowing deep down that the worst was yet to come.

By the beginning of September, the stories we began hearing were harrowing, the kind of news that made your heart race and your stomach turn. Greeks were fleeing for their lives. They spoke of Turkish soldiers swarming the streets, houses set alight, families running with nothing but the clothes on their backs, driven out by terror, killings, and unspeakable cruelty. Their words were a grim preview of what might come to us.

Tensions between Greeks and Turks, had begun to boil over in our town. Shops owned by Greek families were vandalised under the cover of darkness. Turks who had once greeted us warmly on the streets now avoided eye contact, their silence deafening. The world we had known was unravelling, just as my father had feared.

For me, the fear came in waves, moments when it hit so strongly that I struggled to breathe, followed by periods of numb disbelief. How could this be happening? How could everything we had known and built crumble so quickly? I thought of Persephone in the kitchen, of our beloved house, of the festivals and traditions that had filled my childhood with joy. Would all of it be erased?

The arguments between my parents grew sharper. My mother's urgency increased with each new piece of information that reached us, while my father clung to his belief that staying was the safer choice.

"What would it say to the people here if I and the other men of prominence ran away?" he said one night, his voice heavy with frustration. "I cannot abandon everything we have built, everything our family stands for."

But my mother's patience had worn thin. "What good will it do to stand on principle if we are not alive to defend it?" she snapped. "Think of the children, Emmanouil. Think of their future."

Her words struck a chord with me. I wanted to speak, to tell them I didn't care about the house, the cotton fields, or even Sokia itself. All I wanted was for us to be safe, to stay together as a family. But I stayed silent, too afraid to insert myself into a conversation so weighted with consequence.

Smyrni was a beacon of hope in my mother's mind, a place where she believed we could find safety. But even Smyrni, we were hearing, was becoming a city under siege. The Greek army's retreat had turned it into a final, desperate refuge, and the Turkish forces were closing in.

Still, my mother believed that in Smyrni we would find strength in numbers. "There are ships in Smyrni," she said to my father. "If the worst happens, we will have a way to escape. Here, we will have nothing."

But my father could not bring himself to leave. He was too tied to the land, to the life he had built. I wondered if it was pride, or denial, or a mixture of both that kept him rooted in place.

The turning point came one hot, stifling evening when a messenger arrived with news from Aidíni, a town close to Sokia. It had fallen to the advancing Turkish forces. Entire neighbourhoods had been destroyed. Its Greek population had either fled or those who had remained had been brutally slaughtered. The messenger, a boy not much older than I, was pale and trembling as he recounted the news to my father. His words painted a picture of chaos and terror, a world we could no longer pretend was not coming for us.

The men of Sökeli Cafer Efe, the feared leader of the *Zevbekides*, together with the Kuva-yi Milliye—the irregular fighters we called *Tsetes*—pushed forward to reclaim their land. By September 1922, these fighters swept into Sokia, bringing with them the same violence and retribution that had already scarred neighbouring towns. Some hailed them as liberators, but to us Greeks, they were harbingers of doom. These fighters, hardened by years of conflict, had already built a reputation for ferocity, and now, with victory on their side, they wielded their power unchecked.

Retribution followed swiftly. Greek residents, including families like ours, suddenly found themselves caught in the crossfire of a bitter and vengeful struggle. They were agents of a harsh reckoning, an unforgiving force that sealed the fate of those who called Sokia home. Homes were abandoned in haste, families fled into the night, and the streets echoed with the chaos of a community being torn apart. The defeat of the Greek army brought with it a new chapter in our lives. It was one filled with sorrow and loss, displacement and the breaking of long-standing communities. The memories of those days remain vivid, a reminder of the complexities and human cost of war.

CHAPTER THREE

I will never forget the day their shadow fell over our lives. It was the *Tsetes* on everyone's lips, wielding vengeance like a blade. They rounded up those they deemed responsible for the years of Greek presence in the region. My father was a landowner, a man respected for his integrity and fairness. But that mattered little to these men. For them, he and the others represented symbols of a community that no longer had a place in this land. To them, they were simply Greek, and for that alone, they were condemned. They called themselves heroes of the Turkish cause, but to me, they will always be murderers, and the scars they left on my heart have never faded.

That night, my father sat for hours, his head buried in his hands. Despair filled the surrounding silence. He had waited too long, clinging to the false hope that our family would be spared, and now the heaviness of his mistake bore down on him.

My mother did not speak, but I could see the tension in her jaw, the restrained 'I told you so' that she did not dare voice. When my father finally looked up, his face was pale, his expression one of resignation.

"We will go," he said quietly. "Pack only what we need."

Relief washed over me, but it was tinged with fear. The journey to Smyrni would not be easy, and even if we made it there, safety was not guaranteed. Still, it was a decision, a plan, and for the first time in weeks, I felt a flicker of hope.

Yet, even as we made plans to leave the following morning, it would soon become clear that time would not be on our side.

I could feel the weight of our situation pressing down on me. My father had always been our strength, our protector. But now, even he was powerless against the tide of history. The war had turned against us, and the dream of a greater Greece had become a nightmare. Our home, our land, everything we had known and loved, it was all slipping away. And though my father tried to shield us from the worst of his fears, I could see the truth in his eyes.

We were out of time.

On the 3rd of September, a day after the messenger's warning, the storm we all feared broke over us with unrelenting fury. It began with an urgent knocking on the door, one that sent chills through the house. It was Kerem, a Turkish boy who worked in my father's cotton fields, his face pale and his eyes wide with fear. He looked too young to be burdened with the weight of the news he carried.

"Emmanouil bey," he stammered, his voice shaking as he hastily stepped inside. "You must leave. You must hide. The Turks are coming for you. The order has been given by the Kuva-yi Milliye."

My father stood rooted to the spot, his face impassive even as the rest of us stared at the boy in horror. "Who told you this, Kerem?" he asked quietly.

"My father," the boy replied, his eyes wide with horror. "He heard it being spoken of, and he sent me to come here quickly to warn you."

"You must go, Emmanouil," my mother pleaded, her voice breaking. "Leave for Smyrni or Samos before it is too late."

But my father could only stare at her incredulously, his jaw tight. "Do you truly believe I would leave you here, alone with four children, to save myself? Do you understand what they would do to you if they came and found me gone? They would slaughter you all!"

His resolve was unshakable. He sent Kerem away with words of gratitude and a gold coin, a gesture of kindness even in the face of impending doom. The rest of us, though, were paralysed by dread, the air in the house heavy with fear.

Only two hours later, as we were preparing ourselves to leave, the nightmare began. We were gathered in the main room when we heard the unmistakable clatter of boots on cobblestones, the harsh, clipped commands shouted in Turkish. My father went to stand by the door, his back straight, his face a mask of calm determination. He told us to stay inside, to stay quiet.

But it was too late.

The Kuva-yi Milliye, burst through the door, their rifles slung across their shoulders, barking their orders, their voices cold, unfeeling. I could see my father visibly tense, bracing against the force that was about to rip through our world.

They told him to stand aside. I could see the moment he hesitated, the slight tremor in his hand as he gripped the doorframe. But he obeyed, stepping aside, his eyes darting quickly to my mother and to us, his children. His entire body seemed taut with the need to protect us, to shield us from what was coming, but there were too many of them, their intent clear.

He stepped aside, his hands raised slightly in a gesture of compliance. "There is no need for violence," he said in Turkish, his voice steady.

They ignored him and pushed past him, boots heavy against the wooden floor. He followed, his face pale with terror as he desperately tried to hold on to some semblance of control, but the chaos was already taking over. He didn't know what they were going to do, didn't know what cruelty awaited us in the hands of these men.

We stood to the side and watched helplessly as they rifled through drawers, overturned chairs, and ripped down curtains. It was then that one of them, his face hard as stone, turned to him with a cruel smile. *"Emmanouil Ndaousani, seni tutuklamamıza dair bir emir var!"* Emmanouil Ndaousani, there is an order for us to arrest you!" he said, his tone official, emotionless, and menacing. "You will come with us."

My father's face drained of what little colour remained. He took a step back, the enormity of the words sinking in slowly, as if his mind could not immediately process what it meant. Arrested. Taken away. Away from his family, away from the only world he knew.

In that moment I heard my mother's voice, raw and desperate. She was pleading, begging them not to take him. It was a sound that came from the very depths of her soul, a sound I imagined echoed in the hearts of every woman torn apart by war and loss. My mother screamed as they grabbed my father, their hands rough and unrelenting.

She rushed forward, reaching out to clutch my father's arm, begging them to release him.

"Please," she sobbed, her voice breaking with desperation. "He has done nothing. He is a good man. Please!"

But these men were unmoved. One of them shoved her back, and she fell to the floor. My eldest brother, Dimitri, who had been sheltering us, rushed forward to help her to her feet. My arms were around my younger sister and brother. I looked at Polyxeni. Her attention was fixed on our father. She stood frozen, her body trembling, too young to fully understand the cruelty unfolding, but old enough to know that something terrible was happening. There was a heartbeat of hesitation, her small frame shaking with fear. And then, as if some deep instinct propelled her forward, she ran.

"Baba!" She screamed his name, over and over, her voice rising in pitch, desperate and shrill. She lunged towards the fighters, her little hands trying to grab onto our father, trying to pull him back, trying to stop them from taking him away. Her thin arms wrapped around him, holding on as tightly as she could, sobbing, begging. She was so small, so impossibly small, against the towering figures of these men.

For a fleeting moment, my father's hands reached down, trying to touch her, trying to hold her, to comfort her in some impossible way amidst the chaos. But then came the fighter, a vicious brute who stepped forward, his face a twisted sneer, impatience flashing in his dark eyes. The rifle butt swung up, and then crashed down with brutal force. The sound was sickening.

The crack of the rifle slamming into her skull echoed in my ears, a hollow, nauseating thud that reverberated through me. Her scream, her heart-wrenching, terrified scream, was abruptly silenced by the searing pain. Her small body crumpled instantly, folding like a rag doll as she fell to the floor. The air left her lungs in a choked gasp. She lay there, still and broken, her dark hair falling across her pale face. There was no movement, no sound, just the sickening stillness that followed the violence.

My father began shouting in vain, his voice hoarse as he desperately tried to free himself from the fighter's iron grip. "Let me go!" he shouted, his voice hoarse with desperation. "Let me go to her!"

His body twisted, struggling against them, his face a mask of agony as he looked back, witnessing the scene he was powerless to stop. His eyes were wild as they landed on his daughter, his precious child, lying motionless on the floor. Agony was ripping through him, tearing at his very soul as he watched helplessly.

He let out a strangled cry, a sound I didn't think a human could make. His knees buckled as he was dragged away, his eyes locked on the lifeless form of my sister. His voice, hoarse and cracked, shouted her name over and over, begging her to get up, to move. But she didn't. She couldn't.

And then he was gone. My father, the man who had always been the pillar of strength in our family, the man who, to me, had always seemed invincible, was taken away from us.

My mother's scream was primal, a raw, guttural sound that seemed to come from the very depths of her being. She rushed towards my sister, and collapsed to the floor, gathering her into her arms. At first her body seemed lifeless, slack, and unresponsive, until my mother pressed her cheek to my sister's mouth and felt the faintest breath. That fragile warmth told her she was still alive, and she clung to her as tears streamed down her face.

"Polyxeni!" she cried, her voice breaking with grief. "*Polyxéni, agapiméno mou pethakáki, xýpna, agápi mou, xýpna gia ti Mamá sou.* Polyxeni, my beloved child, wake up my love, wake up for your Mama."

But there was no response.

I stood frozen, unable to move, unable to speak, clutching my younger brother Stamatis, who was crying, his face turned into the skirt of my dress. My sister laid in my mother's arms, her face pale, and her body still. A deep welt had risen, the skin swelling grotesquely beneath the blow. A thin thread of blood slipped from the wound, trailing down across her brow and into her hairline.

My brother Dimitri rushed to our mother's side, his face drained of colour, his emotions barely contained. Persephone was already kneeling on the floor, her arms holding my mother steady as she trembled with shock.

Dimitri dropped to his knees and slid his arms under Polyxeni's limp body, lifting her effortlessly. I saw the emotion in his eyes, grief, anger, and something else. Determination. The need to avenge what had been done to our little sister.

He carried her into our parents' bedroom on the ground floor. My mother and Persephone followed close behind him. I came after them with Stamatis, who clung to my skirt, his small hands gripping the fabric as though it could protect him from the chaos.

Inside the bedroom, my mother then went ahead of Dimitri, pulling aside the bed coverings. He then lowered Polyxeni down onto the mattress with a gentleness that belied his strength. Then he knelt beside her, as my mother straightened her limbs. His jaw clenched as he examined her injuries.

"She needs the doctor," he said grimly, turning to my mother. "I will go and see if Doctor Periklis will come."

Dimitri rose to his feet, his face set with grim resolve as he looked down at Polyxeni's pale, lying there so still, unmoving. My mother's hand shot out, grabbing his arm in desperation. She didn't speak at first, but the tension between them was almost tangible. A silent exchange passed as their eyes locked, both understanding the risks that were involved, but also understanding that there was no real choice.

She finally broke the silence, her voice low and trembling. "It is not safe, *pethi mou*," she said, her words heavy with fear.

Dimitri didn't respond. He didn't need to. The determination in his eyes was answer enough. He placed a hand over hers for a moment, a gesture of reassurance that felt more like goodbye.

They stared at one another for what seemed like an eternity, my mother's face lined with worry and his with steadfast resolve. Then, in a barely audible voice, she told him, ". I Panayía na se proséchei, pethakáki mou.. May the blessed mother protect you, my child."

Without another word, he turned and walked towards the door, sparing not a glance in my direction, his steps steady but heavy with purpose. I watched him go, my heart pounding in my chest as he disappeared. In that moment, a terrible thought took hold. I didn't know if I would ever see my brother again.

The moment Dimitri left, my mother and Persephone turned their full attention to Polyxeni. My sister's forehead bore the cruel imprint of the rifle butt. The swelling had risen quickly, a large bruise already darkening beneath the blood, a sickening shade of purple and black, as if the blow had marked her for death. Her still, pale form was a haunting sight, and the urgency in the room was palpable. I sat on a chair in the corner, my arms wrapped tightly around Stamatis, who had buried his face in my shoulder. My eyes remained fixed on my mother, who knelt beside the bed, with Persephone hovering close by. Her hands trembled as she gently brushed Polyxeni's hair from her bloodied forehead.

My mother looked up at Persephone. "We cannot wait for Dimitri to return," she said, her voice steady despite the fear and anguish in her eyes.

Persephone nodded and hurried from the room, returning with a bowl of steaming water and a bundle of cloths, herbs, and honey from the kitchen. She set them on the bedside table, then disappeared again, reappearing with the small brown bottle of iodine. They knew what had to be done if there was to be any hope of saving my sister. I had watched them many times as I grew older, tending to the cuts and burns of the workers, learning the old ways of Greek folk medicine and the improvised remedies they trusted when no doctor could be found.

"When a doctor isn't near, we do what we can," Persephone always said, her voice steady even in urgency. 'First, we clean it. If we don't, the infection will do what the wound has not yet done."

My mother soaked a cloth in the steaming water, wrung it out, and began gently wiping the blood from my sister's forehead, until the wound lay bare, raw, and angry against her pale skin. Her hands were steady, but her eyes betrayed her fear.

Persephone opened the iodine, and with careful hands my mother dabbed it onto the wound. Then she dipped her fingers into the honey jar, treasured for its soothing, cleansing strength, and spread a thick layer across the gash. Persephone crushed dried yarrow and thyme between her palms, their sharp, earthy scent rising in the room, and pressed the crumbled herbs over the honey. At last they bound it all with strips of clean linen, a fragile barrier against the unseen dangers that waited to claim her.

The remedies that had served us in the past now seemed fragile against the brutality of the moment. We had no way of knowing how grave Polyxeni's injury was, only that the force of the rifle butt could not have left her unharmed. Was her skull broken? Was she bleeding inside? We could not tell. The not knowing gnawed away at me as much as the wound itself. We were helpless, left only to wait and pray, while she lay there deathly still before us.

My mother then sat back, washing her hands in another bowl of hot water, and drying them with the towel that Persephone provided. She reached for my sister's hand, gripping it tightly as if willing her to respond. She then closed her eyes, her lips moving in a final prayer as she leaned forward, pressing a kiss to Polyxeni's cheek.

"We have done all we can," she said, raising her gaze to meet that of Persephone's.

"*I Panagía na válei to chéri tis,*" she replied, crossing herself, a common Greek expression asking for the Virgin Mary's divine help or intervention.

The hours stretched on, and by late afternoon, Dimitri had not returned. My mother began to panic, though she tried her best to hide it from us. She never left Polyxeni's side. Persephone brewed a pot of chamomile tea, its warm, soothing aroma filling the room, though none of us had the appetite to drink it. She brought a small cup to my mother, urging her to take a sip, but she simply shook her head. Her focus was fixed on my sister.

Despite their efforts, the traditional remedies seemed inadequate. Polyxeni remained unresponsive, her breathing shallow, her complexion unnervingly pale. My mother's face, lined with exhaustion, grew more anxious as the hours dragged on. By early evening, my brother still had not returned. My mother began pacing, wringing her hands as she whispered prayers, asking the *Panagia* to be merciful. Persephone tried to comfort her, but there was no comfort to be found.

When the knock came at the door, my heart leapt, thinking it might be Dimitri, but when my mother opened it, it was young Kerem, the same boy who had warned us the day before. His face was streaked with tears, his small body trembling as he stood in the doorway.

"Kerem?" my mother asked, her voice sharp with fear. "What is it?"

He hesitated, his tear stained facing looking up at my mother. "*Hanımefendi,*" he began, his voice breaking. "The Turks they have taken him too."

My mother swayed, reaching out to the doorframe for support. "No," she replied, shaking her head as if denying it would make it untrue.

Kerem wiped his tear-streaked face with trembling hands. "*Hanımefendi,* they took the doctor as well. They have taken them to the jail. There is no one left to help you."

The colour drained from my mother's face, and for a moment, I thought she might collapse. She stumbled back, clutching her chest as though the weight of his words had struck her physically. I rushed to her side, guiding her to a chair as she began to sob.

How much more could our family endure? My father was gone. My eldest brother, too. And Polyxeni, my little sister, was slipping further away with each passing moment. I burst into tears again, the weight of it all too much to bear.

The following day and a half passed in a haze of grief and despair. My mother never left Polyxeni's side, tending to her with a desperation that grew more frantic as the hours went by. But it was clear to all of us, even to my eyes, that my sister was slipping away.

I wanted to scream. My sister, the one who had always been so full of life and energy. How could she be like this? I wanted to shake her awake. I wanted to tell her to stop being so still, stop being so silent. But the words felt as if they were stuck in my throat. I sat there in the corner of the room, feeling powerless. I closed my eyes for a moment and willed myself to stop imagining the worst. But I couldn't help it. What if her injury was severe, something we had no hope of being able to fix? It had been too long since the rifle butt cracked against her skull. We all knew it, but none of us dared to say it out loud.

My mother didn't speak at all. She just sat there watching, as I did. Her eyes stayed fixed on Polyxeni's face, searching for signs that she was still here, still alive. I knew she was trying to hold it together for all of us, trying to be strong, but I could see the cracks in her composure. Her eyes were red-rimmed, her face drawn tight, her mouth set in a hard line. She hadn't moved for hours, hadn't said a word.

"Mama?" I whispered into the silence. She looked up at me, her eyes wide. There was no calmness left in them. "What if she doesn't wake up?" I already knew the answer. We both did. Nothing was certain anymore. All we could do was keep waiting.

She didn't answer immediately. "She will be all right," my mother said at last, though her voice cracked halfway through the words. Her eyes didn't meet mine, and I wondered if she was trying to convince herself more than me.

Persephone glanced at me then, her eyes red-rimmed and filled with sorrow. She had not rested, just as my mother had not. While my mother and I had kept vigil through the long hours, Persephone had done her best to look after Stamatis, keeping him amused, answering his many questions, bringing him in to see his sister who was 'asleep'.

When my brother finally rested, she would return to sit with us in silence, her face shadowed with exhaustion, and I could only imagine the grief she carried within her. Persephone had been there when my mother had given birth to my sister, cradled her as an infant, laughed at her mischief as she grew. I had known her steady hands, her calm voice, her tireless care. She had always been a pillar of strength. Yet now, like my mother, she was a woman bowed beneath the weight of her sorrow. She endured, sitting with us in the silence, holding her grief as she had held us through so many trials, waiting alongside us, for a miracle, or for fate to deal its cruellest blow.

I looked back at my mother, still seated beside my sister, her hands never straying far from Polyxeni. My mother hadn't eaten, hadn't rested. I could see the fear etched into her, the way she fought to hold herself upright while grief threatened to crush her entirely. And I—what could I do? Nothing. Nothing but sit and wait, while my heart was on the edge of breaking.

We had already lost so much. My father. Dimitri. And now, the thought that we might also lose Polyxeni terrified me. What would become of us if that happened? My mother's heart, already raw and strained, could it survive another blow? I had heard stories of hearts breaking so completely that life itself slipped away. The very idea made my blood run cold.

There was nothing left for us to do but wait. Wait and watch as the hours slipped past.

Polyxeni's breaths grew shallower, her skin colder, paler than it should have been. . Her lips had taken on a bluish-purple hue. Her eyes did not open, no matter how softly I spoke her name, and her small body lay still, unmoving. I sat beside her, holding her hand, whispering to her in case some part of her could still hear me.

"Polyxeni," I said softly, my voice breaking with tears. "Please wake up. Please don't leave us."

I pressed my face against her tiny hand, letting what little warmth I had flow into her. Her breaths were shallower now, her skin pale and cold beneath my trembling fingers. I could only pray that my little sister would be spared, that she would open her eyes, and come back to us.

*   *   *

We were caught between our urgent need for Polyxeni's care and the terror of what might befall to Kerem. The young boy sending messages for us was risking everything under the looming threat of reprisal. Each gesture of help carried a danger we could neither ignore nor fully shield him from. And all the while, our dear Polyxeni was fading before our eyes, her life slipping through our fingers, a reality that pressed like a heavy stone on my chest.

I stood quietly, listening to Persephone's conversation with Kerem as he returned once again. "The priest? Have they taken him yet?"

The young boy shook his head, his voice trembling. "No, not yet," he replied, "but my father says it is only a matter of time before they do."

Persephone nodded gravely, then pressed some money into his small hand. She instructed him carefully, urging caution: to go to him, deliver this money, and convey her message. He will understand the urgency, she assured him, as if knowing that Polyxeni would not survive the night.

At that, tears welled up in his eyes and spilled down his cheeks. Persephone pulled him gently into her arms. "You are a good boy," she whispered, her voice breaking. "May you be protected."

On the second afternoon after my father's arrest, we were still keeping vigil at Polyxeni's bedside. I glanced at my mother, seated beside her. The anguish in her eyes was unmistakable. They stayed locked on my sister, her face drawn, the creases deepening with every passing hour. She knew. She had known for hours.

Her voice came ragged, torn by grief: "Please, my darling child. Please don't leave us."

But just as we surrendered to the inevitable parting, that she had left us, much to our astonishment, I saw her eyelids flutter. Slowly, my sister opened her eyes. They focused on my mother. Her lips parted, and in a faint voice came the sound of one word.

"Mama."

Our mother gasped in shocked disbelief, before falling to her knees and cradling my sister's cheek with her hand. Their eyes locked, and for a heartbeat, hope surged through the room.

"My darling child. Your Mama is here."

Everyone rushed closer, disbelief and hope on our faces, thinking this was the turning point, that the miracle we had prayed for had been granted, that our Polyxeni might live after all. My chest ached with a mixture of fear and longing, my hands trembling as I reached for her. I wanted to hold her, to keep her here, to beg the *Panagia* to let her stay.

My mother bent and kissed her face, then brought Polyxeni's hand to her lips, pressing kiss after kiss into her fragile fingers. Their eyes locked once more and the look that passed between them spoke of both love and heartbreak.

Then her lips parted once more. "Mama," she repeated, barely audible now.

And then one soft breath. A final exhale. Her eyes closed. Her small body stilled, utterly and completely. The hope that had gripped us moments earlier, vanished in an instant.

We knew then. She was gone.

It hadn't been the miracle we had all prayed for. What I had just witnessed, it was a parting. A final goodbye, from a daughter to her mother.

That brief moment had also been a gift.

A final act of love.

Then came the sound I will never forget. My mother let out a low, keening wail, a sound of pure, unrelenting grief torn from somewhere deep inside her.

It filled the silence, filled all of us. Persephone wrapped her arms around her, tears streaming down her face as she tried to offer comfort. But there was no comfort to be had.

I closed my eyes and allowed myself to grieve because there was nothing else left to do.

*   *   *

Kerem appeared once more at our door. Persephone quickly ushered him inside and then bent down to speak to him, explaining again what he must do. I could see the fear flickering in his eyes, but he nodded bravely.

With tears clinging to his lashes, he turned and slipped out into the darkness. I watched him go, my heart tightening at the sight of that small figure carrying a burden so much larger than himself, and I prayed that this brave boy's actions would not lead him into danger.

That night, after I had put Stamatis to sleep, my mother, Persephone and I bathed my sister. It was our duty, one born from love and grief, just as tradition had taught us. When someone died, the women of the family prepared the body, their hands moving with a purpose that was equal parts sorrow and devotion. This ritual was more than an act of care. It was a final act of devotion, an offering to the departed before they left us for good.

We used warm water, scented with rose petals and basil from our garden, to wash her body. The steam rose softly in the air, carrying the fragrance through the room. Washing her was not just about cleansing her skin. It was something deeper. It was an ancient ritual meant to purify her spirit, to free her from the burdens of this life so she could cross over into the next. My mother's hands moved steadily, but I saw the strain and the overwhelming grief etched into her face, her lips pressed tightly as though holding back a scream. She wiped Polyxeni's arms and shoulders with a tenderness that broke something deep inside of me.

When we had finished, my mother took a small vial of olive oil in which Persephone had mixed with lavender and gently rubbed it into Polyxeni's skin. Her hands shook as she worked, the oil glistening faintly in the lamplight. Lavender—it had always been Polyxeni's favourite scent. The oil wasn't just for the body; it was a way of honouring her, of preparing her to meet our ancestors. I couldn't stop staring at her pale hands, lifeless now, and the soft brush of my mother's fingers.

Once her body was ready, we dressed her in white. The fabric was simple but beautiful. It was the colour of purity, of new beginnings. That was what you did when someone so young left this world. My mother reached for Polyxeni's gold cross, the one she had worn every day since she was a baby, christened into the Greek Orthodox faith. She kissed it softly, her lips trembling, before tucking it back into the bodice of my sister's dress, close to her heart. I watched with a heavy heart, knowing that no matter how carefully we dressed her, she would never wear the gown of a bride. Her hair was brushed and arranged gently, as though it were to be admired at a celebration rather than on this sorrowful occasion, which was nothing more than a symbol of the life she would never have the chance to live.

My mother and Persephone smoothed the folds of the garment, their movement slow and deliberate, as if they could hold back the inevitable. In her hands, they placed a small sprig of basil, the herb of kings, meant to protect and guide her soul as she crossed over. Then we wrapped her in the white shroud, covering her body as tradition instructed.

When we stepped back, Persephone brought in the *thymiato*, which held hot charcoal and infused with frankincense. The resin burned slowly, its sweet, earthy aroma thickening the air. She handed it first to my mother, who swept the smoker over Polyxeni's body, saying prayers, her voice choked with emotion and unbearable grief. I watched as the smoke rose in delicate spirals, curling around her as if to carry her spirit upward. Then it was my turn, and finally Persephone's.

Polyxeni laid on my parent's bed, wrapped in the white shroud, her face calm and serene. My mother sat beside her. She whispered prayers, her voice breaking only once as she kissed Polyxeni's forehead. Tradition demanded that we stay with her body through the night, and so we did. We sat in silence, the air thick with grief, as the hours passed. No one mentioned sleep; it felt wrong, unnecessary. The oil lamp cast long shadows around the room, as we watched over her. My heart was heavy, my mind tangled in a host of emotions and unbearable grief.

But beneath that grief, there was something else, something dark. I could feel the anger rising in me, a seething loathing for that brutal animal who had taken my sister's life. The hatred burned hot in my chest, consuming me. In the space of a few days, I had lost so much of my family, and I could not forgive them—várvaroi, that was what they were, barbarians. I sat quietly, watching her, holding onto the smell, the silence, the fleeting sense that she was still with us. I knew it wouldn't last. Soon even that would fade, and she would be gone completely.

Outside, the irregular fighters patrolled the streets, a cruel reminder of the limits to our freedom. We understood we could not bury my sister with the dignity she deserved. There would be no procession through to the church, no hymns, sung as the priest conducted the funeral service, no gathering of mourners. They had already taken so much from us, and now they would take this too.

But my mother refused to let them take everything. Each gesture, each prayer, was an act of defiance. They could deny us the rituals, but they could not take the dignity my mother gave Polyxeni in her last moments. Amid our grieving, as we kept vigil for my sister, there came a knock on the door. We all froze, eyes wide with horror, as we looked at one another, and I could feel my heart begin to race with fear. Had the Turks now come for us too? For a moment, none of us could move, unsure of what to do. The thought was unbearable, more loss, more violence.

But when the door creaked open, we almost broke down and wept with relief. It was the priest from our church, accompanied by Osman, Kerem's father, and several other Turkish men who were long-time employees of our family. They entered quickly and quietly, carrying a simple coffin between them. My breath caught in my throat as they placed it gently inside. The priest bowed his head and offered his condolences to us, and the men did the same, their voices soft, respectful. It was a strange moment, this collision of grief and fear, but in the end, these were men we had known for many years, offering their sympathy, a fragile thread of humanity amid the chaos unfolding amongst us.

The priest's voice broke the silence, urgent yet calm. "We must hurry now, Mariegó, if we are to bury Polyxeni with any dignity," he said, his words carrying both reverence and urgency. He then directed his attention to Persephone, asking her to bring the *thymiato* so he could begin the funeral service.

My heart tightened as the men moved swiftly, lifting my sister from the bed, and handling her with the utmost care, placed her in the plain wooden box. My mother moved quickly and placed an icon of the Virgin Mary into the coffin. The priest began the service, his voice steady as he chanted the prayers, the words reverent and sorrowful as they filled the room, offering what comfort he could in the face of such loss.

Once the brief service was finished, the men turned to my mother. I could see in the depths of their eyes that they too were deeply affected by our loss. These men had worked for us for many years.

"Hanımefendi, we must leave now," they said with urgency, alert to the danger outside. "The Kuva-yi Milliye are not patrolling during this hour, but we cannot be sure how long we have."

My mother nodded silently, tears streaking down her face. Persephone, her face pale, stepped forward. "I will stay behind," she said quietly. "Stamatis is asleep. You go with Eftihia and be safe."

With that, those same loyal souls, the priest, my mother, and I moved towards the door, carrying the coffin to the cemetery. We moved under the cover of darkness, our small procession silent except for the occasional muffled sob that escaped my mother.

When we reached the edge of the cemetery, the men led us to where a plot of earth had been freshly dug. My heart was heavy as I watched my mother, fragile and bent with grief, bid her final goodbye. Her voice trembled as she knelt over my sister's coffin, her hands shaking as she leaned forward and pressed her lips to my sister's forehead. The words she spoke were soft, reverent, but I knew them by heart— "*Kaló parádeiso, agapiméno mou paidi,*" she whispered, the prayer for a peaceful paradise to her beloved child, for her soul to rest without fear. But I heard the sorrow, the brokenness in the words she spoke. "You are my blood, my soul, my life. I don't know how I am going to live without you. I will always love you, and I will keep you in my heart forever. Until we meet again."

I wiped my tears away, but they kept coming, faster now, as I looked at the faces of the men standing around us. They stayed silent, their eyes glistening in the dim light of the lantern they had brought, their expressions a mixture of sorrow and respect. The gravity of the moment settled over me, and I realised that even in their silence, they shared in this loss. Some of them looked away, as if unable to bear the weight of my pain, while others stood motionless, their grief written clearly on their faces.

My mother turned slowly, her face etched with grief, and beckoned me forward with a trembling hand. Her eyes, red-rimmed from the tears, searched mine with a silent plea. She didn't need to speak; I understood. She was asking me to say my final goodbye, to release my sister, to let her go.

The weight of that moment crashed down on me. I walked towards the coffin on unsteady legs, as if the earth itself was pulling me down. My breath came in shallow gasps, my chest tight, as I knelt down and bent over the coffin. The tears blurred my vision, but I could still see her face, peaceful now, as if she were merely sleeping, though I knew that was not true. I placed my hand on the edge of the wood, and then, I leaned down, my lips trembling as I pressed a kiss to her cheek.

"*Kaló parádeiso, agapiméni mou athelfí.* Good paradise, my beloved sister," I whispered, my voice cracking.

The words felt too small for the grief I carried, but they were all I had left to give. I stayed there for a moment longer, holding onto her in silence, my heart heavy with everything we had lost. Then, with a final tearful glance at her, I rose to my feet and stepped back, knowing that she would always be with me, in my heart, in my soul, never truly gone.

The men gathered around the grave began to move. I watched as they replaced the lid, sealing her away from the world, preparing to lower it into the earth. The weight of that moment pressed down on me, like the very soil that would soon cover her.

"*Aionía i mními,*" my mother said, a quiet prayer for her eternal memory, her voice breaking, as the coffin disappeared into the freshly dug grave. The priest offered final prayers as my mother knelt beside the grave, her tears falling onto the freshly turned earth, her sobs muffled.

I felt a coldness settle in my chest, grief, yes, but something else, something darker. And as I stood there, watching her lose her daughter and my sister, I wondered if she too felt the anger, the loathing that burned in me for what had been taken from us. For everything that had been lost to us in a single, brutal day.

Before we left the cemetery, Osman, Kerem's father, stepped forward and gently but firmly stopped my mother. His face was grave, shadowed with worry, and he held her gaze with a weight that left no room for argument.

"*Hanımefendi,*" he began, "it grieves me deeply to say this, but the Turkish soldiers march towards Sokia. I beg you to take heed. For the women who remain, those who have lost husbands, brothers, sons, there will be little mercy." He paused, as if measuring each word against the reality that loomed. "I offer my sincerest regrets for the suffering that comes to your people, and I pray you take every precaution. Do not linger. Go now, before the town is no longer safe."

My mother's hand trembled as she gripped his, and I could feel the urgency in his stance, the fear of what was coming pressing upon us all. The cemetery, quiet and solemn a moment before, seemed suddenly heavy with the knowledge of what awaited us.

When we returned to the house, Father Michael stayed behind briefly. His voice was low but firm, tinged with urgency.

"*Mariégio, mázepse ta kai fýge.* Gather your things and leave. It is no longer safe for us here in Sokia."

My mother nodded, her face pale and drawn, though her eyes betrayed the storm raging inside her. She said nothing. There was no time for questions or hesitation, only action. I watched as she left the room and with trembling hands pressed some keys into the priest's palm.

"Take these," she said, her voice low and strained. "The carts are in the barn and so are the mules. You know the men who can help us." Her hands trembled as she passed him the iron keys to the *stablos*, the outbuilding where the carts and mules were housed. The priest nodded, his face a mask of quiet resolve. His hands closed around the keys, but for a long moment, neither of them spoke. The silence between them was heavy.

"Father Michael," my mother continued, her voice tight, "gather together the women of the men who worked for us who want to leave. We cannot meet at the square. The barbarians are still hunting."

The priest nodded solemnly. He knew the gravity of her words. The town was full of both *Zevbekides* and the *Tsetes* (Kuva-yi Milliye). We had to leave, but we had to do so quietly. We would not gather where the eyes of the Turks could fall on us, where the rumours would spread before we could escape.

"We will meet at the outbuilding," she told him, her tone firm, resolute. "Just before dawn breaks. Speak to Osman. Give him this for the risk he and the others will take to help us to flee," she added, putting some gold coins into his palm. "Ask them to prepare the two carts. The smaller one to carry our food supply and our meagre belongings. Ask them to fill the clay pots with water. And the larger cart with the canvas top. The women must come swiftly and silently."

The priest bowed his head slightly. "I will make sure they are ready," he said, his voice low but certain. "They will meet you at first light. Mariegó. May God protect you."

Then I heard my mother's voice soften, almost break. "And what will become of you?"

He remained silent. We all knew what awaited him. Soon the Turks would come for him too. At last he spoke, his words quiet but steady. "My fate is in God's hands," he said. "For now, I must do what I can to help those who wish to save themselves."

She nodded, though I saw the sorrow in her eyes. In the brief silence, I realised she carried the weight of his fate along with our own.

CHAPTER FOUR

The preparations had begun. The priest would ensure the others knew where to go. They would be familiar faces, women who, like us had also lost so much. Our carts would be ready by the time the first light broke carrying our water and supplies, enough to keep us moving, to keep us alive for the first stretch of the journey. They would be pulled by the mules, sturdy and sure-footed, though I could not shake the thought of how long this journey would take us, and the challenges we might encounter before we reached safety.

I turned to my mother. Her face was set in a quiet mask of determination. Her eyes, though, betrayed the exhaustion of the last few days. The *Tsetes* had swept into Sokia, taking my father, my elder brother. And our Polyxeni, my beloved sister, had been taken from us in the most violent of ways. Now, we too were leaving. Fleeing for our lives.

We worked quickly, gathering what little we could into small suitcases. We moved with a sense of purpose that belied the chaos within us as we focused on the essentials—clothing, blankets, food to take with us. The clay pots in the cart would be filled with water for the journey and replenished where we would find drinking water.

Before long, my mother gathered all the valuables that remained—jewellery, land titles, money—items that had escaped the soldiers' notice when they had ransacked our home. Persephone joined her, and I watched as they pried up a plank of wood underneath the staircase, revealing a hollow space below. They placed the valuables inside, packed them in tightly, covered them with a cloth to protect them and then replaced the plank.

"We will retrieve them when the *kakó* is over," she told us. "We will come back for them."

Kakó. The word lingered in the air. The evil. Would it ever end? Would there ever be a time when we could return to our home?

I watched as Persephone took an extra precaution. She fetched a needle and thread from the kitchen drawer and carefully sewed pockets into the inside waistband and bodices of the dresses we would wear to keep the money close to our bodies and less likely to be lost or stolen. I watched as her fingers moved quickly and steadily, a grim determination in her every stitch.

"Just in case," she said quietly, not looking up. "If we need it on the way, or if we cannot return."

The sight of her bending over the fabric, weaving safety into every stitch, spoke of her need to protect what we had left. The thought of leaving everything we couldn't carry with us was too painful to dwell on. I focused on the quiet determination in their eyes as they prepared for what felt like the impossible. We would be leaving everything behind and stepping into the unknown.

Even now, *agapi mou*, decades later, the memory of those few days is still etched vividly in my mind. It was the time our family was broken beyond repair. I remember thinking how swiftly life could turn from hope to despair, how quickly familiar streets could become places of fear. And beneath it all, an unspoken knowing settled in my chest. Evil, once it comes, leaves nothing untouched.

As the first light of dawn crept into the sky, my mother placed a hand on my shoulder.

"It is time," she said softly.

And so, with heavy hearts and trembling hands, we prepared to leave the only home I had ever known, not knowing if we would ever return, not knowing what awaited us. But we had no choice. The world we had known was gone, and all that remained was the hope that somehow, somewhere, we might find safety.

At that moment we had no inkling that what we had experienced that day, was only the beginning. The storm that swept through our home would soon engulf us all, leaving destruction and loss in its wake.

*   *   *

As the day dawned, we prepared to leave Sokia behind. My sister's grave was still fresh in the earth, a cruel reminder of the loss that had shattered our family. There was no time to linger at her grave, no time to give her the mourning she deserved. The Turks had taken my father and older brother, Dimitri. Their fate was still unknown to us. That uncertainty weighed heavily on us and especially on my mother, but it was Polyxeni's death that had broken her.

Persephone still moved steadily, but she looked haunted by exhaustion and grief. My mother moved slowly, her shoulders hunched beneath the weight of the heavy burden she carried of everything we had lost.

Stamatis clung to his toy horse, too young to understand fully but old enough to sense the fear that hung in the air. The house was eerily silent as we gathered at the door, preparing to leave our home. My mother hesitated, her hand resting briefly on the wooden frame, as if saying goodbye to all that had been. Then she turned to us, her voice steady despite the tremble in her hands.

"We will make our way to meet the others," she said.

With heavy hearts and with what little we could carry, we left behind not just our home but a part of ourselves we would never recover. When we arrived at the outbuilding, there were women and children with bundles of food and blankets, preparing to leave. Their faces looked haggard. Each of them had lost something precious in the last few days. Husbands, brothers, fathers. Yet here they were, ready to face the unknown.

Amongst the group stood some elderly women who had chosen to stay behind, unwilling to abandon their homes, fearing they might burden us, or perhaps they understood they would not survive the arduous journey. Their choice carried a quiet resignation, a bittersweet acceptance of their fate mixed in with the tears and anguished goodbyes. For the young children, their faces were filled with confusion and fear. Some remained silent; others were crying as they clung either to their mothers or to the grandmothers they were leaving behind.

A debate then ensued. Should we head west to Kusandasi and find passage to Samos? Or should we go north to Smyrni?

Some argued passionately for the safety of the sea. "The islands are close," one woman said. "We can find boats in Kusandasi. Samos is under Greek protection."

But others believed in the safety of Smyrni. At that moment, it seemed like a city that promised refuge from the chaos that was consuming our towns. It was a place of commerce and culture, where Greeks, Armenians, Levantines, and Turks had lived and worked side by side. Smyrni, with its bustling port and elegant homes, seemed untouchable, protected, somehow, from the violence sweeping through the countryside. It was the crown jewel of Ionia, and surely, no one would dare destroy such a place.

"Smyrni is a Greek city," one woman said confidently. "The Turks won't harm us there. We can find shelter there until this madness is over."

My mother stood silent, her face pale and gaunt from nights without sleep. She was caught between two impossible choices. I could see that the only thing holding her to the thought of Smyrni was the faint hope—perhaps a futile one —that if the Turks did release my father and brother, they might somehow find their way there. That, against all reason, we might be reunited.

We clung to the hope that the port would offer us an escape. Word had reached us of foreign ships anchored in the harbour, their presence a reassurance. The women convinced themselves that these ships, symbols of European power, would intervene if the situation became dire.

"The Europeans won't let Smyrni fall," said one woman with calm conviction, as though speaking it aloud could make it true.

The British, the French, and the Americans, had consulates in the city, investments, and interests to protect. Surely, they would not allow its destruction. Beyond that, Smyrni was familiar. It was a city where Greek culture thrived and where many believed safety could still be found.

Yet as I looked at my mother, I could see the doubt lingering in her eyes. Perhaps she too was recalling my father's warning.

"Do you think the British, the French, or the Americans care about us?" he had asked bitterly one evening. "They will support us only as long as it serves their interests. The moment it does not, they will abandon us to our fate."

Finally, when the voices grew quieter, the choice was determined. We would go to Smyrni. We carried our hopes with us as we left Sokia, even though fear lingered in the back of our minds. Smyrni was where so many had gone to seek safety. Surely, it would be safe for us too. Or so we believed.

As the first faint light of dawn crept over the horizon, our makeshift caravan began its march. Two carts pulled by sturdy mules, formed the backbone of our journey. The first, heavily laden, carried our small suitcases, blankets, and essential supplies. Leather bags and clay pots of water were carefully stored to keep them cool, and the cart's wooden frame groaned under the strain. The second cart, shaded with a fabric cover, would be used as a refuge for when the children became too weary to take another step and to shield them from the heat that would soon follow.

The plains stretched out endlessly, broken only by the occasional cluster of trees or a distant village and the sound of the cicadas, which filled the air, their droning song a reminder of the oppressive heat to come.

The first hours passed in relative silence. Stamatis walked beside me, his small hand clutching mine.

"Will Baba, Mitsos and Polyxeni be waiting for us in Smyrni?" he asked, his small hand now gripping mine.

I hesitated. "Maybe," I said, not wanting to tell him what I truly thought— that our father and Dimitri were unlikely to meet us anywhere in the foreseeable future. As for Polyxeni? The weight of that memory crushed me. The pain of losing her was unbearable, and it would be a wound that would never heal. My father was in prison, but Dimitri's fate was still uncertain. They were gone, and so was any sense of normalcy for us. I wasn't even certain that they would still be alive by the time we reached Smyrni. I could not bring myself to put a voice to the truth.

As we began our journey, my mother, whose face had always been a picture of composure, walked with a strange, hollow look in her eyes. The weight of grief and fear seemed as if it was suffocating her, and yet, she did not falter.

Her will was strong, but in the quiet moments, when no one spoke, I saw the raw pain in her features.

Our group was small. There was Chrysanthi. Her husband Vangelis had been taken away in the violence of the past few days. He had worked for my father for years, and now he was gone. Foteini had lost her husband, brother and father, the horror that had unfolded in their home clearly visible in her eyes. Theodora, a woman with three children under the age of seven, had been dragged from her home as her husband was taken away. She walked alongside the cart, and the look in her eyes spoke more than words ever could. Each of us had lost someone, and every step we took felt like an eternal reminder of that loss.

Around us, the other women were equally burdened. Katerina, who lived near us, walked ahead. Her husband, Vasilis, had been taken. Her two older brothers, who had been working in the fields, were among those who never returned. She said nothing, but her heart, like my mother's, was heavy with the weight of loss. She had two young children with her, aged six and eight years.

Evangelia had buried her husband earlier in the week as the chaos had unfolded, as well as her father. He had been elderly, but the Turks had killed him anyway, claiming he was a threat simply for being alive. She, too, carried her grief with her, her eyes red and swollen from crying as she walked beside us with her son, who was only twelve years of age.

The women in our group showed remarkable strength and endurance. We talked to one another in hushed tones, sharing moments of conversation before turning our focus back to the road. For the children, the journey was especially gruelling. Their small feet kicked up dust, and their cries punctuated the silence. Some walked hand in hand with siblings, while others clung to the hands of their mothers. Those too young to walk for long stretches were lifted into the second cart, where they nestled among the bundles of blankets. Their presence was a reminder that their lives depended on the success of our journey. The older children bore a different burden. Their faces, streaked with tears, betrayed their fear and uncertainty. Yet they kept moving, fuelled by the resolve of their mothers.

The route we had elected to take was kind at first, winding through fields of cotton and olive groves. The road itself was a challenge with its dusty surface, and the journey was not without moments of despair. Sometimes it seemed endless, when the weight of exhaustion threatened to crush our spirits. But in those moments, the group found strength in one another. Whenever someone stumbled, a hand reached out to steady them with words of encouragement. When a child cried, someone would soothe them. The journey was exhausting, each step weighed down by the knowledge that we were heading into the unknown, with no promise of safety or shelter ahead.

Sokia was behind us now, the village fading into the distance as we pressed forward on the dusty road to Sazlı. The land here was open and wide, the plains stretching out before us, bordered by the distant hills. To our left were the fertile fields of the *Koiláda tou Maíandrou* Meander Valley, which were nourished by the river winding unseen through the heart of the land.

The mules pulled our carts, their hooves kicking up puffs of dry earth. Persephone and my mother walked beside them, murmuring encouragement that seemed to soothe the animals. Thankfully, the road was easier here, on the valley floor, where the path was level. At times, the wind brought us the scent of the *Maiandros Potamós* Büyük Menderes River, a cool and earthy scent that reminded us it was nearby, though it was hidden beyond the fields. We skirted its valley, passing by the canals and irrigation ditches that spread like veins through the farmland. Some farmers still worked in the distance, their heads bowed under the scorching sun. Some paused to watch us pass, their faces unreadable as they straightened to lean on their tools.

By late morning, the sun beat down on us mercilessly. The village of Sazlı came into view as we trudged along the dusty track, its cluster of houses small against the backdrop of the hills beyond. Compared to Sokia, it was modest, yet it had once thrived, its Greek population primarily farmers who tilled the fertile fields that stretched out on either side of the village.

As we drew closer, an unsettling quiet greeted us. No sounds of daily life reached our ears, no voices calling out, no clatter of carts, no bleating of goats. The stillness was unnatural, and the air felt heavier because of it. The women in our group stopped instinctively at the edge of the village, their eyes darting between the shuttered windows and the narrow streets.

"It's too quiet," said one of the older women, her expression cautious.

My mother cast a wary glance towards the village. "It is small. If something had happened, we would have seen signs of it. Smoke, destruction."

"They have abandoned the town," Persephone offered.

The thought of entering, even briefly, made us feel uneasy. The risk was too great, and our journey too urgent. Instead, my mother pointed towards a copse of plane trees near the village boundary. "We will stop there. Just long enough to rest."

We spread ourselves out under the trees, a welcome respite from the heat of the morning. Their broad leaves offered shade, and the soft rustle of the branches in the breeze provided a semblance of peace. My feet ached, and the sweat had soaked through the back of my dress. These moments of respite were brief, dictated by the urgency of our situation, but they were essential. Everyone took a moment to sit, their bodies sinking into the ground with sighs of relief. Persephone unpacked a few of our provisions—bread, dried figs, and walnuts—and passed them around together with cups of water to quench our thirst.

For a while, we simply sat in silence, the weight of the journey pressing down on us. The soft hum of cicadas filled the air. I looked around me at the women who sat there; some of them had their gazes fixed on the horizon. Perhaps they were looking for signs of hope, or perhaps they were remembering the lives they had left behind, silently mourning the loved ones they had lost and what could never be regained.

Though the shade and water offered some comfort, none of us fully relaxed. The silence of Sazlı lingered in our minds, a reminder of how precarious our situation was.

"We should move on soon," my mother finally said, her tone leaving no room for argument. The others nodded, and one by one, we began gathering our belongings. The plane trees had given us what they could, but now we would have to continue.

*   *   *

Agios Theodoros (Ortaklar) was a small rural settlement. The village, though modest in size, served as a waypoint for farmers and traders moving goods such as cotton, olives, figs, and grains along the valley's routes. To the east, the land began to rise, the hills dotted with wildflowers and shrubs. To the west, the plains opened wide, their fertile soil nourished by the nearby *Maiandros Potamós*. It was a land of beauty, now shadowed by uncertainty.

The town was a cluster of homes, built of stone or whitewashed, their red-tiled roofs blending into the landscape. Stone-paved streets wound between them, converging at a small central square where the rhythm of village life played out. It was a village of farmers and tradespeople. The Greek Orthodox Church stood at the edge of the square and was the centre of community life.

By the time we reached Ortaklar, the sun was beginning its slow descent towards the horizon. The air had cooled slightly, but the heat of the day still lingered in the earth beneath our feet. We had walked long and hard, and the weariness was evident in everyone's eyes, especially the children. The town was a shadow of its former self, and we soon discovered that most of its Greek community had already fled. The remaining townspeople were the elderly, who were trying to maintain a facade of normalcy amidst a backdrop of fear and uncertainty.

A man stepped forward from the group gathered near the square. He was slight and stooped, his back curving under the weight of years. A linen cap was perched on his head, and his face was weathered from years spent under the sun and age. He greeted us with a nod, his eyes kind but tinged with sorrow. He looked us over quickly, his eyes landing on the mules and carts.

"You will want to leave them somewhere safe," he said, gesturing towards a narrow lane that led to an open yard behind a cluster of homes. "Come, I will show you."

We followed him, and the yard he brought us to was small but orderly, with a low wall enclosing it where there were a few other carts. It smelt of hay and livestock, and the familiar sounds of mules snorting, and stamping greeted us.

"You will go to the church," he said in Greek, his voice calm and authoritative. "The priest and some of the women are taking people in. It is crowded, but there is food and shelter there for you and the little ones." He paused and then focused his attention on the mules. "I will see to these. I will give them water and some fodder. They will be safe here."

I could see my mother and Persephone exchange glances, reluctant to hand over the care of the mules, but his steady presence left little room for argument. "*Pigénete, íste óli kourasméni kai chreiazéste xekoúrasi, eidiká ta mikrá.* Go, you are tired and require rest, especially the little ones," he added softly, nodding towards the carts. "Go on now."

Relieved and grateful, we began gathering our belongings from the carts. The man took the reins from Persephone with a reassuring nod, unhitching the mules before leading them towards the watering troughs where a few other animals were already tethered. "I will secure them here," he called over his shoulder. "They will be well cared for."

As we made our way towards the church, I looked back once. The man was already at work, untying bags of fodder and pouring water into the trough, his movements practiced and efficient despite his age. The mules seemed calm in his care, their ears flicking as they bent their heads to drink and refresh themselves after the long and arduous day.

When we arrived at the church, we were greeted by an elderly priest, Father Athanasios. His deep, weathered voice carried a warmth that seemed to ease the weight of our long journey. "Come, my children," he said, his eyes soft with understanding. "Here, you will find others like yourselves. Rest, and we will offer you what we can."

The scene inside was one of quiet chaos. The stone walls, which normally echoed with the sound of hymns and prayers, now absorbed the murmur of voices—soft conversations, the quiet sobs of mothers, the restless movements of children. Groups of weary travellers had already gathered in the church, their faces drawn with exhaustion, their clothes dirtied by the journey. But there was a kind of solidarity in the air, a quiet understanding between us all.

In the courtyard, an open fire crackled, its smoke curling upward into the night sky. Around it, a handful of elderly women bustled, stirring a large pot suspended over the flames, and the warm scent of *fasoulatha*, bean soup, filled the air. It was a simple dish, but in that moment, to us it seemed like a feast. The elderly women had gathered what others had left behind when they had fled, and now they were offering it to us.

We were so exhausted, on the edge of collapse. We huddled together, passing the soup around, and sharing some of the food we had brought with us. For a moment, the sharp pang of hunger softened, and the children's spirits lifted as they were fed. The soup was thick, nourishing, and hot. We ate slowly, too tired to fully savour the taste of it, but the relief on our faces was unmistakable.

I glanced around the room. There were others here, families who had been driven from their homes, their lives upended by the violence and turmoil. Their faces, like ours, were lined with exhaustion and worry. For a moment, I felt the weight of it all, the loss, the uncertainty, the endless road ahead of us, but then, something small and fleeting would pass between us all. A smile, a word of encouragement. It was the language of survival.

As the night wore on, we settled into a corner of the church, the warmth from the soup still lingering in our stomachs. The children fell asleep, exhausted from the journey, their small bodies curled into tight little balls. We tried to make ourselves as comfortable as possible, though comfort was a distant memory by now. In that quiet, fragile moment, there was a sense of peace. It wasn't much, but it was enough. The kindness of the people of Ortaklar reminded me that even in the darkest of times, there was still room for compassion. And for that, I was profoundly grateful.

People began sharing their stories, of homes left behind, of the chaos and uncertainty of the road, and of the retreating Greek army.

An elderly man with a thick moustache and a mournful expression spoke first. "I saw them," he said, his voice heavy with sorrow. "The soldiers retreating, their faces hollow. They had no strength left, no supplies. The Turks were closing in, and they, like us, are just as desperate to reach Smyrni."

Another woman, younger but with an equally haunted look in her eyes, nodded. "In my village, we heard the gunfire in the distance, saw the flames as houses burnt. We knew it was only a matter of time before the Turks came for us, too."

Another elderly man leaned forward. "There are groups of *Zevbekides* who are armed and ruthless," he said, his voice grave as he spoke. "They have been attacking Greeks who are fleeing, robbing them, even worse. We must be careful."

The *Zevbekides*, or Zeybeks as the Turks called them, were armed groups. Some said their name meant 'young warriors' or 'the brave', though no one seemed to agree if the name they were given was Turkish or Greek. In quieter times, the *Zevbekides* were men dressed in their vibrant vests, baggy trousers, and heavy belts studded with weapons. They had stood against oppressive landlords and roving bandits. However, as the Ottoman Empire crumbled and chaos engulfed the land, their loyalties shifted. Bands of them turned to raiding, answering to no one but their leaders.

The Turks celebrated the Zeybeks in their music and dance in the steps of the *Zeybekiko*. We Greeks also adopted the dance as our own, its slow, solitary movements a reflection of dignity and pride. Even in the darkest times, their cultural influence was a reminder that history is rarely simple. Heroes and villains often wear the same face, depending on who tells the story.

Over time, the Zeybeks had become something darker. Some joined the resistance against foreign occupation; others turned to preying on the vulnerable, including refugees like us. In the chaos of those years, their name to me would always remain as a symbol of the barbaric violence that had overtaken our world. Even now, I can still feel the raw anger that burned in my chest, the hatred that took root each time I heard their name. They were once protectors of the land, but in our eyes, they became the face of fear, cruelty, and a reminder of how quickly men could turn into monsters when given the taste of power.

*   *   *

Our first night on our journey had been spent in the church, the cool stone walls offering a fragile sense of security against the uncertain world outside. Our group had huddled together, conversing amongst ourselves, until exhaustion pulled us into an uneasy sleep. Now, with the first pale light of dawn filtering through the windows, it was time to leave. The air was crisp, but we knew it wouldn't last. We needed to be well on our way before the sun's relentless heat slowed us down and drained our momentum.

Other groups were already preparing to leave. The low murmur of voices and the shuffle of hurried movements filled the space. Families worked quickly to pack away what little they had brought with them, folding blankets, and rousing their children gently from sleep, their drowsy protests soothed with soft reassurances.

"Let us go, *korí mou*," my mother said, her voice one of firm resolve as we walked together to exit the church.

When we stepped outside, the scene was one of quiet urgency. Some had already loaded their belongings onto carts, the creak of wheels breaking the morning's stillness, while the owners coaxed their reluctant mules into motion. My mother and I made our way to where we had left our carts the previous night, leaving Persephone behind to tend to Stamatis, who was still asleep. We moved with purpose, the weight of the journey ahead of us pressing heavily on our minds. But when we rounded the corner, we stopped in our tracks.

The carts and mules were already prepared and waiting for us. The mules stood patiently, their coats brushed clean, their reins secured to the post. It was as if an unseen hand had prepared everything for us while we slept. Even the water containers, which had been nearly empty the night before, were now filled to the brim. My mother gasped softly, her hand flying to her mouth.

From behind the carts, the old man appeared. His stooped figure moved with quiet deliberation. He greeted us with a nod and a smile.

"You have done all this for us?" my mother asked, her voice trembling as she stepped closer to him.

The old man shrugged modestly, his face calm. "The world is heavy enough for you without adding another burden," he said simply, his voice low and steady.

My mother clasped her hands together in gratitude. "*Efcharistó kire*," she said, her words soft but brimming with emotion. "You have been kind and generous. How can I repay you?"

The old man shook his head slowly. "There is no debt between us, *kyría*. Only the road ahead."

His words stirred something in me, a mixture of sadness and gratitude that settled heavily in my chest. I looked at his face, at the deep lines etched by time.

My mother undid a small knot in her scarf and drew out a small gold coin. She stepped forward, her hand trembling slightly as she offered it to him. "Please," she said. "Take this. For all you have done."

The old man held up his hand in refusal, his lips pressing into a thin line. "No," he said firmly, though not unkindly. "I have no need of it. Keep it for yourselves. The road ahead will ask much of you."

My mother hesitated, her hand still outstretched. "But—"

"Please," he interrupted gently. "Hide it well. You may need it. Remember, not all you meet on the road will have kind hearts."

My mother nodded slowly, pulling her hand back and knotting the coin into her scarf once more. Her eyes glistened with unshed tears as she murmured her thanks, though I could tell no words felt adequate.

The old man turned his gaze towards the village. "*To mikró mas chorió,* our little village," he said softly, almost as if to himself, "was once alive with children's laughter, women gossiping by the well, men singing as they went to work in the fields. Now it is filled with emptiness and the grief of those who have been left behind."

"Where have they gone?" my mother asked.

He sighed, the sound heavy with grief. "Some went to the coast, hoping to find boats to take them to the islands. Others to Smyrni, though what they will find there…" He trailed off, shaking his head. "I am an old man. I have lived through wars, famines, peace, and more. But never have I seen our people fleeing for their lives like this."

His words pierced my heart. Thoughts of my father, my brother, Polyxeni, the home we had left behind, and the uncertainty of what we would find in Smyrni swirled in my mind, making my throat tighten.

The old man straightened as best he could, his hands resting on the edge of the cart. "You should go," he said, his voice regaining some strength. "The road is long, and the sun will not wait."

My mother stepped forward and placed a gentle hand on his arm. "You have given us more than we could have asked for," she said. "May God watch over you."

"And over you," he replied, his voice soft again. He paused for a moment, then added, "May your journey lead you to a place where the earth is kind, and the people are kinder."

My mother and I each took the reins of our carts and began leading the mules back to the church to collect the others. As we pulled away, we turned to look back and saw the old man raise his hand in farewell. When we arrived back at the church, another group of women had heated milk for us to drink and *paximathia* (rusks) to eat, before we set off. The warm liquid felt like a small blessing as we sipped it, its comfort steadying us for the journey ahead.

*   *   *

The road to Ayasoluk, (Selçuk) was not difficult, but every step felt heavier as the day stretched on. The land around Ortaklar had been flat, its wide-open plains easy to traverse, but as we pressed on, the ground began to rise and fall in gentle waves. I remember the *Küçük Menderes* River, or as we called it, the Kaystros, coming into view just south of the town. Its waters sparkled as it wound its way lazily across the plain. When we reached its banks, we decided to stop and rest. We had been walking for hours, the dust clinging to our clothes and our skin sticky with sweat. Here, at least, we had water.

We found a secluded spot near the river, sheltered by a cluster of trees. For the first time since we left Sokia, we bathed ourselves and the children, washing away the dirt and weariness that clung to us. The water was cool and invigorating, as I scrubbed my body before changing into fresh clothes. This simple act brought with it a fleeting sense of renewal.

Afterwards, we settled under the trees to enjoy some of the fruit we had gathered during our journey, sweet figs, ripe apricots, peaches, and clusters of grapes that burst with juice as we bit into them. It was a small indulgence, but it lifted our spirits. The mules were led to the water to drink, their thirst as urgent as our own, and we then began preparing ourselves for the next leg of the journey.

The terrain grew easier after we left the river, the flat expanse of the plain stretching out before us, but the sun was relentless, beating down on us as we trudged forward. The sight of Ayasoluk on the horizon gave us a renewed purpose. The town was situated near the great ruins of Ephesos. To us it was Ayasoluk, the old name that carried the memory of Agios Theologos, Saint John the Apostle. The Ottomans renamed it Selçuk, but many people still used the older name. Ephesos itself referred only to the ruins, silent and abandoned, not to the living town nearby.

We walked in near silence, conserving our energy for the final push. As we neared the town rising prominently in the distance, we could see the the *Lófos tis Aiassoulóukis* Ayasoluk Hill ahead, with the *Kástro tis Aiassoulóukis* Ayasoluk Fortress and the *Vasilikí tou Agíou Ioánni* Basilica of St. John at its top. To the side, on the flat plain, stood the remains of the *Naós tis Artémidos* Temple of Artemis—just a few columns and scattered stones. As we pressed forward, much of the ancient city lay hidden in the valley, beyond our immediate sight. Our focus now was on reaching the town before nightfall.

When we finally arrived in Ayasoluk, the streets were a chaotic crush of humanity. Refugees like us crowded into every available corner, their faces weary and hollow. The town's resources were clearly stretched to their limit, and the makeshift camps that had sprung up in every available space left no doubt that we would have to look elsewhere for shelter.

We veered towards the outskirts of the town, following a narrow path as we left the noise and crush of people behind. The fields here were dotted with small structures such as barns, storage sheds, and the occasional house. It was near one of these that we found an outbuilding, which looked to be abandoned but was surprisingly intact with its sturdy stone walls and timber roof. The floor was lined with rough-cut wooden planks, slightly warped in places but serviceable. Inside, we found scattered signs of its former purpose—fodder for the animals, farming tools leaning against the wall, and a stack of wood stored for winter and oil lanterns, which we quickly lit.

Grateful for the shelter, we unloaded the wagons, carefully setting our belongings aside. We spread out what bedding we had, arranging it on the wooden floor to make the space as comfortable as possible. The mules were fed and watered, their tired movements matching our own. We then set about building a small fire just outside the entrance, using some of the wood.

That night we cooked some lentil soup, to which we added a few fresh vegetables we had foraged along the way, and the bread we had brought from a village bakery. We also had the watermelons we had found lying forgotten in a field. It wasn't a feast, but it was enough.

As the fire burned down to embers, we spread out on the floor of the outbuilding. The distant hum of the crowded town reached us even here, a faint reminder of the world's turmoil. Yet, for that night, we had shelter and food. It was enough to carry us through to the next morning.

It was still dark when my mother woke me, even before the other women had stirred. She whispered that she and Persephone would walk into the village to see what they could find for us and the children. They slipped out quietly, leaving me listening to the slow, restless breathing of those still asleep.

An hour passed, maybe more. The other women began to wake, rubbing sleep from their eyes. Someone coaxed the small fire back to life, and the smell of coffee rose into the damp air of the outbuilding. My worry grew heavier with each passing minute.

Then at last, they returned. They had been fortunate enough to reach the market before the crowds had begun to press in. They carried several loaves of bread, a large *kalathaki* of still warm mizithra cheese and milk for the children.

We sat together on the wooden floor, the walls of the outbuilding sheltering us from the morning chill. Outside, the town stirred to life. Ayasoluk groaned under the weight of so many souls, displaced and afraid. We heard raised voices, the creak of carts as people prepared to leave and press on with their journey.

Yet as we sliced the bread and passed around the cheese, sprinkled with the honey we had brought with us, there was a moment of shared comfort. Warmth from the fire, the softness of fresh cheese and the sweetness of the honey on our tongues, served to momentarily dull the press of fear and the uncertainty of what still lay ahead.

*   *   *

The sun was merciless as we reached Torbáli, just after one in the afternoon, and its harsh light seemed to accentuate the strain etched on every face around us. The town was teeming with refugees, a desperate, restless sea of humanity that filled the streets and squares. Women carried children who were too tired to walk, while others clung to bundles that contained all they had left. Men, their faces hollow with fatigue, hauled carts laden with hastily gathered possessions. The air was heavy with the mingling sounds of misery, babies' cries, voices raised in desperation, and the constant shuffle of feet on dusty ground.

As had been the case in Ayasoluk, we soon realised the town was not prepared for the flood of refugees passing through. We were part of a growing crowd, exhausted souls who had travelled miles under the scorching sun, some with nothing but the clothes on their backs and a few belongings stuffed into bags or onto carts. Torbáli, with its narrow streets and humble stone houses, was strained to its limits, its resources stretched thin by the influx of strangers.

The people there, kind as they were, could offer little. People were crowded into any available space. There were not enough shelters for so many, and the air was thick with the stench of bodies, sweat, and the unmistakable odour of desperation. The sanitation was poor, and the heat made everything worse. I remember the tension that hung in the air between us, the refugees, and the villagers, who were already struggling with their own hardships. Some of them helped, offering us bread or water, but there were no simple answers. We were all just trying to survive.

I overheard snippets of conversation, rumours of Turkish soldiers and *Zevbekides*, tales of violence in nearby villages, and the endless hope that Smyrni would be a haven.

"They won't harm the city," said one man. "It is too important, too many foreigners there." I clung to those words, letting them fill the void where hope had long since been extinguished.

However, the talk in Torbáli, was heavy with the news of the Greek army's retreat. It was hard to escape the sound of it. We heard words such as 'defeat', 'desperation', and 'destruction' so often, as though they were the only words that could describe it. The army wasn't withdrawing in any kind of orderly fashion; no, it was a broken mess of men fleeing for their lives.

We did not see them ourselves; the soldiers took different roads than ours. They moved through Ousakeion, Philadelpheia, and Magnesia, leaving destruction in their wake. Burned fields, smouldering homes. The land itself bore the scars of their retreat. Some villagers spoke of soldiers who had taken their last steps far from home and had collapsed on the roadside, too weak to continue, while others described the trails of abandoned carts and supplies scattered along their path. The Greek soldiers, once proud and strong, had turned into shadows of themselves, starving and exhausted.

Smyrni was all any of us could think of. The soldiers, we heard, were heading there too, desperate to reach the harbour and board the waiting ships the Greek government was sending for them. They would find chaos, we were told. Refugees were now flooding into the city, hoping to escape before the Turkish forces arrived.

But these were just words, passed from one frightened mouth to another. Surely Smyrni would be safe. Surely we would find shelter there with our cousin Konstantinos. I did not know then what Smyrni held for us, only that we had to reach it. Whatever awaited, it was better than what lay behind — or so we thought.

Torbáli, we soon realised, was too crowded for us. My mother and Persephone had pushed through the throng of people, searching for a corner, a gap, any space where we might find shelter. However, there was no relief from the suffocating press of bodies, each face carved with the same hunger and fear that we carried with us. We exchanged weary glances and made the only choice left to us. We would press on to Belevi, praying it would offer what Torbáli, could not.

The journey ahead was not long in distance but daunting in our condition. We gathered ourselves, tightening the scarves we wore on our heads against the sun and walked. The road out of Torbáli stretched wide, and it felt endless. Dry fields flanked us, their muted greens and yellows blurring into one another as our tired eyes fixed on the horizon. Persephone, always pragmatic, rationed water carefully, ensuring the children, their faces flushed with the heat, had enough to drink.

As the day wore on, the countryside changed. The rolling hills near Belevi rose before us, and the waning light, cast a coolness over the path that made the final stretch bearable. We arrived at the town in the early evening, with its stone houses and red-tiled roofs clustered at the base of the hills. The hum of crickets replaced the cacophony we had left behind in Torbáli.

Belevi, though small, was not untouched by the turmoil. Refugees had also come here, setting up camps on its edges, their presence a reminder that there was little escape from the tide of displacement. Yet the village's rural quiet and smaller size seemed to buffer it from the chaos we had encountered earlier in Torbáli. A few villagers stood watching as we entered. An old man, leaning heavily on a cane, informed us that the town was already overcrowded, and we could not stay. He told us about an abandoned outbuilding and gave us directions on how to find it.

We thanked him, but before we could leave, he placed a weathered hand on my mother's arm and asked softly if we had young children with us. When she told him yes, he nodded, the lines on his face deepening, and beckoned her and Persephone to follow.

He led them to a small house just inside the edge of the town. In a low, tired voice, he explained how they were bracing for the worst. He was an old man now, and his own family had fled the advancing Turks, just as we were doing. His wife had died, he said, but it was the emptiness left by the departure of his children and grandchildren that weighed most heavily on him.

"I slaughtered some of my chickens today," he said, his voice rough with sorrow, almost breaking. "I kept a few for those who might reach the town later, though by now most of what we had is gone. Take these. Feed yourselves and the little ones, while we still have something to offer you."

Much to my mother's shock, he handed over several chickens, but he refused to accept payment. His voice was gruff, but his generous offer of shelter and food was a kindness we gratefully accepted.

Once again, we made our way towards the outskirts of the town. We were exhausted in every sense of the word, mentally, physically, and emotionally. Every step we took felt heavier than the last. Just when we thought we could not go on any longer, Persephone, who had been walking a little ahead of the group, paused and turned back towards us. She pointed to something off in the distance, a cluster of trees partially obscuring what looked like the outline of a building.

"There," she said, her voice carrying a note of urgency.

We watched as she made her way towards it, weaving through the shrubs and brittle grasses that lined the path. We watched as she pushed open the wooden door and stepped inside to inspect it.

"It is clean," she called back, relief evident in her tone.

"Let us move on and see if we can find the road that leads to it," said my mother. I could hear the tension in her voice ease as she exchanged a glance with me.

We walked further up the road, and sure enough, we found it. A narrow, well-worn track, wound its way towards the outbuilding. As we drew closer, the structure came into view. It was small but intact, with sturdy walls and a pitched roof that had withstood the years surprisingly well. When I stepped inside, I saw what Persephone had meant. The interior, though bare, was serviceable, with smooth stone floors that had been swept clean, and there was a faint smell of wood and earth rather than rot or decay. Outside, just a short distance from the building, was a small stone well.

That night, we built a small fire to cook with, the flames flickering in the dark as we gathered around it. We were all so tired of soup, and the thought of something different lifted our spirits. Using some of the oil we had brought with us, we fried the chicken and boiled some rice, savouring the aroma as it filled the air. Afterwards, we finished our meal with some fruit, a welcome treat that added a bit of sweetness to the evening.

Exhausted, the children were the first to fall asleep. The rest of us sat in the quiet, the crackle of the fire the only sound, each of us lost in our thoughts, but grateful for the small comfort we had found. When I finally took myself off to sleep, the hardness and chill of the stone floor seeped into my body. I lay there staring at the ceiling, until my eyelids grew heavy, and sleep overtook me.

I don't know how long I had slept before I woke up. The darkness outside was absolute, the kind that blurs time and makes you question whether morning is just minutes away or if there were many more hours of darkness left. I turned instinctively towards where my brother was sleeping, his small, rhythmic breaths a comfort to me. But as my eyes adjusted to the gloom, I realised something was wrong. My mother was not there. Persephone was missing too.

Panic shot through me. Where could they have gone? My heart thudded in my chest as I pushed myself up and crept towards the door. The air outside was cool as I stepped into the night. At first, I saw nothing but the empty expanse of land stretching beyond the outbuilding. And then I heard it, a soft, muffled sound carried on the wind. Crying.

I followed the sound until I saw them. My mother and Persephone were sitting just a short distance away. My mother's shoulders were shaking, her face buried in her hands as sobs wracked her body. Persephone sat beside her, one arm around my mother's shoulders. She was silent except for the tears streaming down her face.

"Mamma?" I said, my voice wavering as I took in her distress.

Neither of them looked at me right away, but Persephone's eyes met mine briefly. She shook her head, as if to warn me against speaking further. But I couldn't just stand there and watch. I walked over and sat beside my mother, my heart aching at the sight of her grief.

I had often thought quietly to myself how she had stoically held herself together over the past few days. Her grief must have been unimaginable, and yet she had never broken down. Her strength had seemed unshakable, her focus unyielding. She had led our small group of women and children with a calm, determined resolve that had left no room for tears or hesitation. I had seen her comfort the younger children when they cried out for their fathers, reassure the women when they spoke of their fears about what lay ahead. But now, under the cover of darkness, her strength had given way and her emotions had opened into a flood that needed to be released.

"Mamma," I said again, this time more firmly.

She raised her head slowly, and I saw her face. It was etched with anguish, her eyes red and swollen, her lips trembling as she struggled to find her voice.

"I made the wrong choice," she said, her voice sounding so broken she could barely enunciate the words. She looked up at the heavens, as if searching for answers in the stars. "I should have insisted we go to Kusandasi. We could have reached Samos by now. I have led us to this—this uncertainty, this danger. What will become of us? Of you? Of the children?"

Her words hit me like a blow, not because I believed them, but because I knew how deeply she believed them herself. It was as if the weight of her decision had finally crushed the facade of strength she had been holding onto.

"Mamma, don't say that," I said, my voice breaking. "You did what you thought was best. You've kept us safe—"

"Safe?" she interrupted, her voice rising. "Do you call this safety? Sleeping in abandoned buildings, not knowing if we will have food tomorrow? What if the Turks come after us? What if Smyrni is not what we hoped it would be? You have heard the rumours, thousands flooding the city. What if the ships won't take us?"

Her voice cracked on the last word, and she turned away, burying her face in her hands once more and sobbing even harder. Now, looking at her, I realised how much that choice had cost her. I didn't know what to say. How could I? I was just as afraid as she was. I had been carrying the same doubts, the same unspoken fears, ever since we left Sokia.

Persephone spoke softly, her voice steady despite the tears in her eyes. "Mariegó," she said, addressing my mother by her name. "You have done everything you can to protect us. None of us could have known what would happen."

My mother shook her head, her tears falling freely now. "It is not enough, I should have done more. I should have insisted we leave," she said, her voice trembling with anguish. "We never had any guarantee that the Turks would spare us irrespective of what my husband thought. I should have given him an ultimatum, taken you all to Samos and left him to his land and his fate with the Turks. But I waited. I waited for him to come to his senses, and by the time he did, it was too late. Now I have lost him, Dimitri, and my precious child Polyxeni lies in the earth in Sokia. Our family has been broken, shattered into pieces that can never be put together again."

Her words stirred something deep within me. I should have spoken up that day in Sokia, insisted that we make our way to the coast, to seek out the relatives that still remained in Samos. Something had warned me against Smyrni. Now, if the rumours turned out to be true, it would become a living hell, a place of death and destruction. What would be our fate if the Turks turned on us Greeks, seeking vengeance for what had been done in the wake of the Greek army's retreat? We had seen it already. In Sokia, we had witnessed firsthand the horror of retribution.

I reached out and took her hand in mine. It was cold, her fingers trembling against my palm. The three of us sat there in silence for a while. I felt the weight of my mother's despair settle over me, the realisation that she was human, not unshakable as I had thought, but fragile and desolate in her grief. For all the strength she had shown us, she needed support just as much as anyone else.

*   *   *

We had not travelled far from Belevi when we encountered the first group of *Zevbekides*. They were sitting by the side of the road in the shade of a cluster of trees, their horses grazing nearby. The surrounding air was thick with the smoke of their cigarettes as they relaxed. They were only a few men, rugged and wild in their appearance. Their clothes were rough, their faces weathered by the unforgiving sun. One of them, a tall man with a thick beard and sharp eyes, stepped forward from the group and raised his hand to signal us to stop. We did so and then watched as he threw his cigarette to the ground, using his foot to stamp it out with deliberate force.

My mother's face hardened with suspicion, but she did not flinch. We had heard the stories of them, their rough ways, their willingness to extort or even rob those who were unfortunate enough to cross their path. They were not soldiers, but guerrilla fighters, loyal to no one but themselves. They often appeared when least expected, and their motivations were impossible to predict.

"Where are you going?" the man asked, his voice rough, yet laced with a curious undertone.

"To Smyrni," replied my mother, her voice steady but guarded. "We had no choice but to leave our town."

The man's gaze flickered over us, assessing our small group. His eyes lingered on me for a moment, and I felt an icy shiver run down my spine.

"You are not the only ones travelling the road ahead," he said, his tone taking on a more sinister edge. "There are others like us who may not be as kind."

I could feel the weight of his words, but we had no choice. We had to keep moving. My mother gave a small nod, her gaze unwavering. "We thank you for warning us."

The Zeybek smiled, though it was not a reassuring expression. He seemed to enjoy the discomfort that passed between us, savouring the uncertainty we faced. But after a long pause, he stepped back and motioned for us to continue on our way.

"Be careful," he said, almost as an after-thought before leaving to re-join his companions. The road ahead stretched long, but we had no choice but to keep moving. Fear was a constant companion. We did not know if we would encounter other *Zevbekides* who would be less kind, less forgiving. We prayed we would reach safety before darkness found us.

We pressed on. Tension now filled the air. We remained vigilant, our eyes scanning the road, but none of us could have anticipated what would happen next.

CHAPTER FIVE

As the day wore on, the road ahead became congested. Families with children pressed forward, clutching what little they could carry, their faces drawn with exhaustion and dread. The cries of the little ones pierced the air—shrill, unending—each one a reminder of the desperation that bound us all. Our group lagged behind, overtaken by others who moved with frantic determination. For a brief while, the road fell silent, eerily so. Then, from the scrub and trees around us, another band of *Zevbekides* emerged. I can still hear the thud of their horses' hooves breaking the stillness. Fear tore through us. In that moment there was little we could do, except pray.

The first group we had encountered had warned us that there were others not as sympathetic to our plight and to be careful. But how could we be? We were traveling fully exposed to any who wished to do us harm. The road stretched endlessly before us, and there was no place to hide, no shelter to shield us from the malice of those who saw us as prey.

This time, there were more of them, at least a dozen, all armed with rifles and knives. Their appearance was startling, a sudden and jarring reminder of the perilous reality we were facing. Their presence sent a shiver down my spine, and I could see the terror in the eyes of the other women and children around me.

I had hoped, foolishly, that we might pass by them without incident. But as they came closer, they formed a tight circle around us, blocking the way ahead. There was no escape. They stood tall in their saddles, their expressions hard and unyielding, like wolves eyeing their prey.

One of the *Zevbekides*, likely their leader, dismounted from his horse and strode towards us with deliberate menace. His dark eyes swept over our group, lingering on the women and children with a mixture of disdain and cruel amusement. His lips twisted into a sneer as he spat out, "Where do you think you are going, eh? Do you think we will let you pass through here without paying your due?"

The others erupted into harsh laughter, their voices cutting through the tense silence like knives. There was something threatening about this encounter. These men did not just want to intimidate; they wanted to dominate, to humiliate.

Another one, younger and brimming with arrogance, sauntered toward us. His eyes roved over our clothes and weary faces, a smirk playing on his lips. "Give us all your valuables," he demanded, his voice sharp and cold. "Everything you have. Now."

We exchanged desperate, fearful glances. The air around us felt suffocating, heavy with dread. What could we offer them? We had so little left.

My mother stepped forward, her chin lifted despite the tremor in her hands. Her voice, though soft, carried a firm resolve. "Our homes in Sokia were ransacked by the Kuva-yi Milliye," she said in Turkish. "They took everything from us, our money, our jewellery. All we have left are the clothes on our backs and the little we carry in the carts."

The leader scoffed and took another step closer to her, his breath hot and foul as he loomed over her. "Lies," he growled, his voice low and dangerous. "Everyone has something. You expect me to believe you have nothing?" His gaze darted to the other women, cold and calculating, searching for valuables.

The women around me began to cry softly, their quiet sobs a counterpoint to the mocking jeers of the *Zevbekides*. The children clung to their mothers, their wide eyes filled with fear. We were completely at their mercy—unarmed, defenceless, and utterly powerless. And they knew it.

I knew we had to speak up, to protect what little dignity we had left. It was my mother who spoke up once more, her voice firm and resolute. In Turkish, she said, "You have already taken everything from us, our husbands, our sons, our livelihoods, our homes. We have nothing left but what you see now."

For a moment, there was silence. The leader, his rugged face framed by the distinct headscarf and moustache, scoffed with bitter anger. "Your brutal Greek army did the same," he growled, his voice laced with bitterness. "Do you think we have forgotten the villages they burned, the men, women, and children they slaughtered? An eye for an eye, that is the saying, is it not?"

He stepped forward, his hand resting on the hilt of his yataghan, its curve sharp and menacing, his movements slow and deliberate. His voice grew louder, cutting through the air like a blade. "You stand here crying for mercy, but where was your mercy when your Greek dogs slaughtered our people, took our land, and burned our mosques? What you deserve, what you all deserve, is the same. We should exact upon you what your men did to our women."

His words hung heavy in the air, laden with blame and bitterness. But he wasn't finished. His voice grew sharper, dripping with venom as he gestured toward us, his eyes narrowing with accusation. "And why should we show you mercy? Your Greek dogs slaughtered our people without hesitation. You, the women, did you not cheer as they marched through our lands, as our homes burned to ash? Tell me, why should we not exact the same punishment on you?"

A murmur rippled through them, their eyes dark with agreement. One of them spat on the ground near us, his lip curling with contempt. My mother stood frozen yet resolute. She drew in a shaky breath, her gaze unwavering despite the weight of their hatred. "We are from Sokia," she said, her voice steady. "We lived side by side with our Turkish neighbours. We did not cheer on our soldiers as they did in Smyrni or elsewhere. Nor did we condone their behaviour. The lands they sought to conquer did not belong to us. Ashes should not have been left in their wake."

I recognised the words my mother spoke. They were my father's words, words he had uttered to us in the quiet of our home long before this moment. Her voice carried his sorrow, his conviction, as if he stood there speaking through her. But the Zeybek, with his rugged face and unyielding eyes, merely smirked at her.

"You are wise," he sneered, his voice thick with mockery, "for a *gâvur karı.*" The insult—a slur for a Christian woman—hung in the air, vile and stinging.

He turned his eyes to the rest of the women, sweeping over us like a blade. "What kind of women are you?" he asked, his tone sharp and cruel. "Are you the kind who prayed for our men as they died? Did you weep for the children left behind or the women they raped and murdered?"

His gaze landed on one of the women who clutched her terrified child tightly to her, her face pale with terror. "And you," he said, his voice cold and cutting. "Do you cry now because you are afraid? Or because you are ashamed? Tell me, did you sing songs of victory when our people bled, or did you stay silent, letting it happen? Silence is not innocence. It is the same as betrayal."

He stepped back and laughed, a sound as bitter as gall. "Look at you all," he sneered, his tone filled with derision. "You clutch your children as if they will save you. You stand here trembling and call yourselves mothers, wives, daughters, but where were your tears for us? Where was your pity then? Do not think you are any better than the men who fought for your king. You are no different. Hypocrites, the lot of you."

The words were meant to crush what little dignity we had left. My mother, though, stood tall, her shoulders squared despite the tremor in her hands.

But he didn't stop there. He stepped closer, towering over my mother as his smirk twisted into something uglier. "Your kind," he spat, his words dripping with disdain, "you think you are different because you lived with Turks in Sokia? You think that makes you innocent? Bah! You are all the same. Arrogant *gâvurlar,* poisoning our land with your churches and your foreign kings. You live off our soil, but your hearts are loyal to the ones who burn it."

His words were venomous, each accusation cutting deeper than the last. He paused, his lips curling into a sneer as he gestured towards a young woman clutching a crying child. "Look at you now. Pathetic. Mothers? Sisters? You have no men to hide behind now. Do you fight for yourselves? Or do you grovel and weep, hoping we will pity you?"

The words landed like blows, each one harsher than the last. I could see some women in our group clutching their children tightly, their heads bowed in silent terror. Others stared ahead, faces pale and drawn, trying to maintain what composure they could. My mother stood her ground, firm and unyielding.

"We did not take your lands," my mother replied, her words cutting through his tirade. "In Sokia, it was your soldiers who struck the first blow. They came into our town, into our homes and tore them apart. We prayed every day that we would continue to live and work in harmony, side by side with our Turkish neighbours." Her voice caught, but she pressed on, undeterred by the weight of his glare. "We did not choose this war. We did not call for it. We wanted only to live in peace. But it was your brutality also that left us with nothing. Do not speak to me of ashes as if you are blameless. We are not your enemy."

The Zeybek barked a harsh laugh, shaking his head. "Not my enemy? Then what are you, *gâvur karılar*? You stand here with your hands empty and your mouth full of excuses. Your soldiers thought they could march into our lands, and now you want to play the victim. You disgust me."

His face darkened, his smirk vanished, replaced by a sharp, volatile anger. Before she could say another word, he struck her across the face with the back of his hand. The sound of the blow rang out in the silence. My mother staggered but did not fall, her hand instinctively rising to her reddened cheek.

"*Kes sesini, gâvur karı!* Shut your mouth, infidel woman!" he barked, his voice a venomous snarl. "You dare speak to me of blame? Of harmony? You are lucky you still draw breath. If you were a man, I would have cut you down where you stand!" His chest heaved as he glared at her, as though her defiance had stoked a fire within him. "Your kind needs to know their place, beneath our feet. Do not forget that. Maybe you think your clever words will save you. But they will not."

He turned to his men, waving a dismissive hand toward us. "They think their tears will save them. But I say they cry crocodile tears, like all their kind. Treacherous, deceitful. If it were up to me, we would send them back to their king in pieces, one by one."

The laughter that followed was cruel and guttural, like the growl of wolves circling their prey. His words struck us like a thunderbolt. The women around me gasped and clutched their children, shrinking back in fear. My mother's face paled, her lips parting as though to speak, but she soon realised the futility of doing so. His dark eyes scanned us, cold and calculating, as if deciding whether to make good on his threats.

The silence that followed was heavy, oppressive, and I could feel the collective dread tighten its grip on us. In that moment, we were not just women; we were symbols, scapegoats for vengeance carried over generations. There was no reasoning with him, not when the wounds of the past had festered so deeply.

He merely stared at my mother, his eyes narrowing. He didn't care about the truth of what she had said. He didn't care about the pain we had already suffered. His voice was a low growl as he demanded we hand over our valuables, jewellery, coins, anything of value we should immediately surrender to them.

Then, with a nod of his head, he gave the order, and within seconds, his men began to ransack our belongings. They pulled apart our cases, tossing out clothes, blankets, those items that were meant to carry us through this journey; everything was scattered in the dust and then trampled underfoot. The women pleaded with them, their voices breaking with desperation, but it only seemed to fuel their cruelty.

And then the beatings began. Evangelia refused to give up her jewellery, and they turned on her with savage fury. They struck her without hesitation, their blows landing heavily against her fragile body. Her cries echoed in the air as she collapsed to the ground. Her young son screamed in terror at the sight, his small hands clutching his mother, trying to shield her from further harm. But there was no shelter to be found from these barbarians.

The men grew angrier. One of them grabbed Theodora by the arm and yanked her to her feet. "You will give us everything!" he screamed, his face twisting in fury before striking her across the face, sending her stumbling to the ground. The other men laughed, but I could hear Theodora's pained cries. The other women Katerina, Chrysanthi, and Foteini screamed as rough hands grabbed them, tearing away any jewellery they wore, taking whatever valuables they had on their person and then beating them without hesitation.

When they reached us, my mother took off her earrings and handed them over with trembling hands. The Zeybek in front of me fixed his eyes on the earrings I wore. I could feel the weight of his gaze, and I knew what was coming next.

"Give them to me, *Gâvur kız* infidel girl," he said, his voice low and threatening.

I hesitated for a moment. The earrings had been a gift from my father, and they were all I had left of him. But I knew I had no choice. He snatched them from my hand, his smile widening as he admired what he held. I held my breath, praying he would not find what Persephone had sewn into the bodices of our clothes.

Thankfully, they were too focused on what they could see to search deeper. They mocked and jeered as they plundered. Their hands were rough, and their glares felt like daggers. They did not find the hidden money, and I knew, that we had been fortunate. But fortune in that moment was relative. What little we had kept hidden came at a price. Their anger boiled over as their search yielded less than they had hoped. That rage was directed at us. My mother, Persephone, and I were not spared their cruelty. They struck out at us with fists and rifle butts, landing on us with brutal force.

I stumbled to the ground from a blow to my shoulder, the pain radiating down my arm, but I kept my lips pressed tightly together, swallowing down my cries. I would not give them the satisfaction of hearing me beg for mercy. Persephone, tried to shield me, but they shoved her aside and beat her as well. My mother cried out as they struck her across the face, yet somehow she stayed upright, her body swaying with the force of the blow but refusing to collapse.

All I could hear were the screams, the children's desperate wails and the mothers' cries of pain. The scene was a blur of violence, terror, and despair. I couldn't breathe, couldn't think. I sat there, watching as these men desecrated everything we had left.

And then they turned their attention to the children. One man roughly yanked Katerina's youngest son from her arms, causing him to cry out in pain. He held him by the arms, shaking him as though he were nothing more than a rag doll. The boy's terrified screams echoed in the air as he called out for his mother, and my heart ached as I watched on helplessly. His mother cried out for them to release him, but the Zeybek only laughed, while another one struck her violently across the face.

"Your children mean nothing to us," he spat out. "They are just as worthless as you," he added, before throwing the child roughly back at her.

The older boys were also beaten, and their arms twisted behind their backs until they cried out in agony. I will never forget the sound of their laughter—the cruel, guttural laughter of men who took pleasure in our pain. They saw us not as human beings but as symbols of an enemy they despised, and they lashed out with all the bitterness and hatred they carried in their hearts.

When their leader barked another command, the men turned their attention to the mules. These creatures had been with us since we left Sokia, carrying our heaviest burdens and helping the children when they could no longer walk. They unharnessed the animals and led them away. Moments later, the sharp crack of gunfire shattered the air. We knew instantly what they had done. The mules — those faithful creatures who had endured this journey alongside us — had been shot, their lives taken out of sheer spite, their bodies left behind as lifeless reminders of the Zeybeks' cruelty.

Tears streamed down my face as I clung to my mother, her body trembling with suppressed sobs, the weight of our helplessness crushing me. And as I watched them go, I prayed, not for mercy, not for us, but for something much darker. I prayed that these Turkish dogs, would meet a brutal death for what they had done to us. For the children who had cried in fear and pain, for the women who had been beaten, for the lives they had destroyed. Their faces, twisted with hatred and cruelty, were burned into my memory, and I knew I would never forget this day. In my mind's eye I could still see the *Zevbekides'* leaders face, but this time I saw his agony as he burned in the fires of hell.

They left devastation in their wake. The mules, our means of transport were gone, together with anything else they deemed worth stealing. The road was littered with the remains of our possessions, and for a long while, we sat in stunned silence, too shaken to move. The weight of what had happened pressed down on us, leaving our spirits crushed.

My mother sat on the ground with Stamatis curled up in her lap. His small body trembled as he buried his face in her shoulder, his cries muffled but heart-wrenching. She rocked him gently, her hand stroking his hair, whispering soothing words, but her eyes kept darting to me. The lines of exhaustion etched deeply into her face seemed even more pronounced now, her eyes shadowed with barely suppressed rage.

I sat nearby, holding my throbbing shoulder, unable to suppress my tears. She looked over at me, her gaze sharp yet tender. "Are you badly hurt, *korítsi mou?* Did that brutal beast injure your shoulder?"

"It hurts, Mamma," I admitted, my voice breaking under the weight of my emotions. "Why must we suffer like this? Why have we lost so much only to endure even more?"

The words spilled out of me, unbidden and raw. My tears came then, hot, and uncontrollable, as the despair I had tried to suppress overwhelmed me. My mother reached out and wrapped her arm around me, pulling me in close. She pressed a kiss to the top of my head, her lips lingering there to comfort me from the weight of my despair.

"*Kourágio, korítsi mou. Den échoume álli epilogí.* Courage, my girl. We have no other choice," she told me.

Her words carried the weight of truth, yet in her voice, I heard her own struggle, her own fight to stay strong for us. My mother, normally so restrained, had her resolve stripped bare by the cruelty we had endured. Her face, bruised and swollen, reflected her fury as much as her pain.

'*Na kopoún ta chéria tous gia aftó pou mas ékanan!* May their hands be cut off for what they did to us," she said, her voice trembling with righteous anger. Then I watched as she did something I had never seen her do before. She spat on the ground in contempt, as if the act itself was an expression of her unspoken rage.

Eventually, the women began to stir. We moved among the group, helping the others to their feet, soothing crying children and tending to the bruises and cuts left by our attackers. The despair among us was tangible. Without the carts, how would we carry our possessions? How would the children manage the gruelling distance to Smyrni on foot? We had another two hours at least to reach Ayrantzilar and then five more hours to Smyrni.

We took stock of what little remained. The water skins, by some miracle, had been spared, and for that, we were grateful. Everything else was scattered, trampled underfoot. Still, we worked methodically, gathering what could be salvaged.

With the carts rendered useless without the mules, we were forced to abandon them. What little we could carry was shared among us, distributed as evenly as possible. The stronger women took on the heavier loads, while the older children carried smaller bundles. I could see the worry etched on every face as we prepared to continue, the enormity of the journey ahead weighing heavily on us all.

*   *   *

The faint creak of wheels and the murmur of voices reached us. We turned as one, and there they were, a group of refugees, their carts laden with their own belongings. As they drew closer, they stopped, and two men stepped forward from the group, their expressions darkening as they approached us. Their eyes roamed over our bruised faces, taking in the scene of devastation around us.

"What happened?" one of them asked, his voice heavy with concern.

"The *Zevbekides* did this to us," my mother replied. "They took everything of value and beat us. Then they shot our mules and left us here."

Anger immediately burned in the men's eyes. "So now they are seeking out defenceless women and children to exact retribution for the wrongs committed by the Greek army. What kind of men are they, that they strike those who cannot strike back?"

"Brutal dogs and cowards," the other replied, his anger palpable. "We thought this road would be safe as the soldiers have not reached this far yet. But it seems the *Zevbekides* answer to no one but themselves."

The men then turned their attention to the carts, their expressions grim as they surveyed the damage. "We do not have a spare mule to tether to your cart," one of them said finally, shaking his head. "But we will make room for what is left of your possessions and for the children. We cannot leave you here. Are you travelling to Smyrni?"

When my mother nodded, he smiled in response. "Good, then we will travel together, and there are now many more following behind us. It will be safer that way."

Safer. The word echoed in my mind, its meaning elusive. Was anywhere truly safe? Were we unknowingly heading into the eye of the storm? Every step towards Smyrni felt like a step into uncertainty, into danger we couldn't yet see. Was this meant to be our fate, to stumble from one peril to the next, until there was nothing left of us?

I heard him continue, his voice steady but laced with resolve. "If they should return, then we have rifles. We may be outnumbered, but it will give me satisfaction to remove a few from the face of this earth."

His words did not reassure me. They only sharpened the edge of my fear. The rifle strapped across his back and others in the group seemed more a provocation than a promise of safety. Was this all we had? A handful of rifles, and a fragile hope of reaching Smyrni unscathed? If I stopped to think too long, I was afraid the fear would root me in my place, and I would never move again.

Without hesitation, they helped us load what remained of our belongings onto their carts. It wasn't much, but it was enough. Their kindness was a reminder that even amidst despair, there were still those willing to share what little they had. Without their help, we would have been in a precarious position, left to struggle under the weight of our burdens and the uncertainty of what lay ahead.

We reached Ayrantzilar in the early afternoon. The sun was high, casting a harsh light over the outskirts of the town, where clusters of refugees had set up temporary camps. The road was crowded and clogged with carts, animals, and weary travellers. Our group stopped on the edge of this teeming mass, close enough to the town but far enough to avoid becoming entangled in its chaos.

Persephone and my mother conferred quietly with the men, then ventured into the town to see if they could find food for the group. Despite the crowds, there was a strange sense of safety here—safety in numbers, perhaps. As my mother and Persephone followed the men into Ayrantzilar, I sat by the carts with Stamatis, trying to keep him entertained while we waited.

The wait stretched longer than expected, but there was nothing to do but rest and watch the ebb and flow of the throng around us. Everywhere I looked, there were faces like ours, drawn, anxious, and tired.

When the others returned with bread, cheese, olives, and a small sack of dried figs, plus a container of milk for the children, there was a collective sigh of relief. The food wasn't much, but it was enough to stave off hunger for another day.

We resumed our journey soon afterwards, with the last stretch to Smyrni ahead of us. The road became even more congested, slowing our progress to a crawl. The throngs of people grew denser, and the noise was almost unbearable, a cacophony of voices, the creak of wheels, and the braying of overburdened animals. The press of bodies on either side was suffocating.

We reached Halkapinar in the evening of the 10th of September. It lay to the northeast of Smyrni, a semi-rural district on the city's edge. A tram line connected it to the centre. Refugees like us, arriving from inland through Aryncilar, entered the city here since it lay on the main road from Sokia and Aidíni. The chaos had deepened. Refugees had surged into the city from every direction, fleeing the advancing Turkish forces. The streets were choked with humanity, a desperate tide of people clinging to whatever hope they could muster. Smyrni groaned under the weight of so many, all seeking passage to safety. Everywhere I looked, there was movement. People were shouting, their voices blending into a confusing din. Children cried, their wails piercing the heavy night air, families huddled together, their faces etched with fear and exhaustion.

The Quay was a chaotic mess. People jostled for space on the crowded docks, their voices rising in a cacophony of desperation and pleading. The air was thick with the smell of sweat and despair, the stench of unwashed bodies and fear pressing down on us like a suffocating fog. I clung to Persephone's hand, afraid that if I let go for even a moment, I would be swallowed up by the sea of humanity.

A woman clutched at my mother's arm as we passed, her eyes wild with fear. "Have you seen my son?" she begged, but she had no answer for her. Persephone pulled me away gently, her expression pained but resolute.

Was this the sanctuary we had hoped for? As I looked around me, all I could see was the desperate, frenetic energy of people clinging to whatever scraps of hope they could find. The area was heaving with people, women clutching their children, the elderly leaning on younger relatives, men shouting names into the chaos. Somewhere in the crush, we lost the others from our group. One moment they were with us, and the next, they were gone, swallowed up by the desperate tide of humanity.

*　　*　　*

Smyrni should have been our salvation. That was what my mother had believed when she had made the decision to bring us here. But now, as we pushed our way through the seething mass of bodies, we understood there would be no refuge in this city. We knew the route we had to take to reach our destination, but we needed to avoid the waterfront at all costs. We climbed inland through the *Elliniki Synoikia* (Greek Quarter) to the residential streets above the commercial district, then onward to the slopes of Pagos Hill and the Asansér area — the higher part of the quarter where our cousin's house overlooked the harbour.

Somehow, we managed to stay together as we made our way through the chaos that threatened to separate us. My mother held Stamatis close, her grip so tight around his shoulder, I feared she might hurt him. Persephone walked beside me, clutching my hand, her headscarf drawn low over her face, as if it could shield her from the horrors unfolding around us.

Shops and homes had been ransacked, their insides gutted. The streets were littered with broken glass, splintered furniture. Upturned carts and looted chests spilled their contents across the ground. Clothing and family relics had been trampled underfoot and told of hurried escapes and lives left behind. The air held the stench of ruin and death.

And then there were those who had not fled quickly enough.

Men lay sprawled in the streets, their bodies twisted unnaturally, their blood pooling in the cracks of the cobblestones. Some had been shot, others butchered where they had stood. Their eyes, stared at nothing. Their mouths frozen in screams that no one had heard—or no one had heeded. The bodies of young women lay on the cobblestones, their dresses torn, their eyes lifeless. And young children and babies, butchered. My mother's steps faltered. I saw the anguish on her face, the silent horror she dared not speak aloud.

She didn't have to. We understood.

The dangers we faced as women in this city were unspeakable. The memory of the *Zevbekides* still clung to us. Those men had swept through the countryside, leaving devastation in their wake. We had barely escaped them once, but there would be no escaping this. If the Turks set upon us, there would be no mercy. Persephone made the sign of the cross over her chest, whispering a prayer under her breath. I wasn't sure if she was praying for the dead or for us.

"We have to keep moving," my mother said, her voice tight and urgent, her grief and fear swallowed down.

We pressed on, half-running, half-stumbling from exhaustion. The further we moved into the Greek quarter, the worse the horrors became. *Tsetes* and Turkish soldiers moved through the city like wolves. I saw them yank women from their homes, ignoring their screams. Some were thrown onto the cobblestones, their fates, like the others we had seen, unspeakable. Others were dragged into alleys, their cries for mercy swallowed by the chaos.

But I had seen. And I would never forget.

A man stumbled in front of me, gripping his side, his white shirt soaked in red. He reached out as if to grasp me, and I screamed. Before I could react, he fell. There was nothing I could do. I couldn't cry. Not now. And so we walked on as fast as we could, past the looted shops, past the once grand homes, past the men whose lifeless bodies bled into the streets, past the women whose fates we did not dare to name.

Our only hope lay ahead, to get to our cousin Konstantinos home, if he and his wife Ourania and their two daughters, were still there. If there was anything left. If we weren't already too late. We clung to the hope that they would be here, that they would take us in, and we would be safe, if only for a little while.

Stamatis had begun to cry. But we had no other choice.

We ran. Through streets we no longer recognised, past the bodies in the gutters, past the women who screamed for help that would never come. The sound of gunfire cracked in the distance. I didn't know how much longer we could keep going.

By the time we reached his house, our bodies were numb from exhaustion, our minds dulled by fear. My mother pounded on the iron door, her voice raw as she called their names. For a long, terrible moment, there was no response.

Then, just as I felt despair creeping in, the door finally opened. Relief washed over me so suddenly my knees nearly buckled. Konstantinos stood before us, his face gaunt with sleeplessness. His eyes widened as they fell on my mother.

"*Christé kai Panagía!* Christ and the Virgin Mary! Mariegó? What has happened? How did you make it here?" His voice broke with disbelief.

His gaze shifted quickly, first to little Stamatis clinging to my mother's hand, then to me, exhausted and unsteady on my feet, and finally to

Persephone standing next to me, her face still pale from what we had witnessed on the streets.

For a moment he seemed unable to take in the sight of us. Then, shaking himself free of his shock, he reached for my mother, steadying her as she swayed. "Come inside, quickly, all of you," he urged, pulling us through the doorway before bolting the door quickly behind us.

My mother stumbled forward, and as she was pulled into an embrace, she finally collapsed.

"Thank God you made it," he told her, embracing my mother tightly as emotion overwhelmed her.

We were safe—at least for the moment.

Konstantinos guided us through the house, where his wife Ourania and their two daughters sat, their expressions mirroring our own fear. He led us to a sitting room where a single oil lamp cast flickering shadows on the walls. The iron shutters and windows had been closed tightly to shut out the world outside, but that didn't stop the sense of impending doom from creeping in. My mind still swirled with the horrors of what we had witnessed.

*   *   *

The scent of warm water and soap clung to my skin, but no amount of scrubbing could wash away the exhaustion or the fear. My mother bathed Stamatis, murmuring soft reassurances while he sat silent and pale, his small hands trembling. Persephone moved with a quiet efficiency, but the vacant look in her eyes betrayed her exhaustion.

We changed into fresh clothes from what remained in the small bundles we carried, to replace the dust and sweat-streaked garments we wore. Then, Ourania pressed us to sit while she served us *revithósoup,* chick pea soup, and set a plate of bread and olives before us. We ate in silence, too exhausted and too traumatised to speak.

When we had finished, Konstantinos gestured towards the small living room, where he motioned for us to sit. Ourania served us coffee. "Tell me everything."

Coffee cups were placed before us, but my mother's hands trembled too much to lift hers. Her face was pale, her lips pressed tightly together, holding back her emotions as if she feared that once she started, she would be unable to contain them. For a long moment, she sat in silence, staring at the dark liquid before her. Then, with a shuddering breath, she began.

"They came. We had been warned, but your uncle refused to leave us," she said, her voice hollow. "He knew, Konstantine. They were taking him away from us. He turned back to reassure us and Polyxeni, realising what was about to happen, screamed. She tried to stop them," my mother told him. "She tried, my brave girl, but they struck her. The rifle came down hard on her head, and she crumpled to the floor."

I shut my eyes, but it did nothing to push away the memory of that moment. The terror in her voice. The way she had thrown herself at them, grasping at my father as if she could hold him back with sheer will alone.

Ourania let out a horrified gasp, her hand covering her mouth. Konstantinos merely sat there, his eyes shadowed in grief.

"We knew we needed a doctor. The streets were thick with fear. Dimitri went to find help, but he never came back. The Turks took him too."

She swallowed hard, her fingers tightening into fists. The words hung in the air, suffocating, heavy. "Polyxeni lingered for a day and a half," she continued. "Her breath grew weaker. And then, she was gone."

My mother's voice broke. She could not go on. I pulled her into my arms, holding her as she wept. Eventually, she straightened, swallowing down her grief, forcing herself to finish.

"We buried her under the cover of darkness," she said, her voice unsteady. "The priest helped us, though he warned me. 'You must leave,' he said. 'They will come again.' We gathered the women, the children of our workers who had been left behind after the Turks took their husbands and brothers. And then we left."

Her hands were clenched in her lap, her gaze distant. "The roads were filled with others like us. The towns we passed through were overcrowded, every space taken by those fleeing for their lives. There was very little food and water. The locals helped wherever they could, but there were too many mouths to feed."

She exhaled shakily. "Four days.....four days we walked, and then the *Zevbekides* found us."

I saw Konstantinos stiffen.

She exhaled shakily. "They beat us, took our valuables, our clothes were strewn in the dust, our water containers smashed into the dirt. Then they took our mules and shot them." Her voice cracked. "Another group found us, and somehow, we made it here."

He sat still, his face turned to the floor, his grief and anger carved into the lines of his features. Finally, he exhaled, a sound heavy with sorrow.

"We thought if we could reach Smyrni safely, then the worst would be behind us." She paused, the weight of it all settling on her. "But we have seen the horrors. Bodies of men, women, and children." Her voice faltered for a moment, but then she continued. "We thought we would be safe here. But now... now I fear it may be worse."

"When we reached the city, the crowds separated us," I told him. "There were too many people, too much panic."

Konstantinos rubbed a hand over his face, his expression dark. "You thought you would find safety here?" He took a deep breath. "But you have walked into hell."

My mother straightened. "And what of Smyrni now?" she asked, her voice tight with fear. "Tell me there is still a chance—"

His eyes met hers, unflinching. "Panic set in as soon as news reached us of the retreating Greek army," he began, his voice low and steady. "Some sensed what was coming and tried to flee. Many gathered at the waterfront, hoping to find passage to the nearby islands or even to Greece itself. Others have sought refuge in smaller coastal towns, hoping to wait out the storm."

I clutched my mother's hand as he continued. "We would have done the same, but we held off, trusting in the news we heard that the Greek government had sought help from the British to broker safe passage to allow our people to leave without bloodshed. The armistice never came. The British have washed their hands of us. And that, I fear, has sealed our fate."

We stared at him, horrified. "So, they have left us with no protection?"

He nodded. "Yes. On the fifth, the refugees started arriving. They began pouring into the city, begging for help. And by the eighth, the Greek officials had abandoned the city. Aristides Sterghiades, the Greek High Commissioner, left that morning. He handed over the keys to the French consul and boarded a ship. Just like that, the city was left to fend for itself."

I felt sick. The Greeks had abandoned us, leaving us to face the wrath of the Turkish forces.

Konstantinos continued, his voice hardening. "On the morning of the ninth, a division of the Turkish cavalry rode in. Their commanders reassured everyone that the city was under control, that there was no reason to worry about our safety. We breathed easier and abandoned our plans to leave the city. We put our faith in the warships in the harbour, believing they would land troops, should the need arise to protect us. What happened was completely different. Other Turkish soldiers and the irregulars were slipping in from different parts of the city's perimeter. The British tried to make peace, to tell them that the Greek officials had gone, and that order needed to be restored. But there was no order. No peace." He shook his head bitterly. "Within hours, the killing and looting began. The Armenians were targeted first. Soldiers and irregulars moved through the quarter with no fear of reprisal. The Italians, the

French, the British. Their ships sit in the harbour. They have done nothing to intervene and stop the violence. The only people they are evacuating are their own."

Konstantinos' eyes darkened, and his voice dropped lower. "The Turkish forces began rounding up people, pulling them out of their homes. It wasn't just soldiers, civilians joined in, taking part in the bloodshed. Young men, old men, women, children, even babies, they were all targets. You saw with your own eyes the bodies lying in the streets, some shot in the face, others in the back. It was brutal. Merciless."

He stopped for a moment, and I saw tears well up in his eyes. "Have you heard what they did to our beloved Chrysostomos, the Metropolitan of Smyrni?"

When we shook our heads, Konstantinos' voice cracked as he continued. "Chrysostomos and Nureddin Pasha were old antagonists. The Bishop had pressed the British for Nureddin's removal in March 1919."

My mother nodded at the memory, her tone heavy with what my father had told her. "Nureddin had been a commander during the Ottoman campaigns against the Armenians and Christians. His methods were merciless. Chrysostomos condemned him publicly, accusing him of atrocities and war crimes. Your uncle and his acquaintances spoke of it often. But it was Mustafa Kemal who shielded him. Because of that protection, Nureddin escaped justice —no trial, no punishment. Kemal valued his loyalty, even when that loyalty came at the cost of mass killings."

"Yes, Chrysostomos had told the British that Nureddin should be shot for his war crimes. Nureddin never forgot that. Late in the afternoon on Sunday, a French patrol called on Chrysostomos to offer him sanctuary at the French Consulate. He declined, saying he wished to remain with his flock. As the French force was leaving the Greek church, a carriage with Turkish soldiers arrived and ordered him to climb in. He was told that Nureddin wanted to see him, and he was taken to the general's office at the Konak. During their meeting, Nureddin reminded him of what had occurred between them in 1919."

Konstantinos paused, taking in a long breath before continuing. "He told Chrysostomos, 'On the last occasion that I had the pleasure of seeing you, you were good enough to say I ought to be shot. I have sent for you, Your Lordship, to tell you that you are to be hanged.' He then ordered the guards to take him out into the street, where a large crowd of excited Turks had gathered. Nureddin came to the balcony overlooking the street and, realising that an alternative to hanging Chrysostomos had presented itself, handed him over to the furious mob—whom he himself had whipped up—telling them to deal with Chrysostomos as they pleased. 'If he has done good to you, do good to him; if he has done harm to you, do harm to him.'"

He paused once more, and the anguish was clearly visible in his expression. "The mob dragged Chrysostomos by his beard to a nearby barber shop where they wrapped him in a filthy barber's apron, beat and stabbed him, gouged out his eyes, cut off his ears and nose. They then dragged his broken corpse through the streets like some cursed beast, a horrific spectacle for all to witness."

The room fell silent, shock hanging thick in the air. Tears stung my eyes. My mother went pale, her lips trembling. Konstantinos' voice grew heavier, raw with grief and rage. "That brutality. How could they? Chrysostomos was a man of faith, a man who lived and breathed for our people. He didn't deserve this. But all his words, all his prayers could not save him from a brutal death, thanks to that barbarian Nureddin."

"But Konstantinos, the British, the French, the Americans. Why didn't they step in?"

He spat the words bitterly. "The French were right there and were furious. They saw everything. Some officers wanted to stop it. Their commanders told them to stand down. Politics was worth more than a man's life. So they just watched—watched him get dragged, beaten, and butchered like an animal."

We sat there in momentary silence. The only sound was the muffled sobs from the other room—Konstantinos' daughters, Anastasia, and Sophia.

Finally, he spoke again, his voice soft but firm. "We are trapped here, Mariegó. No one is safe. Not in this city. Not anymore."

I felt my heart sink, and my whole body went numb with fear and hopelessness. We had come to Smyrni believing it would be our refuge, but it had become a death trap, and there was no escape.

I looked at my mother and saw the despair in her eyes. I knew where her thoughts had gone—to that night when she had sobbed, admitting she had made a mistake. That we should have made our way to Kusandasi and then to Samos. She thought of the other women she had guided, the ones consumed by the crowd when we first entered the city. Where were they now? Were they trapped, pressed against those crammed onto the Quay?

*   *   *

We had barely settled into a fragile routine in Konstantinos' home when the city erupted into complete chaos. The Greek army was gone, having fled in a panicked retreat. There was no order, no defence. Smyrni, had been reduced to a desperate waiting room for death or salvation for the Greek and Armenian minorities.

Thousands of people were rushing towards the quay, hoping, praying, that the Allied ships anchored in the harbour would take them away from this nightmare. But even from the house, we could see them waiting in vain, their frantic pleas met with cold indifference from the foreign vessels that did not move. The docks were already swelling with bodies, refugees packed together like sheep to the slaughter.

Then came the banging on the door. A forceful, heavy pounding that sent a chill through my veins.

"Quickly, into the cellar," Konstantinos whispered urgently.

My mother grabbed my arm, yanking me towards the cellar. Ourania and her daughters followed, Persephone right behind us with Stamatis. The air was thick with terror as we stumbled into the damp, dark space beneath the house. My mother pressed her hand over Stamatis' mouth, Ourania clutched her daughters tightly to her, rocking slightly, mouthing silent prayers to the Panagia. For a moment, I thought my heart might stop altogether from fear. Persephone, clutched my hand as she too whispered prayers for our protection.

Then blessed silence.

The banging ceased, and the boots moved on. The soldiers left without breaking down the door. We did not move even after Konstantinos whispered down to us that it was safe. We remained huddled together, too afraid to breathe.

And so we continued to live—in fear.

Two days passed in a blur and sleepless nights, but none of us dared to leave the house. Outside, the city groaned under the weight of its suffering. We heard the clamour of shouts, arguments, the wailing of a baby, and the screams of women and children. Hoofbeats echoed against the cobblestones, heavy boots pounded the streets, followed by the sharp bark of orders and the occasional crack of a rifle. Doors were being forced open, splintering under the force of rifle butts.

The fear that had settled into our bones only deepened. We clung to the fragile hope that, sheltered as we were behind the heavily fortified iron door and shuttered windows, we would be left untouched by the fate that had befallen so many others.

Somehow, we still believed someone would come. The Allies. The ships anchored just beyond the harbour.

Surely they would not let this continue.

Surely they would step in, reclaim order, and protect the innocent.

The quay was already swelling with people, thousands packed shoulder to shoulder, waiting, praying. We could see what was happening from the upstairs windows. We hadn't joined them yet. We told ourselves it was too soon, too dangerous. But the truth was that we were afraid. Afraid to leave the last place that still felt like shelter.

Then came the 13th of September.

I remember that afternoon in Smyrni with a clarity that refuses to fade. Something shifted. The air felt heavier, the kind that pressed against the chest and made it hard to breathe. We all felt it, though no one spoke it aloud. Something was coming. We just did not know what. Not yet.

Then on that afternoon, everything changed. By early evening, a subtle, almost imperceptible shift in the light began, as if a fiery orange glow had crept over the horizon. At first, we could not be sure whether it was merely the dying sun, but as the hours passed, the glow grew more ominous, more insistent. The unmistakable scent of burning wood drifted in, and fear invaded, making my heart pound.

Konstantinos was gone longer than we expected, and with each passing moment, our dread grew. When he finally returned, his face was ashen, his breath quick and shallow. He had spoken to men he trusted, men who had seen the fire with their own eyes. They, too, were preparing to leave, their homes no longer safe, their choices as bleak as ours. Stay, and the fire would consume us; stay, and we risked being slaughtered by the Turks. There was no refuge left, no walls strong enough to hold back the tide of destruction.

He gathered us together with a voice that trembled as much as it commanded. "We must leave," he said, his tone urgent and final. "The fire is coming, and soon it will be upon us. There is no more time. We have to go now."

Ourania reached out for him then, grabbing his arm, fear in her expression. "Konstantine, why not stay?" she pleaded. "We have the cellar. It could protect us. Let the fire pass over and we will be safe." Her voice cracked, carrying all the fear and desperation we all felt at that moment.

He looked at her incredulously, shaking his head, as if she had not yet grasped the dreadful reality of what she had suggested. "Safe? The cellar could have hidden us from soldiers, yes. But this—this fire will consume the very earth. Down there, it will be like burning alive in the fires of hell. We would not last a moment."

Her eyes widened and her face drained of colour, as her grip on her husband's arm faltered, her hand falling away. A heavy silence filled the room. His words hung in the air suffocating, final. I felt my knees threaten to give way beneath me, as the weight of our situation became clear. The cellar, once a place of refuge, would now become our tomb. There was no arguing with such a truth. There were no more arguments left for us to make. The choice had been made for us.

In a fevered rush, we went about gathering what little we had, placing it into a makeshift bundle, a poor imitation of a rucksack, and then tied it to our backs. Konstantinos and his family had already prepared themselves for this moment, having witnessed the horrors before we had arrived in Smyrni. Their faces were etched with an unspoken acceptance of the worst that might befall us.

Persephone carried one of the water skins we had brought from Sokia, along with whatever dried food we could manage, hard bread, raisins, dried figs, and almonds, anything that could last in the days ahead. Ourania did the same. It was not much, but we clung to the hope that it would be enough to sustain us until rescue came.

We stepped out onto the streets, and we were immediately hit with the full horror of the unfolding nightmare. The city was now an inferno. Flames, wild and unrestrained, leapt up into the sky. Thick, acrid smoke billowed from every direction, blotting out the light and twisting the air into a haze of despair. Everywhere I looked, I saw evidence of devastation—a gruesome reminder of the speed at which death had come for some.

The air was filled with the sounds of terror. Agonised screams, frantic cries, and even the intermittent, jarring sound of gunshots punctuated the chaos. People moved like a writhing tide, a mass of humanity driven by sheer, unadulterated panic. Their faces were twisted in anguish and horror. In that moment, I felt both insignificant and hopelessly trapped in a nightmare that offered no escape.

Konstantinos led the way with grim determination. There were no comforting words, and I saw the terror in his eyes betraying his calm facade, as if he could see nothing but the endless abyss of our doom.

"To the *Prokymaea*," he ordered in a resolute tone that brooked no argument. "We have no other choice. The alternative is to remain and be consumed by the fire."

We hurried along after him, each step taking us closer to the one possible route of escape, even though it meant facing a mass of refugees all clamouring for salvation.

My mother clutched my hand with such ferocity that I felt the desperation of her grip as she struggled to keep us together as we moved through the chaos. Beside me, Stamatis's small hand trembled in mine, his small face filled with fear and confusion. Persephone, walked beside us, clutching, Stamatis's other hand, her face pale and drawn, her usual calm replaced by a haunted resignation.

The full scope of the catastrophe unfolded before us. Flames were spreading along the facades of buildings, consuming what remained of a once-proud city, while the thick smoke choked the air. The heat was oppressive, searing through the very fabric of our being. I looked up, horrified. The inferno was spreading with unstoppable hunger, devouring everything in its path. It was a sight that no words could ever capture: the sky alight with the fury of destruction, and the agonised cries of the doomed.

We moved with the tide of panicked refugees, an endless sea of desperate souls, each one driven by the primal urge to survive. Yet, even in our shared flight, there was no camaraderie, no comfort, only a collective, unspoken despair. Every face was etched with fear and desperation.

Finally, after what felt like an eternity, we reached the quay. The scene that met us there was beyond description—a writhing mass of humanity, a chaotic throng where every individual seemed caught in a desperate struggle against fate. It was no longer a place of commerce or calm; it was a chaotic, suffocating pit of souls jostling for a means of escape. Shouts rang out in every direction, the clamour of thousands merging into a single, dissonant cry of despair.

We paused for a moment, breathless and dazed, amid the crushing mass of refugees. I felt my heart hammer in my chest as I looked around, trying to comprehend the sheer scale of the devastation. Konstantinos, standing a few paces ahead, raised his voice over the roar of the crowd.

"We must try to secure a place on one of the boats." His words, were filled with a grim finality, our only guide amidst the swirling chaos.

All around us, the tide of people surged forward, a relentless force. There was a maelstrom of bodies—men, women, and children pressed so tightly that I could feel the pressure of the crowd, one that threatened to crush us as we pushed forward towards our only hope of escape. We began to wait, shoulder to shoulder with countless strangers, for when an opening might be created to board any ship, which we prayed would come to rescue us.

The quay became a prison with no walls, a place where thousands of us stood shoulder to shoulder, packed so tightly that even the dead could not be removed. Children whimpered at their mothers' breasts, but there was nothing left to give them. The stench was unbearable. There were no private places to relieve oneself. People did so where they stood. Women huddled together, attempting to shield one another, but there was no dignity left in that place.

Human waste collected in the corners where the crowd thinned, mixing with the blood of the wounded and the filth of our suffering. The sea lapped at the edge of our misery. Some desperate for relief, let it take them, choosing the water over the flames, over starvation, over waiting for a mercy that might never come.

The Turks did not simply stand by. Their soldiers moved through the throng like wolves among sheep, firing their rifles into the crowd, beating the helpless with bayonets, seizing whatever valuables they could take. They stripped rings from fingers, ripped earrings from ears. They dragged men away, their fates unknown. Some handed over their last possessions hoping to be spared. Others resisted and were beaten into submission. We saw some soldiers who showed kindness, offering water, but they were rare.

Those who pushed towards the edge of the quay, desperate to board a boat, found themselves blocked by soldiers who struck them down, shoving them back into the panicked mass. Some were thrown into the water, drowning before they could reach the foreign ships. Others, wounded and bleeding, lay where they fell, trampled beneath desperate feet. Women were dragged screaming into the night, their fates sealed in the echoes of their terrified screams. The air was thick with smoke, with the stench of burning wood and flesh, with the cries of the dying and the pleading of the living.

There was no order to the violence, no strategy, only the chaos of unchecked brutality. The fire behind us raged, swallowing the city in an unrelenting inferno, and yet, for many, it was not the flames that would claim them. Death came at the hands of the soldiers who used the confusion to murder, to plunder, to commit unspeakable acts while the world looked away.

We tried to shield ourselves from the heat, though there was no escape. The fire raged behind us, and the air itself seemed to blister our skin. We prayed for rain—not for ourselves, but for mercy, for the flames to stop, for the suffering to ease. But the sky stayed dry. And God stayed silent. We didn't know how we would ever leave this godforsaken hell. It felt as if even He had turned His back on us.

The hours dragged on into the next day. Konstantinos asked around, hoping someone had heard whether Greek ships were coming. No one knew anything. Only rumours. Hopes dressed up as facts.

Later that evening, a ripple of talk passed through the crowd that smaller boats were on their way to evacuate more of us. Those who couldn't wait began diving into the water, swimming towards the anchored vessels — British, French, and American warships already anchored in the harbour.

I watched as Konstantinos stood, scanning the scene, shielding his eyes from the smoke and the glare. His face changed. His mouth opened, but no words came. Then he gasped, a sound I will never forget. He turned to us, his face ashen.

"They are throwing them back into the sea," he said. "Men have reached the ships, but the British, the French they are laughing. The French, they are pouring boiling water on them."

Silence fell over us. Horror. Betrayal.

We saw small boats being launched from the ships, but their destination was at a stretch of the quay far away from where the masses were packed together. For a fleeting moment, our hearts lifted. But the truth revealed itself soon enough. They were not here for us. We watched in disbelief as the Levantines—the foreign merchants, diplomats, and families of mixed European and local descent were evacuated. Many held foreign passports, proof of protection that allowed them safe passage onto the waiting ships. Meanwhile, we the Greeks and Armenians remained pressed against each other in fear and desperation, our fates bound to the chaos surrounding us.

I remember those ships anchored in the harbour. How can I ever forget? While chaos reigned on the docks, crowded with desperate and broken souls begging for help, the crews on those ships, and their officers, dined and played music, indifferent to our suffering. I heard how the music on those decks grew louder when the screams became too much for them to bear, almost as if they wanted to silence the horror that was unfolding.

It was a betrayal that cut deeper than the flames. The British government knew what was happening. Messages were sent, warnings given, yet politics and hesitation kept them from acting. They let Mustafa Kemal's forces block rescue ships from entering the harbour, condemning thousands to starvation and death.

It wasn't the Turks this time. It was the men who once called themselves our Allies. We saw the flags of nations that could have saved us, the same nations that had once promised protection. Yet they abandoned us, left us to the fire, to the brutality of the Turks. They watched us burn, watched us being slaughtered and mocked our desperation.

They were no better than the Turks.

And these men called themselves Christians.

The waiting was its own kind of agony. How long could we last? How long before the flames reached us, or we were trampled underfoot?

In the early hours of the morning, only one ship showed mercy. A Japanese freighter that dumped its cargo to take on as many refugees as it could carry. We had been too far away from where it anchored. We watched it disappear into the horizon, bound for Piraeus, while the rest of us remained trapped, waiting for death by fire, by water, or at the hands of the soldiers.

Some could not bear it. A young woman beside me, her face streaked with tears and sorrow, cradled the lifeless body of her child. She still rocked him gently, whispering words that no longer had meaning. There was nothing left for her here, no future, no mercy, no escape from the agony that had consumed her.

Without a sound, she rose to her feet, her arms still wrapped around her child. Step by step, she pushed through the mass of people towards the end of the quay. The crowd parted in silent understanding. No one stopped her. I watched as she threw herself in. The image has never left me. Even now, after all these years, she lingers in my mind. A mother lost to grief, surrendered to the sea because there was nothing else left.

There was no salvation to be had, only suffering. And yet, we waited, because there was nothing else to do. I recall the heat—searing, unrelenting—a dry, merciless heat that did not just burn the skin but seemed to reach into our bones. The smoke was everywhere. Thick, choking, alive. It poured into our mouths, our noses, our eyes. Each breath felt like swallowing embers. Our lungs rebelled, our throats scraped raw with every gasp. It was as if the sky itself had turned against us, no longer vast or blue but a black canopy of ash and despair, pressing down with a weight that made it hard to stand.

Children cried. Mothers tried to shield them with their bodies, wet cloths, trembling hands, futile gestures against a force that devoured everything. The stench of burning wood, oil, flesh clung to us. It filled our hair, our clothes. There was nowhere to run, nowhere to hide. We stood shoulder to shoulder on the scorched stone, waiting. Drowning in smoke, in heat, in desperation. Waiting for rescue. Waiting for death. We didn't know which would come first.

CHAPTER SIX

Hours passed in a feverish haze, and with each agonising hour, my dread grew. By the time the first light of the second day arrived, the chaos had only deepened. It was then that *The Maid of Chios* and several other vessels arrived and docked at the quay. Their arrival was heralded by a momentary shift in the tide of the desperate surge of humanity, a brief glimmer of reprieve in the endless nights of suffering. The oppressive atmosphere was punctuated by the cries of the desperate and the shouts of American volunteers trying, in vain, to restore some semblance of order.

Our group was close to *The Maid of Chios*. In the brief interval of the shifting human currents, I watched in horror as Konstantinos and his family were swallowed up by the throng. In the struggle to move forward, they vanished from sight, a silent, wrenching disappearance that left me shocked. I felt my mother's grip tighten around me, her knuckles white with fear, as she desperately tried to hold on to me. I clutched my brother's hand, feeling his small fingers trembling in mine, while Persephone's steady hold on him seemed to offer little comfort in that moment of unmitigated terror.

The crowd surged forward with renewed ferocity, shoving and pushing as they jostled towards the waiting boats. In the chaos, I stumbled, and in the desperate act of righting myself, I felt the horrifying separation. I looked around, eyes wide with panic, and realised with gut-wrenching clarity that my mother was no longer with me, and Stamatis and Persephone too had been swept away. I managed to right myself, my heart thundering in my ears as I scanned the crowd, frantically searching for them.

Then I felt a hand on my shoulder. It was my mother. Somehow she had found her way back to me. I clutched her arm, relief mixed in with a rising tide of despair. Yet in that brief reunion, the horror was far from over. Stamatis and Persephone had disappeared into the relentless crush of the crowd. My mother, her eyes burning with raw panic, called out his name — "Stamati! Stamati!"—but the sound was swallowed up by the cacophony of the desperate mass.

Desperation turned to frantic calls as we tried to follow the flow of bodies being pushed relentlessly towards the boats. She screamed his name, clawing through the mass, but we were being shoved from all sides. I strained to see my little brother's face, or Persephone's in amongst the teeming mass, but there was nothing. The agony of that realisation, of knowing that they were somewhere in that crush, out of reach, and likely doomed, felt as if my very soul were unravelling.

As we neared the boat, the tide of humanity shifted again with a force that left me trembling. There was no fighting it. There was no line, no order. Just a wave of screaming people pushing forward, everyone begging, sobbing, fighting to get close. I saw children being lifted, thrown, passed over heads like parcels. Babies in baskets. Elderly women collapsed on the ground, some trampled in the crush. Greek sailors and American volunteers barked orders over the roar of the crowd, urging us to move along, to get on board.

We made it to the edge just as *The Maid of Chios* was taking on its final passengers. A Greek sailor reached down, grabbing me and then my mother by the arm. We were pulled up and thrown onto the deck like sacks of grain. All around us, people wept, screamed, collapsed. I turned back towards the quay, searching for any sign of Stamatis, Persephone, Konstantinos, and his family. Nothing. Just smoke, fire, and thousands of faces crushed against each other, calling out in desperation.

My mother, her voice raw with grief, screamed out his name. "Stamati! *To pethi mou! To pethi mou!* My child, my child!" Her eyes were wild with horror and despair. Her anguished cries were swallowed up in the chaos, by the relentless surge of bodies and the wails and screams of the desperate around us.

In one heart-stopping moment, she tried to step off, to search for any sign of my brother, but was forced back by the sailors. The ship was already overcrowded, people hanging off the sides, clinging to ropes, screaming for their husbands, their relatives. Men shouted from the water, trying to swim to the vessel. Some were dragged out of the water, others sank beneath the waves. We all knew that the men were at the greatest risk. Those who were left behind knew what fate awaited them.

Turkish soldiers stood back along the edge, rifles slung over their shoulders. They didn't interfere, not yet, just watched. Their silence was worse than gunfire. It meant they could act at any moment.

The vessel was about to depart. My eyes, still wide with shock and grief, scanned the quay, searching for any sign of Stamatis or Persephone, Konstantinos, and his family. But there was nothing. Only the implacable sight of a city being consumed by fire and the desperate cries of those left behind.

In that cruel moment, my mother collapsed onto the deck, her body trembling, her anguished sobs echoing in the air around us. I sank down beside her and wrapped my arms around her. I held her tighter, desperate to hold on to the only connection that remained. Yet even as I clutched her frail form, I knew that a part of me had been torn away, forever lost in the violent, inescapable chaos that had torn our family apart once more.

All around me, I heard the desperate cries of those who had lost everything, echoes of a tragedy so vast and unfathomable that words could barely capture its essence.

In those agonising moments on the deck of the ship, as we were pushed into the open waters of the harbour, I felt the weight of loss settle over me. I sat there, listening to my mother's heartbroken sobs. Her shoulders shook with each breath, the sound more raw than anything I had ever heard. Something inside of me had been hollowed out. The cold I felt wasn't from the sea air or the damp clothes clinging to my skin. It came from within. A deep, gnawing emptiness had settled into my very being.

I felt nothing. In that moment, I understood. Everything had been taken from us. My home, my childhood, our safety, the loved ones who had shaped my world, the bonds of family that had seemed unbreakable. All gone. Erased. Somewhere in that stampede towards survival, precious hands had slipped from mine. Konstantinos and his family had vanished. The human tide that had borne us to this vessel had, in its frantic surge, torn us apart, scattering those I loved. All that remained was despair, and it pressed in close like a second skin. Around me, others sat hunched, hollow-eyed, and motionless, clinging to whatever fragments they had salvaged.

There is no solace in recollection, only the stark, unyielding truth of what we endured.

That journey stripped us of our illusions of safety, leaving behind only raw, unmitigated grief. In the final moments as we were pushed towards the small ship, the world around me became a blur of terror and loss—a maelstrom of anguish from which nothing could be salvaged. I am haunted by the memory of my mother's voice, broken and desperate as she collapsed on the deck, another permanent scar on her soul already shattered by the loss of half of our family, her eyes wide and hollow as if she had seen the very face of oblivion.

"To pethi mou! To pethi mou!" she cried, over and over.

And I remember the crushing helplessness that followed. The anguish of that day is still etched into my very being, a relentless reminder of the fragility of life and the utter indifference of fate. I remember the desolation we felt when Smyrni burned, and the air was thick with tragedy and utter despair.

I heard the sound of the motor as the ship pushed out into open water. It was crowded with women and children, their faces pale and tear-streaked. Some sat in stunned silence, their eyes vacant. Others sobbed openly. I stared back at the shore. Persephone and Stamatis, Konstantinos and his family were somewhere in that sea of people. Would they make it onto another ship? Would we ever see them again?

No one had answers. All we could do was watch the distance grow between us and the burning city. And we had no idea if we would ever be whole again.

The water stretched endlessly around us, the mainland fading into a smoky blur. I wiped at my tears, though they kept coming, and tried to remain strong for my mother. I whispered reassurances I didn't feel, told her that they would be safe, that we would see them again. But inside, the weight of despair pressed down on me. It was both suffocating and relentless.

All the way to Chios, I replayed the moment when we were separated, wondering if I could have done something, anything, to hold onto them. My little brother's small hand slipping from mine, Persephone's desperate cries as they were swept away in the crush of bodies. The panic, the cries, the sheer force of the crowd as it surged towards the ship, driven by terror and the frantic hope of salvation. I had seen people stumble, disappear beneath the weight of so many feet, screams cut short, hands reaching up for help only to vanish. Had they suffered the same fate?

And what of Konstantinos and his family? Had they too been torn apart in that madness, lost in the chaos of thousands fleeing, or had they managed to stay together? Were they still alive? My mind tormented me with the possibilities, each one worse than the last. The thought of Stamatis, so small, so helpless, alone in that sea of fear. I closed my eyes and let the tears fall. The helplessness I felt was unbearable.

And yet there I sat, promising my mother that they would be safe. But how could I know? How could I ever know?

Those short hours at sea felt like a deeper descent into desolation. There was no light at the end, no flicker of determination or the stirring of some inner strength to be found. Instead, there was only the cold, unyielding truth. Our lives had been one long journey from Sokia. Each hardship we had endured, we had borne, hoping Smyrni would bring us salvation, only to find ourselves thrust into the midst of hell.

The faces around me were masks of suffering, each person trapped in their own silent torment. I could not recall a single comforting word uttered during that journey, anything that might have hinted at salvation.

Mothers clutched their children with a grip born of fear rather than comfort, as if loosening their hold for even a moment might mean losing them forever. Some rocked in silence, their vacant eyes staring at nothing. Others whispered prayers under their breath, but their voices carried no conviction, only the hollow echo of desperation.

Beside me, a little girl whimpered softly, her face buried in her mother's chest, clinging to a doll missing an arm. The woman did not speak, did not soothe her, she only held her tighter, her body rigid, her gaze fixed on the horizon as if willing herself not to break.

Nearby, another mother cradled a baby against her chest, her fingers stroking its cheek in slow, mechanical movements. I could not tell if the child was sleeping or if exhaustion had drained the last of its strength. Across from her, a young girl clung to her grandmother, her small frame trembling with silent sobs. No one had the strength to offer reassurances they no longer believed. Children whimpered in hushed voices, too exhausted to cry, their small bodies curled against their mothers' sides. Some had fallen into a fitful sleep, their cheeks still streaked with the dirt and smoke of the burning city. A boy, no more than five, clutched a ragged bundle of cloth, rocking it as though he could gain some comfort from it.

I looked away, unable to bear the sight of so much loss in the eyes of those too young to understand it. There was no wailing, no hysteria. We had escaped one hell, only to drift towards an uncertain fate. Our bodies had been spared, but our souls had been left behind in the ashes. The relentless chaos of that day, the fire, the screams, the despair, had hollowed us out, leaving nothing but raw, unadulterated loss. Our home, our family, our future — all of it had been taken away from us. *Katára épese páno mou.* A curse had fallen on me, one that I could not cast off.

*   *   *

As the ship neared the harbour at Chios, the outline of the island became clearer, and a mixture of trepidation and cautious hope surged among us. This ship had saved us from the chaos of Smyrni, but what now lay ahead for us on this small, overcrowded island? I clutched my mother's hand tightly as we stepped onto the dock. We had made it, but at what cost? The acrid smoke of Smyrni still clung to my clothes, my younger brother, Stamatis, Persephone, and our cousins—gone. Or at least, missing. I did not know which was worse, to assume they had perished in the chaos or to hope they might still be alive somewhere in the crush of survivors.

The air felt heavy with despair, and the crowded port was filled with refugees whose eyes told stories of loss too terrible to speak and those who searched frantically for the loved ones they had left behind. People cried out names that vanished into the noise. Others sat motionless, staring at nothing. We had barely had time to catch our breath before we were swept into the mass of humanity once more, another pair of nameless souls adrift in the aftermath.

Local volunteers stood near the landing dock handing out small tin cups of water and hard rusks. I drank quickly, though it barely eased the dryness in my throat. It wasn't enough, but it kept us on our feet. The first hours passed in a blur of noise and exhaustion as volunteers and officials tried to organise us into makeshift camps.

We were among the fortunate ones. My mother and I were taken to a repurposed schoolhouse where rows of wooden benches and cots had been set out with a few blankets and whatever belongings people had managed to save. Everything was packed so tightly there was hardly room to move. The air smelled of damp. It was crowded, yet it was dry, and for that we were grateful. Many others slept outside or in rough tents. There were almost no proper facilities.

The sounds of grief and uncertainty echoed through every corner of that building.

I helped my mother settle onto one of the thin blankets, her movements slow, as if weighted down by the enormity of our loss. I did not cry. Not yet. There was no time for grief when survival demanded so much. The desperate search for those missing or presumed dead. The uncertainty of our future. The tales of how orphaned children had been taken in by strangers, of those who had perished on the journey. My mother remained quiet, moving through the motions of survival but lost in her own grief.

Those first days on Chios were a strange mixture of relief and dread. There was very little food. Very little water. The island had already received too many of us, far more than it could feed. The old Turkish mosque served as the kitchen. Each day we queued for whatever the local kitchen could manage— thin soup, a scrap of bread. Sometimes not even that. The Red Cross had not yet arrived with organised rations. We survived on what the islanders could give us. We were alive. We had entered a life of waiting—waiting for food, waiting for news, waiting for proof that the people we loved had either lived or died.

Within days, the International Committee of the Red Cross reached the island. We were ushered forward in groups by relief workers towards a large tent where tables had been set up. Here, men and women sat with ledgers open in front of them, their fingers stained with ink, their faces impassive. This was where the registration process documented our identity and familial connections. The process was methodical, impersonal. The sheer number of arrivals had stripped them of everything but efficiency. They required basic information—name, date of birth, place of birth. It felt strange, almost absurd, to be answering these questions in the wake of everything that had happened. As if any of that mattered now. But we complied, knowing it was the only way forward.

We were expected to name everyone, those who had been with us on the quay in Smyrni and those like my father and older brother who had been taken by the Turks. Their names were documented in a separate section within our name record to assist in reunification efforts. The word 'missing' was written next to their names. It was a term that carried such finality with it—no certainty of life or death. We were informed that the Red Cross had set up an office near the main tent, where information about missing persons would be gathered and relayed. They assured us that every effort would be made to reunite families, and we were free to check with them daily for updates. Our assigned shelter location would also be recorded so that if any news came about our missing loved ones, they would know where to find us.

It was only when the American Red Cross arrived that official distribution of food and clothing began. However, this proved to be a challenge. They struggled to provide sufficient rations for everyone. The feeding stations became the heart of our survival. There were lines for food and water. Every day, thousands of us would line up daily for soup and bread. We depended on this daily act for survival. The Red Cross worked tirelessly to ensure no one went hungry. But it was never enough.

The soup was thin—sometimes lentil, sometimes beans, or a simple broth with rice, broken pasta or barley was added. Salt was all we could hope for, with only the faintest trace of herbs or oil when they were available. It was nothing like what we had known, but it kept us from starvation.

There were also milk stations. Without them, babies would not have survived. At one station alone, we learned that thousands of children were fed in a single month. I often saw mothers leaving with small cups or bottles, relief plain on their faces.

At first, the hunger was unbearable. Our stomachs twisted in pain, growling through the night as we waited for the next ration of bread and soup that never seemed enough. Mothers gave their share to their children, pretending they were full.

But after a while, it was as if our bodies surrendered. The gnawing ache dulled, our stomachs seemed to shrink, and we moved through the days in a strange, hollow rhythm. We grew thinner, our faces sharper, our clothes hanging loose on our frames. Hunger no longer shouted. It reminded us quietly that we were still alive.

The air was thick with the stench of unwashed bodies and waste, and there was little relief from the filth that surrounded us. Clean water was scarce, and proper sanitation was almost non-existent. The toilets, if they could even be called that, overflowed. Disease outbreaks were a constant threat, exacerbated by cramped living conditions and limited access to medical care. We did our best to keep our small corner of the camp clean, but the smell of refuse was heavy in the air.

For us women in the camps, those days of the month were extremely difficult and often humiliating There were no proper things to use—only rags, bits of old fabric, or torn clothing we folded and reused. Clean water was scarce, and when we could wash them, it was always at night, in secret, so no one would see.

There was no real privacy. Hygiene was poor and led to frequent infections, rashes, and discomfort. The washing areas were few, and soap was a luxury we rarely had. I often felt unclean, uncomfortable, and ashamed. Women often had to wait until night to clean themselves discreetly. In traditional Greek and Anatolian communities, those days of the month were not openly discussed. Women suffered quietly, trying to preserve their dignity in degrading conditions.

For the younger girls, it was worse. Some had their first bleeding there, terrified, and unsure of what was happening. It was another humiliation to bear, another quiet suffering in a life already filled with loss.

It did not take long for disease to take hold. Coughs echoed through the tents, and fevered bodies lay limp beside their families, who could do little more than watch and pray. The American Women's Hospitals sent doctors and nurses to help, and they worked tirelessly, but there were too many of us, too many in need. People lined up for medicine, but the lines never seemed to shorten, no matter how many were treated. Every day, the fear grew.

Yet amidst the hardship, a sense of community emerged. Families bonded together, and children found ways to play amidst the chaos, turning discarded items into makeshift toys.

Each day my mother and I went to the tent where the names of the missing were updated, scrawled in chalk, grouped by arrival dates and locations. Our eyes darted over the list, my heart pounding as I leaned closer, scanning each line, hoping to see the names of the ones we sought. But there was no Stamatis. No Persephone. No Konstantinos, Ourania, or their daughters.

A woman placed a hand on my mother's shoulder. "New names are added with every ship or small vessel that arrives," she said gently. "Do not lose hope."

Hope. A dangerous thing to hold on to when so much had already been taken from us. We did not know if they were dead or alive. But we would not stop searching. Not yet.

Perhaps they had been forced onto a ship bound for another island, Lesvos, or Samos. The evacuation had been chaotic, with thousands desperately seeking passage to safety in those frantic hours. Or maybe they had been taken to Piraeus and were now lost in the chaos of thousands arriving every day. If they had survived, where were they now? How long would it be before we found each other again? Weeks? Months? Longer?

I clung to the thought that somewhere, in some overcrowded camp, they were asking the same questions about us. Would we see them again? I didn't know. But I held onto the possibility, clinging to it like a lifeline. It was the only thing that kept me standing, the only thing that kept my mother from collapsing completely.

In the following days, every moment was an agonising wait for news. We lingered on the quayside, straining our eyes as each overcrowded vessel drew near. The decks were crammed so tightly with people that it was easy to miss a familiar face in the press of bodies. Still, we searched desperately, hope surging with every arrival, only to break again when they were not among the disembarking. The uncertainty was torture. Each ship carried with it both a chance of reunion and the crushing weight of loss.

The Red Cross worked tirelessly amid inadequate resources, doing all they could to log every report of missing persons and to coordinate search efforts. I watched as my mother's eyes filled with fresh tears every time a name was called out, of lost members being reunited with their families. Yet as the days passed, the promise that our family might be made whole again seemed as elusive as ever.

Suddenly, a glimmer of hope finally pierced our despair. A volunteer rushed towards us, his face lined with urgency and cautious relief.

"*Kyria Ndousani?*" My mother and I stood up in unison, our eyes fixed on him as he approached. "We have found a boy who we believe is your son," he continued. "He has been brought here to us from the eastern camp."

"Stamatis?"

In that moment, my mother's trembling hand gripped mine even tighter, her eyes wide with cautious hope and beginning to mist with tears. The volunteer led us into a small, makeshift infirmary, where a child lay wrapped in a blanket. As we stepped closer, I could scarcely believe that the frail figure before us was truly Stamatis.

His eyes, heavy with exhaustion, flickered open and then, suddenly, widened with recognition. A whimper rose from his throat, his small body trembling as he rasped, "Mamma." His voice was weak, but the raw longing in it cut through me.

My mother let out a broken cry and collapsed beside him, gathering him into her arms as if she could shield him from everything he had endured.

"Stamati mou, agapimenomou pethaki, Stamati my beloved child" she sobbed, rocking him, pressing frantic kisses to his tangled hair.

I knelt beside them, my own throat tightening, as the volunteer softly explained that he had been found among a group of refugees who had cared for him. But all I could focus on was the way he clung to our mother, his small fingers grasping at her as if afraid she might disappear again.

His voice trembled as he began to recount his ordeal and the journey that had brought him back to us. He spoke of the quay in Smyrni, when he had been separated from us, and then from Persephone, who had been swallowed up in that sea of desperate humanity, of being jostled and pushed, finding himself lost amongst faces he could not recognise. I understood now that it was by God's mercy, that he had been placed on a boat bound for Chios, though he could easily have been sent to another island, where he might have been lost for months until the Red Cross could reunite him with us. He spoke of the strangers who had looked after him on the journey to Chios and then in the refugee camp. They had been very kind, he told us.

As I listened, my heart ached as I remembered the terror I had felt at that moment when I realised he had vanished in an instant, swallowed up in the chaos and the masses of fleeing families. I had imagined him alone and frightened, and the thought made my body shiver once again.

Our mother held him close, rocking him gently, whispering soft reassurances, promises that she would never leave him again. My throat tightened, tears slipping silently. And in that moment, the weight of fear and separation was eased by the miracle of his return, by the hand of the *Panayia* Blessed Mother, who had guided him safely back to us.

The news, however, was bittersweet. There was still no word of the whereabouts of Persephone, or Konstantinos and his family.

For days after Stamatis's recovery, our small refuge on Chios was filled with cautious optimism intermingled with a persistent dread. The Red Cross continued its tireless work, their efforts to locate those missing becoming a constant source of conversation and quiet despair among the refugees. We visited bulletin boards where missing persons' names were listed and visited the

Red Cross office with every new arrival into the harbour, our questions met with sympathetic, yet often futile replies.

As Stamatis slowly regained his strength, the hope that we had been holding on to had waned. We learned that the chaos had scattered the refugees widely and with thousands upon thousands evacuated, there was no way of knowing for certain where they had gone. The other possibility was far more harrowing—that they might not have survived, that they might have vanished beneath the merciless current of humanity on that fateful day or even worse. The thought was too much to bear.

*   *   *

Word spread quickly through the refugee camp on Chios. On September 16, 1922, Nureddin Paşa had issued a brutal decree: all Greek and Armenian men between eighteen and forty-five were to be treated as prisoners of war, with no chance of escape. Fathers, brothers, husbands became trapped as the city itself burned. For the women, children, and elderly, there remained a window of hope. They would be permitted to leave the city, but only until October 1. After that, anyone left behind faced deportation into the Anatolian interior, a deadly journey from which few returned.

Mustafa Kemal himself reinforced the order.

I hated those men with every fibre of my being — Nureddin Paşa, with his cold, merciless decree, and Mustafa Kemal, hailed by the Turks as a hero. To me, they were nothing but murderers, the architects of the first genocide of the twentieth century. Men who condoned the slaughter of thousands of our people, who watched as flames consumed our homes, our streets, our lives, without a shred of mercy.

That was their legacy. Not greatness. Not honour. Genocide. Their names should be spat upon, cursed for eternity. I will never forgive them. Never. I carry their crimes inside of me, a wound that never healed. Our army may have faltered, may have made mistakes we did not hold with pride, but nothing, nothing, compared to the deliberate, calculated extermination they unleashed upon us. It was methodical, cold, and remorseless.

Let the Turks call them heroes if they wish. Let the world debate the politics, the victories. But in my memory, and in the memory of all who survived the horrors of the Great Fire of Smyrni, we will remember them for what they truly were. And we will carry that truth, as heavy as grief itself, for the rest of our lives.

*   *   *

As more refugees arrived, they told harrowing stories, tales of terror and loss that silenced even the strongest among us. The great evacuation from

Smyrni had begun only after an international outcry, and days after the fire, when so many had already perished—burned, slaughtered, shot, or drowned. By then, it was already too late for many. There had been no swift Allied command, no coordinated rescue when the flames first rose and the quay became a sea of despair. We heard names and spoke of our gratitude—an American relief worker, a U.S. Navy admiral. It was their pleas, their insistence on decency, their pressure on Allied and Greek leadership, that finally forced action. Not swift diplomacy. Not duty. Only humanity. Only later would we understand the depth of what these two men had done to save our people.

We listened to the reports. They confirmed what we already knew. We had survived not because the world cared and acted, but because it had hesitated, and then tried to bury the truth of their inaction. The Allies had been there. They had watched it happen. Warships from the world's great powers sat in the harbour while Smyrni burned. They saw the crowds crushed against the quay, heard the screams of women and children. They saw men dragged away, executed, thrown into the sea. And they did nothing.

Their governments called it neutrality. Protocol. A refusal to interfere. But we knew it for what it was.

Cowardice dressed as diplomacy.

We were not citizens worth protecting. We were not valuable enough. They stayed aboard their ships, polishing brass, playing music to drown out the cries. When desperate souls tried to climb aboard, the crew poured boiling water over them. Then they turned their faces away.

Later, they denied what we had seen. Issued statements that downplayed the fire, the massacres, the chaos. Said there was no proof. Claimed the situation had been exaggerated. Some even blamed us, they said we had panicked, set our own homes alight, invited our fate.

We carried that bitterness with us. It sat on our chests like a stone. The knowledge that the world could watch such horror unfold and choose silence. That the truth could be swept away just as easily as bodies in the harbour. That we were expected to be grateful for the rescue that came far too late for so many.

They tried to write a different story. But we were there. We saw and remembered everything. The world remembers other wars, other tragedies where thousands died, but who remembers us? Has the world ever acknowledged the genocide perpetrated against us? The Allies tried to hide the truth to cover up their shortcomings. Had there not been an outcry, thousands more would have perished while British and French soldiers continued with their tea and music, oblivious to the desperate cries of those left to die.

We were not a footnote in history. We were its victims, its witnesses.

Some still sought to pretend there was doubt about who set Smyrni ablaze. There is no doubt. We saw it, we lived it. George Horton, the American Consul, told the truth when others would not. The British Consul, Harry Lamb, had warned him to stay silent, that it was not 'expedient' or 'obligatory' to tell the whole truth. Horton refused. He named it plainly—Kemal's gangs burned only the Greek and Armenian quarters, carrying out the cry of 'Turkey for the Turks.' The world may still argue, but I know what I saw. I know what was done. And until my last breath, I will name it for what it was.

It was genocide. A calculated policy of extermination. A truth like that can never be denied. I will never forgive them.

*　　*　　*

In the camp on Chios, we spoke often of the horrors we had seen and what we had lost. Yet among the tales of despair, there were also stories of courage and humanity, reminders that not all hearts had turned cold in those days of horror.

One story was passed from mouth to mouth until it reached us too. It was of the Japanese cargo ship, the *Tokei-Maru*, anchored at Smyrni during those days when the Kemalists were slaughtering us without mercy. The Allied vessels stood by and did nothing, their captains bound by orders of neutrality.

But the Japanese captain of the *Tokei-Maru* chose differently. Even when his ship was already full, loaded with valuable cargo, as he saw the wild massacres and the appeals of the refugees, he was so moved, he ordered it thrown overboard. The sea carried away his wealth, but in its place, he took on 825 souls—men, women, and children who would otherwise have perished on the quay.

I remember hearing how he sent out all his lifeboats, commanding his crew to bring back as many as the boats could carry. The Kemalist soldiers, furious, surrounded the lifeboats and threatened to sink them. We were told that the captain himself stood firm, warning their officers that if even a single hair on the heads of his passengers was harmed, he would treat it as an insult to the Japanese flag, and his government would demand reparation. Faced with his resolve, the soldiers backed down, and the refugees boarded in safety.

It was then I realised, this was the very ship my family and I could not reach, the one that had berthed too far from where we stood with thousands of others along the quay. With a growing sense of despair, we had watched it sail out of the harbour.

The Greek newspapers wrote of it, praising the bravery and philanthropy of that man. To us in the camp, it was more than a story. It was a light in the darkness, proof that even when the world had turned its back on us, there were still men of honour who would risk everything to save strangers.

We remembered his name, even if only as *'o Iáponas kapetánios'* 'the Japanese captain.' His act was a reminder that not all nations had abandoned us, that somewhere across the sea lived people who valued life above profit.

Yet with that hope came bitterness too. Many cursed the great powers, who had stood idly by while we were butchered and burned. Some spat on the ground at the mention of their names, saying that it took a man from the farthest corner of the earth to do what our so-called Allies would not.

*   *   *

In the end, Chios became both a refuge and our purgatory. It sheltered us from immediate danger, offering food, water, and shelter, but it also forced us to confront the unyielding truth. Our loved ones might be lost to us forever. Their fate remained a mystery, a cruel and final injustice in a world that had already taken so much from us. It was also a constant reminder of the fragility of hope in a world shattered by loss.

We had already been in the refugee camp for a month. The days seemed to blur into one another, each one indistinguishable from the last. Makeshift shelters stretched as far as the eye could see, each one cramped with people whose lives had been shattered. It was international aid that kept the worst from becoming a complete collapse. The American Red Cross took on the responsibility where the Greek Government was yet to concern itself with our well-being. They moved with an urgent sense of purpose to meet the needs of the thousands of refugees who had nowhere else to turn. Their charity, however, could not erase how exposed we felt.

Inside the camp the old distinctions evaporated. Aristocrats who once hosted salons found themselves sharing space with farmers, shopkeepers, seamstresses, children who had never known hunger. In the camp, there was no difference between rich and poor, young, or old. We all stood in the same lines for soup and bread, our stomachs aching the same. It was an awkward democracy of need—one the world had forced upon us. I saw mothers who once had servants, fathers who once owned land, now waiting beside us, because hunger does not care for who you were. Every day it reminded me that survival makes us all equal. Coughs passed through rows of beds, lice found new homes in hair once carefully dressed. Overcrowding and the struggle for survival shaped the first month for all refugees across the island.

The Red Cross even took photographs of us. At the time, we did not understand the purpose. Perhaps an official record, but later we would see ourselves in those black and white images. They were a way for us to look back and remember not just who we had been, but what we had endured, and, how we had survived.

One morning I sat on the step outside our corner of the building, my arms wrapped tightly around my knees. Inside, Stamatis was well and resting. But it was the fear of sickness that haunted us now. Dysentery and typhoid were beginning to spread through the camp, claiming lives. The American Red Cross prepared tents to isolate anyone who fell ill, to prevent the outbreak of an epidemic. Two isolation wards were set up, overseen by the women of the American Women's Hospitals. My mother had done all she could to keep us safe, but even she knew the danger was growing. It was only a matter of time before disease claimed more victims.

"We cannot stay," she had said that morning, as she came to sit beside me on the step. She stroked my hair gently with her hand. "Samos," she continued, "we have cousins there. They will take us in."

I knew it was true, but it was hard to admit. I looked at the faces of those around us, the people who had once had homes, families, lives, and I saw the same fear in their eyes. Hunger gnawed at us all, and the Red Cross, despite their efforts, could only do so much. The islanders themselves could do little for us. Now, with disease spreading through the camp, we had no choice but to leave. We clung to the hope that our cousins on Samos might offer us shelter at least until we could find a way to begin anew.

I turned and looked at my mother who sat beside me, staring at nothing, her hands limp in her lap. She had carried herself with quiet determination, but now, suddenly, she broke. A sob tore from her throat, raw and unexpected.

I instantly turned to her, wrapping an arm around her shoulders. "Mama, why are you crying?"

She looked at me, her dark eyes shining with sorrow. "I dreamt of them last night," she told me. "The women, the children and our Persephone." Her voice trembled. "Why did I allow myself to be convinced to take us to Smyrni? Your father's words echoed in my mind, but I ignored them."

Her words came in a rush, her grief spilling over. "I led them there, Eftihia, after everything they had already endured in Sokia, on the long, difficult trek we made to reach Smyrni. I led them straight into the chaos that awaited and then into the inferno. I saw them in my dream, all of them, fighting for survival." Her breath hitched. "What has happened to those poor women and the children? Where are they now? Are they safe, or am I responsible for their deaths?"

I swallowed against the tightness in my throat. What could I say to ease her pain when I, too, had wondered about them?

She wiped at her face with trembling fingers. "Now we are bound for Samos. Why didn't I take us there from the start? And what of our family there? How long can we depend on their kindness before we are forced to move on again? We have only the gold sovereigns we carry with us. How long will they last?"

I squeezed her hand. "Maybe when this horror is over, when peace is negotiated, we will be able to go home."

She turned to me then, cupping my cheek with one warm, trembling hand. Her eyes darkened with something heavier than sorrow—something closer to fury. "Eftihia, the Turks will never allow that. Sokia is lost to us. We must now make a new life for ourselves, one very different from the one we knew."

She let out a bitter laugh. "Did you see the ships from our so-called Allies? They stood idle in the harbour, watching as our people suffered, as they were slaughtered, as the city burned, as men, women, and children threw themselves into the sea to escape the flames. And they did nothing." Her fingers tightened slightly against my skin. "No, they gave the Turks what they wanted. The extermination of the infidels."

My mother let out a shaky breath, lowering her hand from my cheek. "I cannot lie to myself, Eftihia," she said, her voice brittle with grief. "I cannot pretend the Turks would have spared your father or Dimitri. Only God knows where their bodies now lie or if they were even granted a moment of mercy in their final hours."

Her composure crumpled once more, and fresh tears streamed down her cheeks.

"They took everything from us. Everything. I should have left, taken you far away, and let your father face them alone. Perhaps then, at least, all my children would have been safe." Her fingers twisted in her lap, her anguish spilling over. "But now I am haunted by thoughts of what my beloved husband, your father, must have endured. What my poor Dimitri—my son— must have endured." Her breath shuddered, her words breaking apart. "And Polyxeni, my precious child. She did not deserve to die so young, to die the way she did."

Her voice gave way then, breaking beneath the weight of her sorrow. "We have lost them all, *agapi mou*." She swallowed hard, her gaze locking onto mine with raw despair. "You, Stamatis, and I. We are all that is left of our family."

My throat burned, but I refused to cry. Not now. Not when she needed me to be the one holding her together. Instead, I leaned into her, resting my head against her shoulder, my arm tightening around her. It was all I could do, as if that alone could keep us from being swept away by the tide of sorrow and despair from all we had lost.

The decision was not made lightly. Chios had been a place where the Red Cross camp was both a temporary refuge and a stark reminder of our plight. The island was bursting at the seams with refugees, each of us carrying our own personal tragedies from Smyrni and beyond.

Samos beckoned. The name stirred something deep inside of me. It was a hope that maybe, just maybe, there was a chance for us. The Red Cross could send word to our relatives. It was a risk, but it felt like the only choice we had. To stay was to wait for sickness to take us, to leave was to gamble on survival.

Later that day, we stood before the Red Cross official, a man whose exhaustion showed in the shadows beneath his eyes. He listened as my mother explained our decision, nodding as he wrote down our names.

"We can telegraph the Red Cross in Samos to notify your family," he assured us. "There is a vessel leaving at dawn in four days. It is carrying others who also wish to go to Samos. Be ready."

Relief and fear mixed within me. Leaving the camp meant stepping into the unknown, but at least it was a choice of our own making. His final words *'be ready'* echoed in my mind. There was nothing for us to prepare for our departure. All we had to our names was the small bundle of clothing we had left Smyrni with and the ever-present weight of the fate of those whom we had lost. These were the only things we would take with us.

The morning of our departure arrived, and the dock was crowded with those desperate to leave, their expressions tight with anxiety. The vessel was a former cargo ship, its hull weathered but sturdy. On the deck, wooden benches had been placed where some chose to sit for part of the journey. Below deck, bunks had been fitted for women and children who wished to rest or who were vulnerable to the motion of the boat.

One by one, we climbed aboard, the crew of sailors keeping order amongst us. We found a space on one of the benches, Stamatis pressing close to my mother as we waited for departure. As the vessel pulled away from the shore, I watched the camp fade, the silhouettes of tents dissolving into the morning light. Yet in that moment, I understood that leaving Chios was a necessary risk, a grasp at a future that might still be salvaged.

The Red Cross volunteers moved among us with solemn determination, distributing food and blankets they could spare to keep us warm while we sat on the deck, their faces etched with compassion and their reassurances.

The three-hour journey to Samos would be nothing compared to what we had endured fleeing Smyrni, when we had been packed tightly on the deck of the boat with the others, suffocating in the press of bodies and languishing in the sorrow and desperation that had gripped us during our escape from the inferno.

A new chapter now awaited us. The sea was carrying us forward, yet once again, it offered us no sense of certainty. I had tried to picture Samos in my mind, to recall the stories our cousins had told us in letters, but words could not conjure up what we had never seen. My mother sat beside me, her fingers curled tightly around Stamatis' shoulder, holding him close, as if afraid that, even now, she might lose him.

*   *   *

As the boat sailed into the harbour of Vathy, the town unfolded before us. It curved around the bay, its whitewashed buildings rising in tiers. The waterfront bustled with activity. Small fishing boats bobbed near the docks together with the larger vessels, which were moored and where dockworkers were unloading crates under the watchful eyes of the crew and merchants.

Men hurried along the waterfront, balancing sacks of grain and barrels of olive oil on their shoulders, their voices blending into the hum of the town. Groups of traders were deep in negotiation, their hands gesturing over wooden crates. Fishermen were selling their morning's catch from small fishing boats, women balancing baskets against their hips. But beneath the rhythm of daily life, there was something else, a tension in the way people paused to glance at the new arrivals.

A long boulevard ran along the curve of the waterfront, lined with low buildings, shops, bakeries, their awnings casting patches of shade onto the street, where men in flat caps lingered by doorways, and in the *kafenio*. Behind the shops, the town rose in tiers up the hillside, houses stacked one upon the other, their terracotta roofs glowing in the sunlight. Narrow, winding alleys twisted between them, stone steps climbing steeply where the earth was too steep for roads. Balconies jutted out over the streets, draped with drying laundry, their railings lined with pots and trailing vines.

Church domes gleamed white against the sky, their bells silent for now, as they stood watching over the town as they had done so for generations. Beyond them, the hills rose sharply, covered in olive groves and cypress trees, their green slopes a stark contrast to the bustling life below.

The sharp scent of salt air and tobacco filled the air. Tobacco factories stood near the docks, their doors swinging open and shut as workers came and went. Further along, other buildings housed olive oil presses, which turned out the island's famed oil.

Our gazes travelled away from the town itself where it gave way to the countryside, the land dotted with small homes and farmsteads. Olive groves stood in neat rows, and beyond them, patches of land were given over to agriculture.

Beside me, my mother adjusted her hold on Stamatis, who had fallen asleep against her shoulder. We had made it to Samos. For a moment, I allowed myself to believe that perhaps, here, we would find a place to rest, a place to begin again.

The moment my feet touched solid ground, my legs wavered, not from the lingering sway of the boat, but from sheer exhaustion pressing down on me. Around us, Red Cross workers and local volunteers moved with quiet urgency through the tide of weary, displaced souls, guiding people to makeshift stations where names were recorded, details confirmed, and instructions passed on.

When it was our turn, we explained we were waiting for family. My mother gave our names, along with those of our cousins, to the woman seated at the table. After scanning the pages of her ledger, she nodded and looked up at us. Her expression was both kind and efficient.

"Ah yes," she said gently. "You are already registered. Your family has been notified. They are coming for you."

The words should have brought relief, but my mother only nodded, gripping Stamatis tighter. I wasn't sure if she was afraid to hope too soon or simply too drained to react. We were led to a small waiting area, where we sat on wooden benches beneath a canvas awning. My eyes drifted towards the water, towards the ship that had carried us here, empty now of its human cargo.

We already knew that refugees had begun arriving on Samos as early as mid 1921. They were fleeing Nicomedia, modern day İzmit, an ancient city on the north-western coast of *Mikrá Asía* (Asia Minor), a major commercial and administrative centre during the Byzantine and Ottoman periods. I remember the way my father spoke about Nicomedia. He had followed every report, each one darker than the last. By late June 1921, it was said the Greek forces and the men fighting beside them had set Muslim neighbourhoods on fire, looted homes, and left elderly people dead in the streets with their hands tied. Villages along the gulf had been burned to the ground. Then came the worst of it. It was reported that the Muslim districts of the cities of Akroinos (Afyonkarahisar) and Eskisehir, as well as a large number of villages were systematically burned. In some places, all the inhabitants, including women and children, were burned alive inside the mosques. Foreign missionaries and officers confirmed it, describing scenes no one should ever witness.

When the Greek garrison withdrew from Nicomedia on the night of 27 June, they evacuated their own people and left the rest to the flames. The region came under Turkish control once more and for many of the Greek and Armenian inhabitants, exile became the only way to survive. The safest escape was by sea. Samos became a destination for those who could make the journey.

When my father heard these accounts, he reacted with horror. He had believed the Greek presence in *Mikrá Asía* would protect us, not bring more suffering. The idea that our own people had committed such acts — against civilians, against the helpless — shook him deeply. It shattered whatever hope he still held that the conflict might spare the innocent on either side. For the first time, I saw real fear in his eyes — fear not only of what might happen to us, but of what this war had already turned our world into.

I remember how he had looked at me for a long moment before he spoke. "Eftihia," he said, his voice low, trembling, "listen carefully. Both sides have done things no human should ever commit. The cruelty isn't only with the Turks. Old men, women, children… tied, slaughtered, trapped inside mosques set aflame. And it was our own soldiers—Greek hands committing these horrors." He paused, his chest heaving, eyes clouded with shame. "War poisons everyone it touches. We have no right to feel justified. Every atrocity that is committed stains us as well."

I drew in a shuddering breath and stepped out of the labyrinth of my thoughts. My father—beloved, steadfast, so full of wisdom—had been wise in ways I could never match. Yet even his foresight had failed him. Not wise enough, not quick enough, to flee in time, to escape whatever cruel fate had claimed him. The ache of that knowledge, the silence of his absence, settled once more heavy in my chest.

By the time Smyrni fell, tens of thousands of refugees had arrived in Samos in a matter of days. The island had quickly filled with families seeking shelter, temporary or permanent, in towns and villages from Vathy to Karlovasi and beyond. Towns and villages had struggled to shelter them all and the refugees had been spread across twenty-seven villages. Samos did what it could, yet there was never enough space. Families slept in schoolrooms, storerooms, abandoned sheds, any corner spared to them. Every village held as many as it could.

Sometimes I couldn't help but wonder if things might have been different had we too gone to Kusandasi and crossed to Samos earlier. Perhaps if my father had listened, if we had fled to the coast before the violence escalated, our family might still be whole. Then there was the decision to lead the women and children to Smyrni. I knew my mother still struggled with it, blamed herself for the fate of those she had guided into the chaos. But how could we have known? We had already witnessed too much, endured horrors no one should. Reflection was pointless. Hindsight could not undo what we had lived through or what we had lost.

We had been sitting for an hour when a Red Cross worker approached with two men following close behind. They moved with a steady urgency, their eyes sweeping over the seated families as though searching for someone they feared they might never find. The moment their gazes locked on us, they quickened their pace.

"Mariegoúla!" one of them called out, his voice hoarse with emotion.

I stared at them both, my breath catching. I knew those faces. My mother had a photograph of them taken years ago, two proud young men standing shoulder to shoulder in their uniforms taken during their compulsory army service, their eyes bright with youth. But the men before me now were older, their faces lined and weathered. Vangelis's hair, once thick and dark in the photograph, was now streaked with grey, his skin deeply tanned and roughened. Stelios bore the same sharp eyes I remembered from the picture, but they sat in a face worn thin, his cheeks hollow, his jaw shadowed with stubble. Time had left its mark on them both.

My mother gasped, her hand flying to her mouth before she rose unsteadily to her feet. "Vangelis? Stelios?" Her voice cracked as she spoke their names.

Tears filled their eyes as they reached us. My mother sobbed, her body trembling as she clung to them. Vangelis gripped her shoulders, his face taut with anguish. "Where are the others?"

The question shattered what little composure she had. A strangled sob escaped her, and her knees buckled. I reached for her, but Vangelis caught her first, holding her upright with steady hands.

"They are gone. We have no way of knowing, but we fear the worst," she replied in an anguished voice and then began to sob.

Vangelis cupped the back of her head and brought her into his embrace, his own eyes glistening. "Mariegoúla *mou*, no words are enough to comfort you after what you have lost, what you have endured."

For a long moment, the three of them stood in silence, the weight of grief pressing down on all of us.

Then Stelios turned to me. His gaze swept over my face before softening, a sad smile breaking through the heaviness in his eyes. "Eftihia *mou*," he told me, taking hold of my hand. "The last photograph I saw of you, you were just a small girl. Look at you now. You have grown into a fine young woman."

The warmth in his voice caught me off guard. He must have seen the tears misting in my eyes, because he pulled me into an embrace. His voice dropped to a gentler tone. "You are safe now. We will look after you. All of you."

His words settled over me, and I wanted to believe him, to let that promise take root inside of me and drive out the fear that had been my constant companion. We had suffered and lost so much. Still, in that moment, I felt something I had not allowed myself to feel in weeks. Hope, something fragile and uncertain, but hope all the same.

"And this must be Stamatis," Stelios said, crouching in front of my brother. Stamatis hesitated, shrinking slightly against my side. His small fingers gripped my hand, his wary eyes flickering between the unfamiliar men and our mother.

My mother wiped at her eyes and turned towards them. "He and Persephone were separated from us," she said, her voice trembling. "For days, we didn't know if we would ever see him again. We were reunited on Chios, but there is still no word of Persephone or my husband's cousins, Konstantinos and his family who were with us."

Vangelis' face darkened, and he reached out, his hand gentle on Stamatis' shoulder. "Brave boy," he told him. "You have been through more than any child should."

Stamatis hesitated for a beat longer before finally stepping forward, allowing himself to be enveloped in the strength of his cousin's arms.

"Come," Vangelis said, rising. "We will take you home. You can tell us everything." He glanced at my mother, his voice laced with sorrow. "The stories we have heard, Mariegó, from what has been written in the newspapers, from the refugees flooding into Samos. They have spoken of horrors beyond words."

Stelios nodded grimly. "But now, you are with us. We will look after you."

There was nothing left for them to gather but the few bundles we carried. We followed them past the crowded relief station and along the edge of the harbour, where a horse-drawn cart stood waiting. It was a simple thing, with wooden benches on either side, but to me, it might as well have been a carriage. Vangelis helped my mother up first, then lifted Stamatis into her lap. I climbed in on my own, gripping the edges of the bench as Stelios took up the reins.

As the cart lurched forward, I stole one last glance at the harbour, at the sea that had carried us here. We were safe, but I knew our journey was far from over.

*　　　*　　　*

We left the harbour behind and began the climb to Ano Vathy. The road twisted upward, pulling us away from the bustle of the port and into a different world. The village unfolded around us, its cobbled streets narrow and winding, leading to small squares where old men sat on benches, their eyes following us with quiet curiosity. Houses lined the steep paths, their walls whitewashed, others the colour of sun-bleached stone, their doors painted in blues and greens. Wooden shutters, some open, some closed, framed the windows, and here and there, a cat stretched lazily in a patch of sunlight.

We would stay with Vangelis, the older cousin, and when we reached his home, a modest, double-storey whitewashed house perched high in the village, Vangelis's wife, Angeliki, met us at the door with open arms. There was no hesitation, no questions, just tears and warm embraces.

They had prepared a room for us. My mother and Stamatis would share a bed, and a single one had been pushed against the wall for me. We also had a chest of drawers. It was simple, but it was more than what we had in the refugee camp.

Before anything else, they urged us to wash. There was a dedicated wash area at the rear of the house, a luxury by the standards of those days, where a large metal tub had been filled with water that had been heated over a wood-fired stove. The effort of fetching it from the communal well, carrying heavy pails inside, and warming it over the fire was not lost on us.

After the journey we had endured and the filth of the refugee camp, the chance to bathe was a gift beyond words. The camp had reeked of unwashed bodies and damp earth. Flies clung to anything still, buzzing over the open drains that ran between the crowded tents. The warm water against my skin loosened the grime, soothed the aches, the exhaustion buried deep in my bones. My mother washed Stamatis, pouring water over his small frame. He barely protested, too tired to do anything but sit in the warmth. When we emerged, washed, and dressed in clean clothes, a new kind of relief settled over me.

The feeling of being human again.

We joined our cousins in the sitting room, where Stelios' wife, Theodora, had arrived, bringing with her a tray of sweets she had baked for us. The rich scent of cinnamon and honey filled the air, mingling with the freshly brewed coffee that sat steaming in small porcelain cups.

A little while later, we all settled in the dining room to enjoy a meal. The table was laden with more food than we had seen since fleeing from Sokia. They had gone to great trouble to prepare it all—dishes of roasted meat, fragrant rice, olives glistening in oil, fresh bread still warm from the oven. Everything looked delicious, a feast laid out before us. At first, we ate—the simple pleasure of proper food too comforting to interrupt. Coming from the refugee camp, where we had queued for hours each day for a ladle of soup and a crust of bread, the sight of a full table felt almost unreal. I remember how our cousin Vangelis urged us to eat, to take more, his voice full of warmth and pity. Yet, though our eyes were hungry, our bodies were not ready. Our stomachs had shrunk from eating rationed meals, and even the smallest portion felt too heavy.

We wanted to eat as we once had—to taste without guilt, to fill our plates and our bellies—but it was impossible. The first mouthfuls brought comfort, then pain, a dull reminder of how fragile we had become.

Still, we forced ourselves to eat a little more each day, as though rebuilding strength could also restore what we had lost. Yet no amount of food could quieten the memories of hunger—the long lines at the camp, the smell of thin soup, the sight of children licking their bowls clean. We had survived it, but it had changed us. Hunger had taught us restraint, humility, and a strange kind of gratitude that never left us.

After the meal ended, Stamatis was fighting against sleep, his small body curled against my mother's side, his breaths growing heavier with each passing minute. The bath, the food, the sweets, and the sheer weight of exhaustion had finally won. They carried him to bed, tucking him in and then closing the door softly behind them.

Only then did my mother begin to speak of the worst of it. At first, her voice was measured, hesitant, but soon the grief poured out of her, raw and unrelenting, as she revisited the nightmare we had endured. They listened, their faces shadowed with sorrow, their hands gripping ours in quiet solidarity. And when she spoke of my father and brother, of Polyxeni's fate, their restraint shattered. They wept openly, without shame.

"Stamatis, he still asks for them," my mother told them, wiping at her tears with hands that trembled. "How do I tell him?"

No one spoke. No one could.

Then she recounted everything, the journey from Sokia, the attack by the *Zevbekides*, the horrors of Smyrni, the desperation on the Quay. The moment we were torn apart from Stamatis and Persephone, from Konstantinos and his family. How the Red Cross had searched tirelessly for them, how fear had gnawed away at us. And how, with each passing day, desperation had begun to hollow her out, leaving only the unbearable thought that she might have lost Stamatis forever.

Vangelis reached across the table, his hand closing over hers, solid and warm. "Mariegó, you are here now," he said gently. "And we will look after you. You are family, and that is what we do in difficult times."

For the first time in what felt like forever, I let myself believe him. We had a roof over our heads and food at the table, and that night I slept without the fear of what tomorrow might bring.

CHAPTER SEVEN

We arrived in Samos in late October 1922. We had been weary and stripped of all that had once belonged to us. Not long afterwards, news arrived carried by men who had come from the port. Greece was in chaos. The news and the shame of our army's defeat had reached us. Word had spread that the king had abdicated, forced out by his own officers, and that trials had begun in Athens. They called it justice, but it felt more like desperation, a frantic attempt to blame someone, anyone, for the catastrophe that had befallen us. The suffering our people had endured was beyond anything one could imagine.

In Ano Vathy, we gathered in the narrow streets, listening to the men read aloud from newspapers, their voices tight with anger. Six men, they said, the prime minister, ministers, generals had been dragged before the courts, condemned, and shot before the month was out. Vangelis shook his head, muttering that dead men could not undo the past. The war had been lost long before they faced the firing squad, and no execution would bring back the thousands slaughtered, displaced or those who had drowned in the waters of Smyrni's harbour.

Even after the executions, the unrest did not settle. Greece was divided, torn between those who had lost faith in the monarchy and those who saw these deaths as nothing more than vengeance. The military coup, led by Colonels Nikolaos Plastiras and Stylianos Gonatas, had sought to restore order, but it only deepened the divisions. The executions were meant to placate public anger, but instead, they left a lingering bitterness in the hearts of many.

The newspapers insisted it was justice. They printed bold headlines declaring the end of an era, claiming that Greece would now rebuild, stronger and united. But there was little unity on the streets of Athens. Royalists spoke of their grievances, while others, desperate to believe in change, clung to the hope that the sacrifice of these men would somehow undo the disaster we had lived through.

Years later, we would learn that the men who were shot had not been the real architects of our ruin, that the truth had been buried along with them. But in the autumn of 1922, the truth mattered less than the desperate need for retribution. And so we continued on, carrying our grief as best we could, uncertain of what would come next.

Then came the newspapers from Greece, carrying hard truths for the world to read. Bold headlines that hollowed us out. The words lay cold on the page, yet the images they conjured were unbearable. They told of the poor, unfortunate souls who had not escaped before Mustafa Kemal's October 1st deadline. What followed was slaughter and despair.

They called them *'forced marches.'* Tens of thousands, perhaps even a hundred thousand, men, women, and children were driven into the interior. Few ever returned. Hunger, thirst, disease, and the brutality of soldiers claimed them one after another. Those who stumbled were beaten. Those who faltered were shot, left to rot where they fell. Mass shootings. Bodies were thrown into mass graves.

"A march of corpses, a march of death across Anatolia," wrote one woman from the Near East Relief Agency. Her words etched themselves into my memory.

I remember the newspapers filled with names of the missing, desperate relatives searching for those who would never be found.

And where was the help? The Allied powers stood by in shameful silence. Just as their ships had remained idle in Smyrni's harbour, they again did nothing, ignoring the horrors until the rest of the world began to publish the truth. Even then, they tried to conceal the true horror of those death marches, never revealing the full extent of the suffering endured by the thousands.

Yet, there were those who valiantly tried to answer the cries for help. The Red Cross and the Near East Relief Agency, few in number and stretched thin, made desperate attempts to reach the survivors. But their efforts were feeble against the scale of the horror. For most of the survivors, there was no sanctuary, no succour, no salvation. No rescue. No relief. No hope.

That silence — that deliberate, damning silence — is something I will never forgive. It was one of the greatest cruelties of those dark days.

And yet there was something else more disturbing and distressing they didn't write about in the papers. Not the Greek ones anyway. The headlines which reported the catastrophe spoke of the fire, the panic, the evacuation. But not the other things. Not the worst of it. Whole horrors were left out between the lines.

They wrote nothing of the grim harvest gathered from the harbour in Smyrni.

But those of us in the refugee camps, we heard them. All of them.

The stories had come across the sea, into the tents, into the buildings they had turned into camps to shelter us. No one knew who had said it first. It was passed along, said it was witnessed by foreign aid workers.

They said the bodies floated in the harbour for days after the city burned. That the water was full of them. Men, women, children. Some had jumped to escape the flames, others had drowned trying to reach the Allied ships. We had witnessed this with our own eyes.

But it wasn't just the deaths of those individuals that made the story unbearable.

It was what came after.

There were men, locals, they said, who came with poles, wire hooks, boats. They pulled the dead out of the water. Not to bury them. Not to bless them. But to take what they could. Rings stripped from fingers, earrings cut from ears, whatever they could find. The dead, already robbed of life, were robbed again of whatever gold and dignity remained.

They didn't call these men monsters. It was a refugee, an old man from Phocaea, who had given them the name.

'*Lafyragogi ptomaton*' he called them.

We knew what that meant.

Plunderers of corpses.

He had survived an earlier wave of ethnic violence in the Massacre of Phocaea in 1914, long before Smyrni burned. *Bashibazouks*, he called them. Men with wild eyes and a hunger for violence, had swept through his town, slaughtering the Greek population, setting fire to houses, the smoke covering the sky like a dark shroud. He had fled to the sea and to Chios. Then, when the worst was over, he returned, and tried to rebuild his life. This time he had fled before the Turks had arrived. He had lived through this trauma twice.

The papers Vangelis brought to us in Samos were still filled with stories of the catastrophe that had unfolded in Smyrni. The *Eleftheros Typos* —the *Free Press*—was openly critical of the Greek government's failures and of the international community's indifference. As the truth was being written, it only confirmed what we had heard in the refugee camp, and the names of those who had shown courage and fortitude to save the lives of so many.

They wrote about an American, Admiral Bristol, the United States High Commissioner, in Constantinople, who had sat idly by. His private writings had revealed his disdain, for Greeks, and for Middle Eastern people. As the crisis in Smyrni worsened, he paid scant attention to the human suffering, seeing it instead as the inevitable result of Greek ineptitude in the war and believing that the Greeks deserved their fate. While the city burned and a humanitarian catastrophe unfolded, he sipped tea and played tennis.

This man's response, marked by neglect and bias, drew criticism both in the United States and in Greece. In our papers, the general sentiment was one of outrage and disbelief. How could a man entrusted with such responsibility stand by as so many of our people suffered and died?

Unlike that *Vromóskylo Amerikáno* (filthy American dog) Bristol, in Constantinople, the newspapers spoke of the heroism of individuals who could not turn away from the suffering before their eyes. It was then we learned the names of those we had spoken of in the camp. Asa Jennings was one of them, a missionary who had long been involved with American schools in Smyrni. He became, one of the great heroes of the catastrophe.

Faced with the unimaginable crisis, he found an ally in Captain Theophanides, the commander of the Greek battleship *Kilkis*, which had been purchased by the Greeks from the Americans in 1914. The captain agreed to help. Jennings began writing messages at the ship's station, which Theophanides translated into Greek. These messages were then taken to the radio room, encoded, and sent to Athens. The reply that came back was almost absurd: the Prime Minister was sleeping. He could not be disturbed.

The first response denied his request for ships. But Jennings, in partnership with Theophanides, pushed back. He threatened, with the authority he did not truly possess, that if the Greek government refused, the next message would go unencoded. The world would know that Greece had allowed the Turks to slaughter hundreds of thousands of Greeks. It was audacious, yet it worked.

Commander Halsey Powell, the American officer in Smyrni, was negotiating with the Turkish authorities to allow the refugees to leave the city safely. The refugees had to be taken out of Turkey—not just for their own survival, but to bring some measure of peace to the Turkish people as well. Mustafa Kemal, a man whose life had been shaped by war and who had seen the devastation of his country, agreed. However, he imposed strict conditions. No Greek flags could fly on the ships, for fear that it would inflame the Turkish population. And no men of military age—between seventeen and forty-five—could leave. The Turks did not want them returning as an invading army.

This condition would prove devastating. Most of those men were never seen again. Only a few escaped. Entire generations of Greeks and Armenians were lost, extinguished in a single, cruel sweep. It was a crime against humanity, one that haunted every account we read.

In that moment, those two men became the great heroes of the catastrophe. We realised they risked not only their lives but also their reputations to aid the impoverished, the sick, the parched, the beaten, the psychologically traumatised people still waiting to be rescued from the Quay as Smyrni still burned.

The Greek government finally relented, ordering twenty-six ships to be placed under Jennings' command. The Greek flags were taken down and replaced with the American flag to signal that these were American vessels. Yet we read in disbelief that even then, the commanding officers of the Greek ships hesitated. Many refused to sail to a Turkish port. Captain Theophanides took decisive action. He ordered every captain on the Greek ships to prepare to sail immediately, warning that anyone not ready by midnight would face court martial and execution on the fantail of the *Kilkis* the next morning.

Captain Theophanides was the genuine hero of that operation, a man all Greeks should honour, yet no one knows his name. If we had not read that article, we would not have known about this man. It is a travesty. He risked everything for his people and acted with courage when the Greek government hesitated.

As the flotilla of Greek ships entered Smyrni's harbour, Jennings stood at the helm of the first vessel. Twenty-six Greek ships, flying American flags, entered the port. Powell, who commanded the American destroyer, led them in. The Quay was lined with the desperate, the dying, the sick, the children, and the old. When they saw the ships with the American flag coming into the port, there was great jubilation. They cheered and wept openly.

Seven days. That was all they had. The Turks allowed only women, children, and the elderly. The Turkish army insisted on examining everybody, forcing them to pass in single file before allowing them to board the ships. Over those seven days, Jennings and Powell orchestrated a rescue that seemed impossible. Ships shuttled continuously between Smyrni, Mytilene, Piraeus, and other Greek islands, carrying nearly two hundred thousand refugees. By the last day of September, the rescue was complete. Thousands had perished, but many more survived because of these two Americans, who risked life and reputation for the helpless.

Later, the papers would write about the honours both Asa Jennings and Halsey Powell received. Jennings was awarded Greece's highest civilian honour, the Order of the Redeemer, and the Medal of Military Merit. Halsey Powell received the Distinguished Service Medal from the United States for his actions in Smyrni. Their courage had been celebrated, their names recorded in history. And rightly so. They had saved thousands, had risked everything for strangers in a foreign land.

And yet, our hearts ached when we remembered Captain Ioannis Theophanides. The man who had ensured the Greek ships sailed, who had threatened court martial and execution to save lives, whose decisive action made the rescue possible. His name is absent from official honours, absent from the public memory of Greece. No medal, no recognition, no ceremony. Just silence.

It seemed an injustice so profound that it lingered with us as we read about him, as we tried to imagine the courage it had taken to stand firm while the world around him hesitated. Two heroes honoured and remembered, one hero forgotten—how strange that history could be so selective.

*   *   *

The winter of 1923 found us in Samos, a place we had come to out of necessity. Our relatives, had taken us in, provided shelter and food, and helped us piece together the fragments of our existence. But we knew it was not a long-term solution.

Life on the island was difficult. Though our family offered us what comfort they could, we knew we were a burden and our future uncertain. The people of Samos were kind, but the island itself had suffered in the wake of the catastrophe. Refugees like us had flooded its towns and villages, pushing its resources to the limit. The tobacco factories in Vathy provided some employment, but competition was fierce. Many of the refugees were men who had lost everything and sought whatever work they could find to provide for their families.

Then, in the middle of February 1923, news arrived that would change everything. The Greek government had offered refugees the chance to resettle in Macedonia, in homes vacated by Turks who had left under the terms of the population exchange agreement signed in January. This was not merely a rumour, it was an official plan, one that offered land and a new beginning to those who had fled and had nothing.

The Greek government had promised resettlement, land, and a future, but what that meant in reality, none of us knew. The Refugee Settlement Commission had taken over the task of dispersing thousands of us across the country, some to Athens, others to Thessaloniki, and many, to rural Macedonia. We listened carefully to the accounts of the officials. They spoke of villages with empty homes, of fertile land waiting to be cultivated, of an opportunity to rebuild a life of dignity and self-reliance.

At first, my mother hesitated. To uproot ourselves again was daunting. But staying in Samos meant remaining dependent on the kindness of others. With our Red Cross registration and previous records, the process of official verification was easier. We were asked about our past, our skills, and the number of people in our family. My mother signed for all of us, herself, Stamatis, and me, her hand steady despite the hesitation in her eyes.

By the time we were offered resettlement in Macedonia, we understood that our past no longer mattered—except for what strength it could lend us in starting over. To begin again in a foreign land was daunting, yet there was no alternative. The decision was made. We would go. There was no certainty, no promise that our lives would be better. We would not be alone. A dozen other families would make the journey north with us. It would take nearly a week, made harsher by the cold. Transport had been arranged by the government, with the aid of foreign agencies, but the process dragged on slowly.

*   *   *

The day we left Samos, the sun was high, though the air was crisp, and the sea sparkled beneath a clear sky. My mother held Stamatis' hand tightly, and I could sense the tension she held in her shoulders. I felt it too. But as I walked beside her, feeling the quiet strength of her hand in mine, I knew that our journey, though long and fraught with hardship, was far from over. We would keep moving, keep searching for a place where we could rebuild what had been lost, and perhaps, one day, find a home that was truly our own.

The vessel waiting at the dock wasn't large or luxurious, but it was sturdy and familiar with its purpose. A small coastal passenger ship, it had been adapted to carry not only goods but also people like us, seeking refuge. It wasn't a grand liner, but its modest accommodations would get us to where we needed to go. The focus was functionality, ensuring we were all transported safely between the islands and along the coast.

It had been hard to say goodbye to Vangelis and Stelios and their families. The night before, both families, together with friends we had come to know during our stay, gathered for a farewell dinner. There had been warmth, laughter, and the quiet weight of parting in every embrace. The following morning, when they took us to the port, their kindness made it even harder to leave. Once again, they reminded us we were welcome to stay for as long as we wished. Their words lingered with me, knowing the road ahead was uncertain but comforted by the knowledge that such generosity still existed in the world.

Stamatis was only five years of age and had already lost so much—his father, Dimitri, Polyxeni and Persephone, who had been like a second mother to him. Each had been a steady, anchoring presence in his young life, and their absence had left him adrift. Perhaps that was why he had formed such a close bond with Vangelis, who had offered him warmth, safety, and a sense of belonging in a world that had turned uncertain and harsh.

Now, faced with parting from him, Stamatis clung to Vangelis, his small arms wrapped tightly around his neck, refusing to let go. When he realised we were truly leaving, his cries tore through the air, raw and desperate, calling out for the man who had become a figure of safety to him. Vangelis held him close, one large hand cradling the back of his head, his eyes fixed on the ground as if looking at us might break his resolve. He whispered gentle words in Greek, promising that Stamatis would see him again, though both of them knew such promises might never be kept.

When my mother reached for him, Vangelis hesitated, tightening his hold as if one more moment might make the parting easier. It didn't. His eyes were red when he finally let go, placing Stamatis in my mother's arms with a tenderness that made my throat tighten. My mother spoke to him in the same gentle tone she once used to soothe him to sleep, though her breath caught as she turned away, shielding her face from Vangelis so he would not see her cry.

As we began to board, Stamatis twisted in her arms, stretching his little hands out towards Vangelis, calling out his name as he sobbed out his misery. His cries sounded deeper than the sorrow of parting, as if he sensed more than he could ever say. At times I have wondered if, had we stayed on Samos, our story might have unfolded differently.

The ship's engine thrummed beneath us as we eased away from the dock. Stamatis cried out in earnest for Vangelis, his anguished cries heart wrenching. We turned back, catching sight of our relatives still waiting on the Quayside. Wiping our own tears, we waved, and they waved back, small gestures but they carried the weight of everything we were leaving behind. Samos shrank into the distance, but instead of fear, I felt a quiet sense of hope. There was no longer a sense of desperation. This journey was different. We were not fleeing. The unknown lay ahead, yes, but it promised the possibility of peace, a new beginning. With the Red Cross at our side, even the uncertainty felt a little gentler, a reminder that we were not entirely alone.

We noticed the quiet efficiency of the crew. They showed us the wooden benches for seating and directed us to simple cabins where passengers could rest and sleep. It wasn't much, but it was enough for a journey of this length. The Red Cross workers were the most comforting, moving around, ensuring we had what we needed. There were supplies—bread, water, food, milk for the children, to keep us going. At each port that we stopped at along the way, more provisions would be brought on board, replenishing what had been used.

The steady rhythm of the ship's engine and the routine of the crew provided a sense of normalcy. The air was filled with the conversation of other families, some quiet, others talking more loudly to one another. The journey was long, but not the worst we had endured. Other families who had also made the same reluctant choice filled the boat. Some spoke of their old homes, the fields and estates left behind. Others, and rightly so, spoke openly of their fear.

What if the promises were empty? What if there was nothing waiting for us? What if the assurances of the Greek Government turned out to be just as empty as the sense of betrayal and abandonment we had felt during the burning of Smyrni?

We had believed we were part of something—part of Greece. But when the fire came, no one came for us. No army, no leadership. Aristides Sterghides, the Greek Consul, had fled at the first sign of danger, slipping away to safety while we stood helpless before the flames. His departure was more than the loss of a man; it was the stripping away of any illusion that Greece would stand with us. The banners, the speeches, the promises of protection, what did they amount to when we were left to face ruin alone? We were not citizens to them, not brothers and sisters in a greater homeland, but expendable, left to burn with the city. That knowledge cut deeper than the fire itself.

We heard many stories of how the refugees were being spoken of in Athens and other cities. Not with compassion, but with suspicion. They called them *Mikrasiátes*—Asia Minor Greeks—when they wanted to sound polite. More often, they were just *prosfiges*, refugees. A word that clung like dirt, as if their presence alone was a burden.

Worse still were the whispers of *Turkospóroi*—seeds of the Turks. As if decades, centuries of living under Ottoman rule had made them impure. As if they were less Greek. Less worthy. It didn't matter that their families had kept the language alive, kept the faith, built churches, run schools, raised their children to dream of Greece as their homeland. When they finally arrived, desperate and broken, they were seen not as kin, as survivors, but as intruders.

There were reports of overcrowded refugee camps, hastily built shacks outside the city, entire families packed into filthy rooms with no sanitation. Disease spreading fast. Of rations that barely arrived. Of insults muttered in markets, landlords who refused to rent, jobs that vanished at the mention of them being *Mikrasiátes*. They were seen as poor, diseased, untrustworthy. A burden on a country already struggling under its own weight. That they should be grateful for whatever scraps they were given.

The children bore the heaviest scars. Many had lost fathers, sometimes both parents. Poverty marked them—their bare feet, torn clothes, the way they stood out from the Greek-born children. The shame of being a refugee silenced many of them. Survival came first.

From our previous haven on Samos, we were not immune to their suffering. In Athens, the refugees, our own people, faced cruelty and greed at every turn. In the chaos, corruption flourished among those meant to help them. Public servants, even politicians, fattened themselves on their desperation. Officials demanded bribes for shelter and basic necessities. Women suffered most of all and fell prey to exploitation. With no male to protect them, they were often left to care for children and the elderly in hovels, forced to pay exorbitant rents, humiliated, and exposed to dangers no woman should endure. Many were forced to barter more than just money—their dignity and their safety to keep their families alive.

It was spoken of in Samos, in the conversations with friends, with those gathered in the square.

"They made a committee in Athens to help the refugees," someone explained, "but it is nothing of the kind. It is riddled with corruption." Voices then lowered, heavy with bitterness. "The money for houses, for food—it never reaches the people. The officials line their own pockets while families beg and go hungry."

Corruption, theft—none of it surprised me, though it sickened me all the same. But when the last words came, I froze. "They make the women pay in ways too shameful to speak of".

To hear that the Greeks, our own countrymen, were forcing such degradation upon women who had fled in desperation, it was beyond cruelty. These poor women were being stripped of their dignity, made to suffer again at the hands of those who should have sheltered them. I was trembling inside with a bitter fury I could not contain.

Many years later, we would look back and feel a deep sense of pride at what the refugees had achieved. To arrive carrying little, with the only possession of the skills honed over generations. In Nea Ionia, the sound of looms soon filled the air; carpets and textiles woven in *Mikrá Asía* found new markets in Athens. Entire streets turned into workshops where families worked side by side, tailors, weavers, cloth-sellers—transforming knowledge into survival.

New settlements rose quickly. With the help of the Refugee Relief Fund, thousands of houses were built in places like Vyronas, Kaisariani, and Nea Kokkinia. The plain *'Prosfygika'* blocks, though stark, became the framework for new lives. They were not grand or beautiful, but they were a place where the refugees could rebuild and create a community. Bakeries, shoe shops, cafés, and small factories opened, and slowly, a sense of ordinary life returned.

In Nea Smyrni, the naming of streets after lost towns became a quiet act of defiance. What began with tents grew into a suburb of craftsmen, teachers, and shopkeepers. Civic life, once consumed by the flames, was slowly rebuilt.

They had done more than survive. They had altered Athens itself. Small businesses fed the city's hunger for textiles, food, and services, reshaping its economy for generations. Women bore much of this labour—widows and wives running shops and workshops, holding families together, forming co-operatives and councils.

What had begun in sorrow became a testament to endurance. From ruin, they built new neighbourhoods, new livelihoods, and a new identity, proof that while Smyrni and the towns of Ionia were lost, its people had not been broken.

*   *   *

We arrived in the port city of Kavala, a town already overflowing with refugees like us and were directed to a makeshift refugee centre where officials assigned families to different villages. Our destination would be Antiphillipi. The name meant nothing to us, yet it was to be our new home.

We learnt that only a year earlier the town was known as *Dranich* in Macedonian, *Dranítsi* in Greek. Its people had been Muslim, Turkish-speaking families who had farmed the same fields for generations. After the compulsory exchange of populations between Greece and Turkey, their houses, their fields, were left behind for strangers to inherit. Now, like so many villages across Macedonia, it was being repopulated with Greek refugees carrying what little remained of their lives.

A convoy of carts took us inland. The countryside rolled away in gentle hills, fields stretching endlessly. It was beautiful, but it did not feel like home. When we arrived, it was clear that it had once belonged to others. The houses, though sturdy, carried an air of abandonment. By the time we arrived, the village was in the middle of becoming something new. The officials had promised us we were to have a share here, a plot to farm and a place to build again. It was a strange thought, that another family's loss had opened the door to allowing us to begin anew.

And as I stood there, I couldn't help but wonder—somewhere now in Turkey, in towns far from here, perhaps even in Sokia, Turkish-speaking families who had been sent away, were also looking at the homes of strangers and thinking exactly the same thing.

Relief workers greeted us. They were kind but efficient, their voices calm as they explained what would happen next. Officials addressed us as a group, their voices carrying across the square. They spoke of integration, of rebuilding, of making this place our own. They told us that this was home now, that we must work the land, strengthen the village, and forge new lives from the pieces of our old ones.

The first order of business would be to assign us our homes. The government had promised supplies, and some had already arrived. A communal storehouse had been set up in the centre of the village, to sustain it until it could stand on its own.

Here was where we could collect our rations. There were sacks of flour, tins of olive oil, and crates of dried legumes. Water was drawn from a well that had served the village for generations. There were stacks of blankets folded with care, and piles of donated clothing in all sizes, remnants of generosity from foreign relief workers who assisted in the resettlement efforts.

My mother listened in silence, her expression unreadable. Perhaps she did not yet believe them. Perhaps none of us did. But for now, there was food, shelter, and the promise of stability. That would have to be enough.

The house we were assigned was modest but solid, offering just enough space. There was a small kitchen, a sitting area, and two bedrooms. A courtyard stretched behind it, where a neat stack of firewood had been left, dry and ready for use. We also had an outbuilding where the previous occupants had kept their livestock. The government had also provided us with land on which to cultivate tobacco, the crop that dominated the landscape of the area. Tobacco, they said, would be our lifeline, a means to make a living from the very soil that had once been farmed by families much like our own.

Inside the rooms were not entirely empty. A wooden table stood in the centre of the sitting area, surrounded by sturdy chairs. The kitchen held a wood-fired stove, its surface worn but serviceable, with pots and utensils still in their places. In the cupboards, supplies of everyday staples had been left behind, enough to provide some comfort.

In the bedrooms stood iron bed frames, their mattresses thin but intact, a place to rest that did not have to be fashioned from the hard floor. Some bed linen remained folded in the wooden chests. A small washing area had been built at the back, complete with a hearth where water could be heated for bathing.

Perhaps those who had lived here before had left in the same manner we had, taking only what their arms could carry, told that another home, just like this one, awaited them elsewhere. The thought settled over me, and I felt an ache in my chest. The home we now stood in was more than we had owned in months. It was far removed from the luxurious rooms of our home in Sokia. There was no grand parlour, no sumptuous furnishings that spoke of a life lived in comfort and abundance. And so, without a word, we set to work, scrubbing the floors, wiping away the dust of absence, letting ourselves believe, if only for a moment, that we could begin again.

The Greek government and the Refugee Settlement Commission had begun organising the land distribution. Farming families were given plots of land to cultivate. Those with skills could find work in the towns. Since my family had been an agricultural one in Sokia, we were granted a plot of land to work. This commission focused not only on housing and employment but also on providing social welfare. My mother, as a widow, was fortunate enough to receive a small pension, which provided us with some security as we started anew. We had experience in growing and exporting tobacco, and this knowledge became our greatest asset.

We worked the soil, planting the tobacco that we knew so well, learning to adapt to the new environment. It was not the life we had once known, but we were no longer living on the charity of others. We were forging a new life, however difficult it was.

As the months passed, the village changed. More refugees arrived, and the empty homes were filled with voices, with laughter, with the sounds of people beginning again. Some men, those with the strength left after all they had endured, ploughed the fields, sowing wheat and various crops for the coming season. The government had provided us with some livestock—chickens, goats, horses, and mules.

Stamatis was among the first to find joy in this new life. He ran among the other children, his laughter breaking the stillness of the village. A small school was eventually set up for the children, and Stamatis could attend. It was a simple one-room schoolhouse, where a teacher, himself a refugee, tried to bring some semblance of normalcy to their young lives.

For my mother and me, it took longer. Though proud and determined, she had once been a woman of means, a lady who managed a household with grace and efficiency, but the weight of our loss was not so easily dispelled. I lay awake, listening to the distant hoot of an owl, thinking of the sprawling cotton fields, of the scent of tobacco drying in the sun.

There were moments, too, of wistful reflection. I would sit on the steps of our home, looking out at the fields and imagining the life we had once known in Sokia—where our days had been filled with laughter, music, and the ease of wealth. The contrast was stark and painful. Here in Antiphillipi, every joy was hard won, and every small comfort was tempered by the relentless reminder of what we had lost.

In quiet moments, I would think about the house that once belonged to our family and speculate as to who now called that place their home. Perhaps a Turkish family, with traditions and a family history of their own, now lived in that grand residence, their lives intertwined with what we had left behind. I also couldn't help but wonder who might have occupied these very premises we now lived in. A Turkish family with their own dreams and memories, now forced into exile as the tides of the population exchange reshaped our world.

We were not alone in our grief. Everyone in Antiphillipi carried their own stories of escape and loss. But together, we built something new. We planted gardens and established a market where goods could be traded. The church, a simple whitewashed building, became our gathering place, where prayers were offered for those who had been left behind and gratitude was given for the chance to begin again.

As the seasons changed, so too did our prospects in Antiphillipi. The tobacco plants grew slowly but steadily, nurtured by our hard work and the resources we had at our disposal. The community of refugees from Samos, Chios, and Pontos that had gathered here forged a network of support. Neighbours shared what we had, and we envisioned a future where our struggles might give way to a life of dignity, even if it was a life far removed from the splendour of what we had known in Sokia.

My mother, ever the pragmatic soul, tried to make sense of our new life. "We may have been reduced to this," she would say softly, her eyes filled with both resignation and determination, "but at least we have a piece of land where we can rebuild. We can work the soil, grow tobacco, and earn enough to survive."

The move to Antiphillipi was marked by both heartache and harsh realities. Each day carried the weight of our displacement, the sharp contrast between the life we had left behind and the one we were now forced to build. Yet, in the rhythm of cultivating tobacco, in the patient work of tending soil that was not ours but now sustained us, I saw another truth. Loss had followed us here, and exile still lived within us, but so too did the will to endure. We were no longer merely refugees; we had become settlers who had planted roots in this modest town, shaping a future from the fragments of our past, and readying ourselves for whatever lay ahead.

*   *   *

The scars of the past were ever-present, though. There was always that haunting gap, a silent space where my father and brother once were. So too, the fate of Persephone, Konstantinos, Ourania and their two daughters remained unknown, and our hearts ached for their lost presence. The Red Cross still had not located their whereabouts. We had resigned ourselves to the fact that we would never know their fates, though deep inside, we knew the worst had likely befallen them.

News continued to filter through to us in articles written in newspapers, which made their way into our town. What stung more than the smoke that had burned my lungs that day in Smyrni, was that the British did not just stand by while we burned, they tried to bury what happened. They took the truth and smoothed it over like a wrinkle in a tablecloth.

The first newspapers began printing details of the horror. Survivors spoke. Missionaries wrote reports. Even some British sailors tried to tell what they had seen from the decks. Murder, fire, the slaughter of civilians, Turkish soldiers dragging women away, raping and then murdering them. But then came the official statements from London. Quiet. Diplomatic. Empty. They said there was 'no clear evidence' that the Turkish forces had started the fire. No evidence of systematic violence. NO EVIDENCE.

As if the scorched and slaughtered bodies left behind weren't enough.

As if the silence of the warships during the massacre hadn't already said everything.

As if witnesses hadn't seen the Turkish soldiers pour kerosene into basements and throw in lit rags.

What shocked me wasn't just the indifference. It was the deliberate softening of the tragedy that had befallen us. The British were careful. Strategic. They knew which way the wind was blowing. Mustafa Kemal was now the future of Turkey, and the British wanted peace. Trade. Oil. Borders drawn in their favour.

And so, they rewrote the fire.

Politicians even started saying that the Armenians might have set it themselves. Or the Greeks. That the fire had 'mysterious origins'. I remember that phrase exactly. '*Apo Mystiriódi Proélefsi.*'

As if Smyrni caught fire all on its own. As if it were a natural disaster.

They said the burning of the city was a 'tragedy'. That was the word they used. Not a crime. Not a massacre. Not an organised campaign to erase us.

A Tragedy. As if we were unlucky, not betrayed.

They blamed our soldiers for the war, as if that made the slaughter of civilians somehow balanced. As if defeat stripped us of humanity.

I have never argued that the Greek army was innocent. But no retreat justifies what the Turks did to Smyrni. And no civilisation worthy of its name should have covered it up.

We had once believed that Britain stood for something. For justice. For law. For order. But what did they stand for in those days when hell was unleashed on the masses waiting desperately for rescue on the quay? They stood still. Silent. And when the ash had settled, they cleaned their hands and said they saw nothing.

That is the truth they did not want to print in The Times of London. That was the truth that was censored in the reports read in their Parliament. They protected their interests. Not the truth. Not the survivors. Not the dead.

They sided with power. In their polished accents, they spoke about peace and order and decency. But I remembered the actions in Smyrni.

The fire may have been hot. But their betrayal burned hotter. And longer.

My beloved granddaughter, if the British were complicit in hiding the truth, so too were the French. A personal emissary of the Republic of France was sent to investigate the fire that had erased entire Greek and Armenian neighbourhoods. His task was to remain supposedly impartial, to determine responsibility. But the ink on that report had dried long before the French evacuees had already arrived on the shores of France.

Their voices had been unified in a single cry. The new regime of Mustafa Kemal was to blame.

And yet, their words were rendered weightless.

The emissaries report, which also included letters from an Admiral, obliterated any testimonies that contradicted the French preferred narrative. The High Commissioner of the Republic of France in the East, also stood shoulder to shoulder with the Admiral, offering official absolution of the Turkish nationalist regime.

Even the French consul in Smyrni, who had been there, who had witnessed the horrors, was contradicted. His report erased.

What followed was not diplomacy, but performance.

The French consul, who had taken refuge aboard one of the battleships in the harbour, wrote his report with a diplomat's restraint but a civilian's outrage. He recorded what he had seen, or rather, 'WHAT HE COULD NEVER UNSEE'.

And in the article they printed what he had written. The French Consul observed that the Turkish authorities insisted to all who would listen that they bore no responsibility for the fire, claiming it was not in their interest to destroy Smyrni. Yet, he noted, such an argument could easily be answered. If it were truly not in their interest, then it was most certainly in their interest to have taken measures to stop the conflagration. In this, he insisted, they had made no effort whatsoever. The army, far from restraining the devastation, participated in the slaughter of innocents—first with rifles, then, so as not to draw attention, with blows from rifle butts—while others looted abandoned houses.

But his truth was not welcomed by the French authorities.

The article told how in October 1922, this man suffered a nervous collapse. It was said that the fire itself, the scale of it, the atrocities he had witnessed had played a part in his mental breakdown. It was no surprise to us. But the indifference of his own government also played a part in that decline. What he had recorded. His letters. His reports. All were cast aside by the French, as if they had no bearing on the matter. As if they had not come from the ashes of Smyrni. It is hard for a man to keep breathing when your truth is treated like poison.

They spoke of how he had been an experienced diplomat, in the service of a country that represented itself as the champion of democracy, of logic, of reason. A nation whose self-image was that of Reason itself. And yet he had to accept something irrational, something cynical and cruel.

Raison d'État 'reason of state.'

I never forgot that word. It sounded so elegant when they read it out. As if politics justified betrayal. That the interests of the state — its security, power, or survival — could justify actions that might otherwise have been seen as immoral, illegal, or unjust. That governments could act outside normal rules or ethics if they believed it served the higher necessity of protecting the state.

What France did was diplomatic cowardice. The British had already betrayed us before the fire. Now the French followed. And the deception did not stop with the diplomats. The truth was suppressed in other ways too.

Later we would also read about the insurance claims from the fire in Smyrni. They were not brought before the courts in Greece, but in British courts because many of the claims were filed by Western merchants and companies insured under British policies. One case was that of the American Tobacco Company. They sought compensation from the British Guardian Assurance Company, for the loss of its warehouses and stock. The case was heard in the London Commercial Court, for the value of the property destroyed was immense—over twenty million pounds by some estimates.

There was evidence enough of deliberate arson. Witnesses had seen Turkish soldiers with torches, moving methodically through the streets, ensuring that Greek and Armenian homes and businesses burned. Yet the courts refused to name those responsible. In their rulings, the fire became nothing more than the result of confusion in a chaotic time.

The courts protected both diplomatic relations by shielding the perpetrators and also protected the financial interests of the British insurance companies, who avoided paying out vast sums to their clients.

To me, it was another betrayal, no different from what we had already endured. The British and French had turned their backs on us in our darkest hour, and now they turned their courts into shields for lies. Not the truth, not the dead, not the survivors mattered—only money and the alliances they wished to keep. They called it justice. Once more it was nothing more than *Raison d'état,* the reason of state.

I hated them for it.

But none more so than in January 1925.

A man from Thessaloniki passed through our town. He went to the *kafenio*. He said little until someone asked him about the British ship that had come into the port of Thessaloniki before Christmas. The newspaper, Macedonia, had barely mentioned it, only that it had arrived from Mudanya. It was called the *Zan*, and it had left for France a few days later. But the name Mudanya held significance for us refugees.

I remember hearing the name when I was a girl. My father would mention it when he came back from trips. It was a port town. I would picture the sea, like in Smyrni. Calm, blue, open. He said the merchants there were friendly and the taverns filled with conversations in Greek, Turkish, Armenian. A town where goods passed through to be exported, spices, fabrics, produce. He told me it was a place where people made deals, drank coffee, raki and then moved on.

To me, it was just a name. Like Ayvalık or Çeşme. Somewhere real, but far away, where life went on, simple and unremarkable. I never had a reason to think otherwise.

But in October 1922, Mudanya was no longer just the name of a port. It was the place where the war ended, for everyone but us. The Armistice of Mudanya was signed. They called it a turning point. A diplomatic success. An end to the war. But I had learned that peace in politics, rarely means justice.

Turkey was there, proud, and defiant, represented by İsmet İnönü, a key Turkish military officer, statesman, and later the second President of Turkey after Mustafa Kemal. He spoke on behalf of the new regime in Ankara. Britain, France, and Italy were there too, the so-called Allied powers who had once promised to protect the Christians of *Mikrá Asía*. And Greece? Greece was not even invited to the table. Like a dog kicked out of a room it had no business being in. Our army had been crushed. The government was collapsing and was later forced to accept the armistice under Allied pressure.

The terms were simple. Greece would withdraw from Eastern Thrace and Turkey would regain control. The Allies would hold on to Constantinople, but everyone knew the city would fall into Turkish hands soon enough. No reparations. No justice. No mention of the massacres, the fire, the hundreds of thousands who had fled, some with nothing but the clothes on their backs.

They said it was a diplomatic victory. For peace, for stability.

For us, it was another betrayal, diplomatically signed, politically sealed and morally forgotten. That was the true meaning of Mudanya.

I can tell you that kind of peace came at a cost. One that people like me, my family and thousands of others paid a heavy price for, but not by the men who signed those papers.

They called it the end of the war, but for us, for the Greek families of Anatolia, it was the start of something worse. From Mudanya came the Lausanne Conference, where the map of the region was redrawn, and from there came the so-called 'exchange of populations'. Three words that still burn in my mouth. That was a polite term they used for throwing people out of their homes, for uprooting centuries of life, for saying, 'You don't belong here anymore.' A solution, they called it, to a crisis they helped create.

The West had promised us protection, had sent our soldiers across the sea, telling us we had history and righteousness on our side until it no longer served their interests.

Every single one of those papers — Mudanya, Lausanne, all of them — they were not signed in ink. They were signed in the blood of the people they abandoned, like lambs slaughtered without mercy, offered up on the altar of politics.

And the world called it peace.

That was what Mudanya had meant for us, until the day the man from Thessaloniki arrived and everything changed. From that day on, I could not bear to hear the name Mudanya without my stomach turning.

The man had looked up from his coffee and said, "They did not print what it carried," he said. "The truth of what that cargo contained would have split the country in two."

He was reluctant to speak about it at first. The distress was clearly evident on his face, they said. But the port workers knew. They were the first to smell it, the dry, bitter scent that clung to the air even before the cargo was opened.

He told them he had seen the wooden crates, dozens of them. When the cargo was revealed, there was no mistaking what they contained. Bones. Human bones. Stacked and packed like firewood. Skulls, femurs, ribs, entire skeletons shattered. They knew what lay in those crates. Tons of human bones bound for France. Swept from the fields and ravines of *Mikrá Asía*, scraped from charred ruins, dug up from mass graves of forgotten massacres. And now they were being sold by the ton and sent west. Some said for fertilizer. No one could say for certain.

But the workers at the port knew what they were looking at. They were the remains of Greeks and Armenians who had perished in massacres and the soldiers held in the prisoner-of-war camps, the camp at Uşak said to be the worst of all. Starvation, disease, and neglect had claimed countless lives, and now the bones were being shipped as if they were mere cargo. He said that the cargo was never publicly declared to avoid distressing the large population of genocide survivors living in Thessaloniki. The authorities were also fearful of the repercussions should the contents be revealed.

The men at the port were refugees themselves, men who had fled Smyrni, Trebizond, Adana. Some wept openly. Others shouted in anger. The workers tried to stop the *Zan* from sailing. They were furious, horrified, and demanded action. But it was too late. The British consul intervened, placing pressure on the local authorities. The captain had papers that had been stamped. The cargo had been 'cleared'. Orders were given.

The ship left two days later for Marseille, its cargo of bones hidden beneath a cloud of official silence. The ship's representatives said nothing. The Greek authorities too chose silence, not to displease the British owners or the French buyers waiting at the other end. Four hundred tonnes of human bones —evidence of massacres that could never be forgotten—shipped away under the quiet complicity of those in power.

What happened at the docks in Thessaloniki over the course of those days, never reached the newspapers. The story was smothered, like so many others. But every man who worked at that dock knew. And the man in the *kafenio* remembered. And from then on, so did we.

And I could not help asking myself, bitterly—were my father's, my brother's, and my cousins' bones among them?

That night, the cold inside me deepened. I already carried grief, but this was different. This wasn't contempt — it was a hard, unyielding fury.

They had turned our people into fertiliser.

That the British had allowed it, no, facilitated it, was no surprise to me. That the French would profit from it did not shock me either. But that the Greek government had ordered silence, had said nothing while their dead were shipped off like cattle bones, that was further betrayal layered on top of our loss. My hatred of the British and the French hardened into something like steel. And the bitterness I felt towards the Greek authorities, raised the bile in my throat. They had allowed the bones of our people to be sold and then crushed into dust.

An ocean of rage swept through my body.

A STOLEN LIFE

CHAPTER EIGHT

Spring of 1924 found us well settled in Antiphillipi. As the warm rays of the sun finally pierced through the cold of winter, the town, once abandoned had rebuilt itself slowly. With its quiet charm, it was here where we found a semblance of normality in the life we were rebuilding. When my mother and I first put our hands into the earth of the plot of land we had been given, it was with a determination forged in loss. Our family, much like the town, was trying to heal, piece by piece. My mother, ever the practical one, knew that we had to adapt, to make things work no matter the circumstances.

Our former life in Sokia was now just a memory. Gone was the beautiful home, and our family had been decimated, their fates unknown. The life I had once envisioned. Gone. Stolen from me, as it had been from so many of the refugees who now occupied this town along with us. Here in Antiphillipi, everything felt different—quieter, humbler. It was not Sokia, yet in the stillness of our new life, I often found myself drifting back to our old home, to the laughter and music that once filled its rooms. Those memories still lingered so achingly beautiful.

Tobacco for us was not just a crop but our future, our survival, the one thing we could grow to help sustain us in this new life. We had no father, no brother to lead us, only the will to endure and the help of those around us.

The cycle of tobacco production began in early spring and extended into late autumn, occupying our attention for over nine months of the year. We began by planting the tiny seeds in carefully prepared seedbeds, covering them with straw to protect them from the cold. Each morning, we watered them, watching as the first delicate shoots emerged. When they were strong enough, we moved them into the fields, planting row upon row until our hands and backs ached. The work was arduous and demanding. The sun bore down on us, but we did not falter. We could not afford to.

Every member of the family, regardless of age or gender, took part in both the cultivation and domestic processing of the tobacco leaves. The days in the fields were long and gruelling. We were not alone in this effort. Every family in the village had a field to tend, and we all helped one another. We worked in groups, taking turns in each other's fields, while the men took on the heavier tasks. It was the only way to manage such an undertaking. We had learned to live together as a community, to rely on each other since the day we first arrived in this town, and that trust carried over into our new lives.

The first leaves were ready by summer. We harvested carefully, taking only the lower leaves at first, allowing the plant to continue growing. The scent of tobacco filled the air as we strung the leaves together, hanging them to dry in makeshift barns. The curing process was slow, but it was essential. A poorly dried crop would be worthless, and we could not afford failure.

Selling the tobacco was another battle. We were acutely aware of the exploitation by intermediaries and merchants, and we lived in constant anxiety, striving to sell our harvest promptly to avoid the peril of storing unsold bales, which risked spoilage or destruction. The merchants in Kavala were used to dealing with larger estates, not refugees with small plots of land. If we sold through middlemen, they would take the profit, leaving us with barely enough to survive. Instead, we came together, forming a cooperative. The men took our dried tobacco to Kavala, negotiating directly with the buyers, ensuring we received a fair price for our labour. It was a bold move, but it worked.

Despite the hardships and the arduous work involved in cultivating tobacco, it held significant economic importance for our households. The income it generated was enough to enable us to look after our families. As the money flowed in, we saw changes and, for the first time, there was talk of a future beyond mere survival. The land had accepted us, and we had made it our own. And with each passing season, I believed more and more that this place could truly become home.

The sorrow of what we had lost never left us, but our future was our own to make.

One afternoon, as my mother and I sat together with the smell of freshly brewed coffee in the air, she told me of a soldier she had met earlier that day. He had arrived on horseback with others, a group of soldiers fulfilling their national service at the nearby base in Pravi, as it was called then. Later it would be renamed Eleftheroupoli, meaning 'City of Freedom', in honour of the ancient Byzantine city near Nea Peramos in the Kavala region. They had stopped at the bakery, and my mother, being her usual sociable self, had struck up a conversation with one of them. She often spoke with strangers, always intrigued by their stories, always eager to know more about the people who crossed her path.

Alexandra, both you and I inherited that trait.

This soldier named Georgios, had caught her attention. As they spoke, my mother discovered that he had been born on Samos. Eager to learn more, for Samos had been where her own family had originated, that connection turned a simple conversation into something far more personal. She asked him if he was from Vathy, but he had replied, no. He was from Chora. My mother, recalling her visits there, spoke fondly of the village and the island's history. As the conversation continued, the soldier revealed more about his life.

He had been born in Mavratzei, a smaller village further inland, before circumstances had scattered his family. His father had gone to America to work as a carpenter. He had been there for three years when tragedy struck. He had fallen to his death while working on a balcony, which ended his life too soon. His mother, Emorfia, could not care for her three sons. Georgios, being the eldest, was sent to live with his grandparents, Alexandros, and Eugenia, in Chora. He had spent his childhood and adult life with them, while his mother remained in Mavratzei with his two younger brothers. She had been young when widowed and had remarried.

My mother had listened intently as he spoke, noting the ease with which he shared his past, the way he carried himself, not with bitterness, but with the quiet acceptance of a man who had already endured much. That afternoon as we sipped our coffee, I could see that she was turning something over in her mind before finally giving it voice.

She suggested inviting him to our home.

At first, the idea surprised me. But my mother, as always, was a woman of action. She reasoned that the soldiers, so far from their own families, must feel the loneliness of their military service. A home-cooked meal, a place to sit and talk, could be a simple act of kindness. Perhaps it was her empathy for him, her desire to make him feel less alone, that prompted her to invite Georgios to our home. It was a decision that would alter the course of my life in ways I could not have expected.

Two weeks later, Georgios arrived.

I had no idea what to expect. My mother had spoken so warmly of him, but I still felt a bit of uncertainty. He was just a soldier after all, a stranger who had crossed our paths by chance. But when I saw him for the first time, the very first thing I noticed was his eyes. They were blue—no, not just blue, but the bluest I had ever seen. His gaze was direct and kind.

There was a quiet confidence about him. He was respectful, reserved at first, yet at ease enough to engage with my mother as though they had known each other longer than just a few brief encounters. He brought sweets, wrapped carefully, a gesture that spoke of the upbringing his grandparents must have instilled in him. My mother welcomed him warmly, and soon the conversation drifted into the natural rhythm of familiarity.

Georgios spoke of Samos, of his childhood in Chora, of his brothers, Pavlos and Angelos, who had remained in Mavratzei, and about his family's struggles after his father's death. As he spoke, I could see how much he had missed them growing up, though he did not say it outright. There was a certain longing in the way he described the details, a connection to a home that had been fractured by his father's death. He was respectful and gentle, and there was no sign of arrogance. He seemed humble, someone who had lived through hardship and had learned to navigate life with a quiet resilience.

His visits became more frequent after that. At first, they were short. An afternoon coffee, a brief conversation before he returned to the barracks in Pravi... But soon, he began staying longer, sharing a meal with us, listening to my mother's stories of Samos, engaging in discussions about the changing world around us. He was always polite, never imposing, but there was a warmth in his presence that settled into the routine of our days whenever he visited.

One evening after he had left, my mother looked at me thoughtfully. There was something knowing in her expression, something that made my stomach tighten with anticipation.

She asked me whether I liked him.

The question caught me off guard, though perhaps it shouldn't have. It was, after all, the logical progression of things. I was twenty now, no longer a child, and in Sokia, my life would have been charted differently. My parents would have chosen a husband for me, someone fitting of our family's standing, a man who could take over the estate when my father was too old to manage it. But here, in Antiphillipi, those expectations had been extinguished. The war had taken so much from us, had rewritten our futures without our consent. And now, there were no arranged matches, no father or elder brother to decide what my life should be.

I thought about Georgios. About the way his eyes brightened when he spoke of his home, the steadiness of his voice, the way he treated my mother with the respect and kindness of someone who understood the depth of her losses. There was something comforting in his presence, something that made the weight of the past feel lighter, if only for a little while.

I told her I did not know.

And that was the truth. I did not know what it meant to like someone in the way she was implying. I had never been given the space to consider such things before. But I knew that when he was near, the world felt a little less broken.

My mother only smiled, as though she had already seen the answer in my hesitation. And as I lay awake that night, I thought of him. Perhaps in this place, where we had forged a new beginning from a past that had been shattered and where a future now seemed promising, something unexpected was beginning to take root.

Over the next two months, life in Antiphillipi settled into a steady rhythm. The new tobacco crop had been planted, and each day followed the familiar routine we relied on. The days were long but predictable, filled with the work that sustained us. Amidst it all, Georgios continued to visit. His presence had become part of our lives, his visits something I expected, though I had given little thought to what they truly meant.

Then, one afternoon, my mother surprised me with a question I had not anticipated.

"Would you consider marrying him?" she asked, her voice steady yet gentle. "I spoke to Georgios about it. He said yes. Now the decision is yours."

I looked at her in surprise, caught off guard by her directness.

That night, I lay in bed, my mind restless with thoughts of what my mother had proposed. We had spoken about it only briefly, but the implications lingered. She had made it clear that Stamatis needed a father figure, that we needed the presence of a man in our household, someone who could provide a sense of stability. It was time for me to think about marriage.

And perhaps she was right. But was Georgios the right man?

There was nothing forced in this arrangement. My mother had made certain of that. She had spoken to Georgios at length, explaining that if we were to marry, he would remain in Antiphillipi. There would be absolutely no question of uprooting me and taking me to Samos. That had been non-negotiable. Only if he agreed would she give her consent for him to take me as his wife.

He had agreed. I tried to envision what life would be like with him. He was kind and steady, and I had grown comfortable in his company. There was no great romance, no fluttering excitement, but there was respect and understanding. Perhaps in the life I now lived, that was enough.

"So, it is decided then?" he asked me one afternoon as we sat outside in the sunshine.

I nodded. "Yes."

There was no declaration of love, no passionate words. Just a quiet acceptance of what was to come.

"I will take care of you," he said simply. "And of your family."

It was not a grand promise, but it was enough.

One week later, Georgios and I became engaged.

The engagement was simple, with little ceremony. There were no grand celebrations, no elaborate displays of joy, just an understanding between us, a quiet acknowledgment that our futures were now intertwined. When he arrived that evening, I noticed the way his gaze lingered on me.

In the days that followed, word spread quickly. The people of the town congratulated us, and though I sensed some curiosity, there was no judgment.

Georgios continued his visits, though now they were different. He was no longer just a friend of the family but my betrothed. It was strange, this shift between us, though he never changed in the way he spoke to me or treated me. If anything, he seemed more careful now, as if aware that I was still uncertain of what lay ahead.

Preparations for the wedding began quietly. My mother arranged most of it, ensuring that everything was in place. There was no dowry, no negotiations to be made as there would have been in Sokia. Instead, there was only the understanding that this was a necessary step for us all.

As the weeks passed, I watched Georgios more closely. He was not a man of many words, or grand gestures, but there was a quiet strength about him, a steadiness that made me feel, for the first time in a long while, that perhaps everything would be all right. He did not try to press his presence upon me. Instead, he remained patient, allowing me the space to come to terms with what was happening in my own way.

Life had taken so much from me, had turned my world upside down more times than I could count. And now, it was offering me something new, something uncertain. I did not know if I could ever love him, not in the way I had once imagined love to be.

As the wedding day drew closer, there was still uncertainty. Georgios had already proven himself to be kind and dependable. Perhaps in time, that would be enough. And so I prepared myself to step into the next chapter of my life with quiet acceptance.

We would be married in early April 1924. Georgios still had two months of military service remaining. My mother busied herself with arrangements, ensuring everything was in order. She would vacate her bedroom and move into the room I had shared with Stamatis, though more often than not, he preferred the security of sleeping beside her.

Georgios visited at every opportunity, bringing sweets or small gifts, humble offerings, as a soldier's salary was meagre. I cherished these tokens of affection, not for their material worth but for the thought behind them. Each gift was a quiet acknowledgment of our forthcoming union, a reassurance that, despite the practicality of our arrangement, he cared in his own way.

As my wedding day drew nearer, my mother took it upon herself to prepare me for the life that awaited me. She spoke in a tone of quiet authority, revealing the expectations a husband had of his wife. When a man and woman came together, she told me, there would be pain, and I would bleed. This was natural, a woman's fate, and it was possible that in fulfilling my duty, I would conceive a child. There was no sentimentality in her words, no romance. She did not speak of love, only of obligation. I absorbed her words in silence, unable to voice the uncertainty that stirred within me.

How different our world was then, my beloved granddaughter. I remember the year when you first came to Samos. Do you remember your romance with Elias? The passion that burned between you both?

Love, desire, passion. These were foreign concepts to me then. I had witnessed the quiet affection my parents had for one another, but my relationship with Georgios was more pragmatic. It was an arrangement, not a grand love affair. And yet, I did not resent it. This was my path, the one chosen for me, and I had accepted it.

I often imagined how it might have been, had I still been living in Sokia, marrying as befitted my station as the daughter of a wealthy landowner. My wedding would have been a grand affair. My gown, exquisite—layers of silk and lace, the bodice embroidered with golden thread and pearls, a mark of my family's standing. The veil, long and sheer, fastened with a delicate comb of pearls. My shoes, custom-made.

My father and elder brother proudly escorting me the short distance to the Church of St. Dimitrios, musicians leading the procession. My bridesmaids, including my beloved sister Polyxeni, scattering rose petals at my feet. Among the guests, those dearest to me—Konstantinos and his family from Smyrni, my cousins from Samos—faces alight with quiet pride and emotion. Persephone would have been there too, her eyes warm and brimming with tears that spoke of years of devotion. Even the prominent families of Sokia, alongside my father's friends and business acquaintances, would have gathered, all of them there to celebrate, to share our joy, and to bless our union.

A feast would have filled long tables, the house bursting with guests offering gifts. Laughter and music would echo through the rooms, the night stretching on in revelry—celebrating not just a marriage but the union of families, a legacy secured.

When the festivities ended, my husband and I would have retired to our own home, my dowry from my father. A fine house, spacious and well-appointed, its rooms filled with elegant furnishings. There within its walls, our new life as husband and wife would have begun. I would not have been alone in my duties; a housekeeper would have assisted me in running the household, as befitted a young woman of my social standing.

I told myself that grandeur did not matter. What mattered was the future I was stepping into, even if it bore no resemblance to the dreams I had once cherished. I could still see that glorious morning in Sokia, Polyxeni and I together, as we had woven fantasies of our own weddings bathed in sunlight, just like Giasemina's with Christoforos. Now reality hit hard. My beloved sister lay beneath the cold earth in Sokia, never to wear a bride's gown. And my own wedding would be a pale echo of those fantasies I had once harboured.

That life was gone. Stolen from me on that fateful day when hatred and retribution had swept through our home in Sokia. The day the Turks took my father and my sister was lost to senseless violence. There would be no procession to the church, no music, no laughter echoing through our home. Only sorrow. The kind that follows loss too deep for words.

But then I reminded myself I had no right to bitterness. My mother, Stamatis and I had survived the catastrophe of 1922. Thousands of others had not. We had witnessed the horrors firsthand and seen enough loss to know that life itself was a gift, however altered from the one we had known. That knowledge did not erase the ache, but it kept it from consuming me.

Instead, my mother, Stamatis, and I travelled to Kavala to choose a simple gown. There were no gilded fabrics, no imported lace, only modest designs, practical and unembellished. The dress I chose was plain, its beauty lying in its simplicity. I remember the excitement in Stamatis's eyes, his small hands lightly stroking the fabric as if it were the finest silk in the world. That joy alone was enough.

*　　*　　*

The morning of our wedding dawned bright, the sky a brilliant blue with the promise of warmth from the sun. We had no family, and so the women who came to help me dress were our neighbours, and they arrived knowing exactly what needed to be done. They moved with quiet purpose, their hands gentle as they brushed my hair and helped me into my wedding dress. My mother placed a small crown made of ribbons on my head, a simple yet powerful symbol of the new life I was about to begin.

As they worked, the women sang softly, their voices carrying blessings for my happiness, my well-being, and a good life with my husband. The songs, familiar yet strange in this new land, filled the room with a bittersweet hope. It was a moment that felt both heavy and fragile, and I could feel the weight of expectation pressing down on me, the finality of what was to come. My mother took my hand, leading me from our home, and with each step, the realisation grew stronger. My life was about to change forever. I was about to step into an unknown future, tethered to a man I hardly knew.

There had been only two other weddings before mine, and the town had gathered to witness the ceremony. Invitations were unnecessary; news of a wedding travelled fast, and no one would have missed the chance to see a bride. They gathered in clusters. The women stood together, old women with their heads covered in dark scarves, young girls clutching their mothers' hands, and the men stood together, some with arms crossed, others twirling their *komboloi.*

Georgios and several of his colleagues waited at the church, standing in disciplined formation. He looked handsome in his uniform, his posture rigid, his expression composed.

I remember little of the service. I was nervous as the ceremony progressed, and once again my thoughts strayed to those who were no longer with us. I sent up a silent prayer, hoping that wherever their souls were, that they were watching this day unfold and hoped they were smiling with pride.

As we emerged from the church, the crowd surged forward in celebration. Rice showered down upon us, the grains bouncing off our clothing. Voices rang out in a chorus of blessings. *"Na zisete!* May you have a long life together." Hands reached out to clasp mine in congratulations. Others clapped Georgios on the shoulder, offering him words of encouragement as he stepped into his new role as a husband.

For a moment, I felt a flicker of something I could not name, not quite joy, not quite sorrow. Had my mother made the right decision? Had I? Only time would tell. But no matter what, from this day forward, my life would be inextricably bound to my husband. That much was certain.

When the next day dawned, everything had changed, though the house, the land, and the daily routine remained the same. I was no longer just a daughter, a sister, a young woman. I was a wife. The bed felt unfamiliar with Georgios beside me, his warmth foreign yet inescapable. He rose early, moving about the house as though nothing had changed, gathering firewood to heat water for our morning bath. I watched him, feeling as if I were observing a stranger rather than the man I had married the day before.

Intimacy had been an expectation, not a desire. I had done what was required of me, yet I could not shake the feeling that I was standing at the threshold of a life I had not chosen. Georgios would have only this day with me before returning to his barracks in Eleftheroupoli. By late afternoon, I would be alone again.

Once he left, my life resumed its familiar rhythm. The livestock needed tending, the tobacco crop required care, and the house demanded the same work it always had. The only difference was the knowledge that I was now someone's wife. Georgios came home only on weekends, a visitor rather than a true presence in my life. We were bound together by name, but not yet by familiarity. Still, he was kind, always helping my mother with the heavier tasks. In this, at least, I was grateful.

Six weeks passed, and then everything shifted again. I was pregnant. Georgios's joy was immediate, and so was my mother's. Even Stamatis, still just a boy himself, was excited at the thought of a baby in the house. But for me, apprehension set in. I had no experience with motherhood. I had always assumed there would be time to prepare for such a responsibility, but now it was here, ready, or not. My mother reassured me she would be by my side, yet a quiet fear remained within me.

With Georgios now home permanently, we moved forward as best we could. My pregnancy progressed as the seasons changed, and by the time the tobacco was harvested and sold, my mother had made a decision. She divided the earnings, giving Georgios and me our share.

"You will need it," she said, her voice firm yet kind. Perhaps she foresaw that we would not always remain under her roof.

On the 7th of February 1925, my first child was born. A daughter. The midwife, with my mother's steady hands beside her, placed her in my arms. We named her Angeliki. Georgios was proud. My mother was overjoyed. She was a calm child, with dark blonde hair and her father's startling blue eyes. I should have been happy, too, and I was, in many ways, but something unsettled me. A shift in Georgios demeanour, a quiet withdrawal that grew more pronounced as letters arrived from Samos.

At first, he said little about them. But I saw the way his expression changed as he read them, the way he lingered in thought, his hands gripping the paper tighter than necessary. When I asked, he brushed off my concern. But my mother saw it too.

"Did you argue?" she asked one evening as we sat by the fire, Angeliki sleeping in my arms. I shook my head. No, we had not argued. But something was wrong.

The answer came three months later. Over coffee, Georgios spoke the words that would fracture our family. We were leaving. His grandparents had written to remind him of his duty, his obligation to them. They had raised him, and now it was his turn to care for them. Without asking, without discussing, he had decided. We would go to Chora.

My mother's rage was unlike anything I had ever seen. She reminded him of the promise he had made, the oath he had sworn, that he would never take me from her. "Had I known this," she told him, her voice and body trembling with fury, "I would never have given you my daughter."

The house, once filled with warmth, grew cold. My mother and Georgios barely spoke. The weight of his decision hung over us, thick and suffocating. But his mind was set, and no tears or arguments would sway him from his decision. And I, as his wife, had no choice. One month later, I left behind my mother and brother.

I hated him for it. But it no longer mattered what I felt. I was his wife. And a wife obeyed her husband.

*   *   *

It took us a week to reach Samos by ship, a journey I had taken once before. The irony was not lost on me. We had left this island behind, setting out for Kavala and then Antiphillipi in search of a new life, a future for my mother, for Stamatis, and for myself. And now, I was returning, as a wife and a mother, bound to this journey not by choice but by obligation. I did not know what awaited me, nor what would be expected of me, only that this was the path my husband had chosen for us.

Georgios had told me that a house had been rented for us. There was no room in his grandparents' home, so we would be living on our own. But it was understood, without question, that I would be responsible for their care while Georgios sought work to support us. The weight of this unspoken duty settled heavily on me.

He spent most of his time speaking with the crew or keeping to himself. He did not ask how I felt about our return to Samos. I doubted he cared. The decision had been made, and my opinion had not mattered.

When we finally arrived at the port of Pythagoreio, the sight of the island filled me with conflicting emotions. The mountains loomed in the distance, their rugged peaks shadowing the coastline. The sky stretched wide and blue over the harbour and the whitewashed buildings of the town gleamed under the morning sun.

We disembarked, weary from the journey, and were met by a man with a mule-drawn cart to take us to Chora. The ride was slow and jarring, causing Angeliki to stir in my arms. I held her close, rocking her gently, though my own nerves were frayed.

The house was near the Church of Agios Dimitrios, close to where Georgios's maternal grandparents lived. I had imagined many things in the weeks leading up to our arrival, but nothing prepared me for the reality of what I would find when we stepped inside.

It was a brick dwelling. The walls were rough and unfinished, patched in places where time and weather had worn them thin, and this would allow the cold to seep through in winter. The kitchen and sitting area were the same, a narrow space containing only the barest essentials—a low wooden table, a few chairs, and a bench along the wall. A small hearth where meals could be cooked and also served to offer some warmth in winter, though hardly enough to chase away the cold that would creep in through the gaps in the stone. It was just liveable.

One large bedroom opened off the main space, its plaster walls cracked. There was a simple bed with a wooden frame and a thin mattress, a chest of drawers and a wooden cot for our daughter. At the rear was a small bathing area and beside it, a basic toilet that was more necessity than comfort. Light filtered in through small shuttered windows. The air inside was stale, heavy with the mingled scents of smoke, oil, and damp stone. Outside, the walls were washed in white lime, though the weather had dulled it, and the roof was of red clay tiles, some shifted and uneven from years of wind and rain. It was shelter, nothing more.

I stood in that space, holding my daughter close to me, and felt my heart sink into the pit of my stomach. Was this the best that could be provided for us? This was what Georgios had brought me to? I looked at him, searching his face for some sign that he understood what he had done, that he saw how impossible it was to expect me to raise our child here. But there was nothing, just the same quiet acceptance, as if this was all normal, as if this was simply how life was meant to be.

If it had been up to me, I would have turned around that very day, taken my daughter, and left. But I had nowhere to go. My mother, my home, my life, everything had been left behind. I was no longer just Eftihia. I was the wife of Georgios Giacoumis. And a wife had no choice but to endure.

I turned to Georgios once more, my voice trembling with anger. "This is where we are to live?"

He nodded, as if my reaction was unnecessary. "It is what we can afford. It will do."

I felt my grip tighten around Angeliki. The air in the room felt thick, suffocating. This place did not feel like a home. It felt like a prison. A place where my thoughts would echo off the stone walls, where my loneliness would fester.

I placed Angeliki in the cradle that had been provided and stood there, frozen, as Georgios brought in our suitcases. He carried no unease, no regret. To him, this was just the beginning of our life together. To me, it was the end of the life I had known.

By the next morning, reality set in. There was no escaping this place, no returning to my mother. My role had been decided.

"They are old, Eftihia. They will need tending to," Georgios informed me as we sat at the table for breakfast. "You will cook for them, help them in whatever way they require."

He spoke as though I should be grateful for the responsibility. As though it were an honour to be placed in service to people I had never met.

I swallowed my anger. I felt the walls closing in. My mother. The woman who had raised me, who had helped me navigate marriage and motherhood, was miles away.

"And what about you?" I asked. "What will you do while I care for your grandparents?"

His expression darkened. "I will work to support us. That is my duty. You have yours."

The conversation ended there. There was no use in arguing. I had no one to plead my case to. I was given no instructions, no formal acknowledgment of my new role. It was simply understood. I would serve them, as I was expected to.

Later the following afternoon, Georgios's grandparents arrived, two small, elderly figures careful in their movements. They greeted us warmly, but their attention focused on Angeliki with obvious delight. They had brought some sweets for us and a tiny gift for the baby. I felt a quiet distance, a polite acknowledgment rather than full familiarity. I was welcomed, but gently— enough to feel included, yet aware that I remained slightly apart.

They spoke with quiet pride of how their daughter Emorfia, after she had remarried, had offered to take them in, yet they had remained in Chora, in their own home. They told me how they had raised Georgios after his father's death, how he had been their comfort through the years, and now that his military service was behind him, how happy they were to have him home again. He had promised he would look after them, and they trusted he would uphold that obligation as though nothing could ever shake it.

"No, not even after taking a wife and vowing he would not uproot her from her family," I thought bitterly. To honour them, he had also broken the vow he had made to my mother. "Obligation to them meant just that. A wife was expected to follow her husband."

I listened in silence while beneath the surface my emotions stirred. They never asked whether that was acceptable to me. My silence they took for agreement. They did not see beyond the polite façade I wore. Behind it, I was holding down the hurt, the anger, the bitterness that threatened to rise, forced to bury it beneath composure.

As the days passed, the loneliness became unbearable. I had no friends, no confidantes. My only comfort was Angeliki, her small face the only light in an otherwise dim existence. But even she could not ease the resentment building up inside me.

Before I left, my mother had urged me to seek out Vangelis and Stelios if I ever needed support, to reach out to the families who had cared for us in Ano Vathy. Yet the house Georgios had brought me to was worse than anything I had left behind in Antiphillipi. I could not even write to my mother and pour out my misery to her. How could I? It had been she who had suggested Georgios as a husband, who had trusted his promises that he would never take me from her or our home. Her fury had burned fiercely until the day we left for Samos. To now tell her what he had done, to reveal this place, would shatter her.

And to invite Vangelis and Stelios and their families here? I could not. This house, barely habitable, could not welcome them. How could I bear the look on their faces, knowing the comfort I had once shared in their homes after leaving the refugee camp in Chios?

One evening, as Georgios sat at the table after a long day, I finally allowed the words to escape. "This is not what I wanted."

He glanced up at me from his meal. "What do you mean?"

"This life. This house. Being taken from my mother. Caring for people who are not my own. None of it."

His jaw tightened. "You are my wife, Eftihia. This is our life now."

"No," I replied, more forcefully than I intended. "This is your life. I had no choice."

For a moment, he said nothing. Then, slowly, he placed his fork down. "You did have a choice. You chose to be my wife."

I did not reply. I did not need to. We both knew the truth.

*   *   *

Word had already spread. The women who stood at their doorways, the men who lingered near the kafeneion. 'O Giacoumis has returned from his national service, and he has brought back a wife, *a Mikrasiatissa,* an Asia Minor woman.'

I knew what that meant. I had heard the stories before, the bitter resentment towards those of us who had been uprooted from *Mikrá Asía*, those who had fled with nothing but the clothes on their backs and whatever dignity they could salvage. Now, I was one of them.

The term *Mikrasiates* was used for both men and women from *Mikrá Asía*. However, these terms were not always neutral; they were sometimes used with resentment or hostility by the local Greek population, who viewed us as outsiders. For us women, there was also the perception that *Mikrasiatisses* were different in dress, behaviour, and customs to Greek women. We were looked down upon as being too proud or too arrogant.

I had to endure that for the first six months on Samos, and how difficult it had been to be accepted.

"*Érthe i Sokiáni na mas kánei tin prévisa.*" The words echoed in my mind. "The woman from Sokia has come to act like the superior one."

It had been a cruel taunt then. No matter that we were all Greek. No matter that we shared the same faith, the same prayers, the same traditions. To them, I was a foreigner.

My husband, for his part, seemed either unaware or uninterested in how the people of the village were viewing me. It was as if he had expected this. But I was not prepared. I closed my eyes, swallowing my anger. This was my life now.

I would have to find a way to survive it.

*   *   *

It was two weeks after our arrival in Samos when my mother-in-law and her husband came to visit. She was a small woman, dark-haired, dark-eyed, and I knew at once that Georgios must have inherited his startling blue eyes from his late father. I was unsure what sort of welcome to expect. The gossip in Chora had already reached me, whispers that her son had married a *Mikrasiatissa.* I couldn't help but think whether she too had heard them.

When they arrived, her welcome was warm. Tears filled her eyes as she spoke to me and embraced me. When she met her first grandchild, Angeliki, her delight was genuine and moving. Her husband, too, was kind-hearted and open, which I had not expected. Like my father, he carried a quiet strength, having married my mother-in-law and taken on the role of father to her two surviving sons. They had brought us gifts.

Yet I could not miss the flicker of shock, quickly masked, as she looked around the house Georgios's grandparents had rented for us. I assumed from her expression, she had been just as shocked and would voice that displeasure to my husband later.

Some women speak of strained relationships with their mothers-in-law. For me, although we could never be close in the way I had been with my mother, and with the distance between us, for she lived in Mavratzei, I felt she truly loved me. Perhaps she understood, more than most, what it meant to have your entire world taken from you by circumstance. After all, her husband had once travelled to America to make a better life for her and their sons, only to meet a tragic death. She was widowed while still young, left with the heavy burden of raising three children on her own.

In that unspoken knowledge of loss, something passed between us. We did not speak of it, yet I felt it in the way her hand lingered on mine, in the softness of her gaze. Two women, bound by different tragedies, each having to learn how to live in the shadow of what had been taken from them.

My mother-in-law visited us often. She always arrived with something, eggs, cheese, figs in summer, sweets from the *Zacharoplasteion*, always insisting it would be unacceptable to come empty-handed. She also brought gifts of clothing for Angeliki, crocheted pieces for our home, and other small household items she thought I might need. My father-in-law, Andreas, for his part, took it upon himself to mend the holes in the stone walls, and to fix the cracked plaster in the bedroom, a quiet gesture of care that touched me deeply.

Georgios's grandparents, too, showed their thoughtfulness. They recognised how much effort it took for me to look after them and often had food items sent from the village for me to cook and to be shared. Their kindness eased the weight of my days, reminding me that my care for them did not go unnoticed.

We also made the journey to Mavratzei to visit my in-laws whenever we could.

The village lay about four kilometres from Chora, a steady climb into the hills. We would travel there by mule cart along the well-worn road, its surface packed hard from generations of wheels and hooves. On foot, the distance could be covered in a little over an hour and a half, though the uphill stretch made it feel longer. By cart, the journey took less than an hour.

Mavratzei sat nestled amongst the hills, its whitewashed houses huddled together as if for shelter from the wind. Cobbled lanes climbed steeply between the homes, shaded here and there by old plane trees. In the cooler months, the air carried the scent of woodsmoke; in summer, the hum of cicadas filled the air. The people there lived simply, tending vines and olive groves, keeping small flocks of goats, their days shaped by the rhythm of the seasons.

My mother-in-law's neighbours, who called in on our visits to greet us, never asked directly about my life before Samos, but I could feel their eyes on me, their curiosity just beneath the surface. I was different. I had yet to acquire the Samiot accent.

*   *   *

I might have been the object of curiosity and disdain in Chora, but not everyone in the village viewed me so. There were two elderly women, Gramato and Vangelia, who took the time to befriend me. They lived a short distance from our home, in modest dwellings that had seen better days, much like the women themselves. Their kindness was unexpected in a place where I felt unwelcome, where every glance seemed to measure my worth and find me lacking.

At first, they approached cautiously. Gramato, the more outspoken of the two, arrived one afternoon with a small jar of *gylko* (spoon sweet). She handed it to me without ceremony, muttering something about how a woman with a young child should not be without some sweetness in her home. Vangelia followed days later, bringing fresh figs and plums wrapped in a cloth. Their gifts were simple but meaningful, a silent acknowledgment that not all in the village wished to see me struggle.

The first time I saw them, I did not know what to make of them. Two elderly women, their backs slightly bent with age, their faces lined with the passage of years, standing at my doorway with a small bundle wrapped in cloth. Their eyes, though worn by time, held a gentleness that I had not yet encountered in this place.

"Come, my child, take this," they would say, handing over whatever it was they held.

I was wary at first. I had grown accustomed to keeping my distance, to protecting myself from the whispers and scorn of the villagers. I did not know what their intentions were. But as the days passed, their presence became something of a comfort. I began to expect them, to listen for the sound of their footsteps approaching the house.

Before long, their visits became more frequent. They brought fruit and vegetables purchased from the vendors who wandered through the village with their carts, calling out their wares. In return for their kindness, I did what I had been taught. My parents had always given to those less fortunate and had instilled in me the value of sharing what we had, no matter how little it might be. I would set aside portions of our meals and deliver them to Gramato and Vangelia. I shared what I could. If I were making lentil soup, I would set aside a portion for them. If there was fresh bread, I made sure they had some, warm from the oven. They accepted my offerings with gratitude, their faces lighting up in appreciation.

And so, a bond formed between us.

Their presence softened the harshness of the world around me. The villagers still looked upon me with resentment, but I had found a small place of solace in these two women. They did not ask about my past, nor did they pry into my sorrows. Instead, they offered quiet companionship, and, perhaps most importantly, they offered affection to Angeliki, who so desperately needed it.

Their own children rarely visited them. Age had left them alone, forgotten by the very people they had once nurtured. In Angeliki, they found something to hold on to, someone to fuss over, to love, to fill the empty spaces in their hearts. And Angeliki delighted in their attention, her laughter filling the small house as they clucked over her, offering her some sweet bread they had brought, and she eagerly accepted the sweets they pressed into her hand.

I watched them together and felt a strange mixture of emotions. Gratitude, yes. Relief, perhaps. But also sorrow. Sorrow that I was expected to make a life here, in a place that did not want me. Sorrow that it was Gramato and Vangelia who delighted in Angeliki when it should have been my mother fussing over her first grandchild, her hands smoothing her curls, her voice murmuring endearments only a grandmother could say. My younger brother should have been the one playing with her, teasing her, chasing her through the house. But my family had been deprived of that joy, and I of the comfort that only their presence could bring.

I remembered the tears my mother and brother had shed when the news had been broken to them, the way my mother had tried to hold back her grief in my presence but could not. At night, when she thought no one could hear, I had listened to her sobs, muffled but unrelenting, a sorrow too deep to be silenced. She had lost so much already, and I had been the last thing she had left to cling to. No amount of pleading with my husband had swayed him from his decision. He had taken me away, and with me, he had taken the last bit of joy from my mother's heart.

There were days when it all became unbearable. Days when I could not ignore the reality of my situation. I had been taken from everything I knew, from the security of my family, and placed in a house that was not a home. I was expected to endure, to carry on as though my will meant nothing. The kindness of Gramato and Vangelia softened the edges, but it did not erase the bitterness that curled in my chest.

And yet, there was nowhere else to go.

The visits continued, the quiet companionship persisting through the passing seasons. In time, I came to trust them. I allowed myself to sit with them, to listen to their stories. They spoke of youth, of love, of loss. They spoke of a time before the war, before the world had changed. I did not tell them my story.

Not in its entirety.

But I think they understood, even without words. It was a small thing. Perhaps that was enough. Perhaps for now, it had to be.

*   *   *

In early January 1926, three days after the Epiphany, a letter arrived from my mother. I could hardly believe the news it contained. My elder brother, Dimitri, had been reunited with her. I read the letter as she explained how he had found his way back to her through the Red Cross. His journey had been a long one, but it was the harrowing tale of his escape that left me shaken.

"It was a miracle," she wrote.

They had been rounded up and placed in prison. Then one day, they were loaded onto a truck, seventeen of them. They did not know where their destination would be, but they had heard that the Turks often took those in prison away from the towns, shot them and buried them in mass graves. However, on the way, a Turkish woman stopped the truck near a *yefiri*, a bridge made of stone. In her hands she carried a *yataghan*, a type of Ottoman Turkish sword or short sabre, carried by irregular fighters and prized for slashing in close combat, its curve sharp and deadly. When the soldiers asked her intent, her reply was chilling. She wanted to kill as many Greeks in the truck as she could. The soldiers laughed at first and but then agreed to her request.

The prisoners were ordered off the truck and lined up. One by one, they were called to the bridge and made to kneel. A soldier would seize each man by the hair, pulling his head back against the low stone wall, while the woman drew her blade across his throat. Their bodies were thrown into the river, the water carrying them away as if eager to hide the horror.

By the time she was finished, fifteen Greeks lay dead. My brother was the second to last. She turned to the soldiers and calmly announced she had had her fill. Without a word, they released him and the last man.

I set the letter down, but the words clung to me. My mind filled with the image of those men, standing in line, each knowing their turn was coming, each forced to watch what awaited them. I could almost see the looks they must have exchanged—the fear, the disbelief, the dawning horror—as they waited for the soldier's grip and the slash of that madwoman's blade. My hands trembled so violently I could barely hold the paper. A wave of sickness rose, sharp and sudden, and I thought I might retch.

The fear. The helplessness. The sheer cruelty. It pressed in on me until I could hardly breathe. With one more sweep of her blade, one more whim of brutality, and my brother's body would have been among those carried away by the river. He had lived where so many had not, but death had stood so close beside him. A single bullet would have been more merciful than the fate those men endured.

I sat with the letter in my hands for a long time. The ink blurred as my eyes welled with tears. For years, I had not known the fate of my beloved father or Dimitri. Now, against all odds, Dimitri had returned to us. But at what cost?

I struggled to understand why the Muslim woman had wanted to kill the Greek men. It was years later that it was explained to me. She had invoked the concept of *takfir*, believing that the Greek refugees were '*kafirs*' or apostates (perceived enemies of Islam) and thus justifying her demand to kill them to fulfill what she saw as a religious duty. She viewed the act of killing them as a means of purifying her soul and securing a place in Paradise, based on her belief that killing non-believers would earn her divine favour.

This interpretation of *takfir*, for me, was a tragic example of how religious beliefs can be misinterpreted and twisted to justify brutal actions, especially in times of war and conflict.

My mother explained further about Dimitri. He did not know where the Turks had taken them. When he and the other prisoner were finally released, dazed, and starved, they wandered for one week through unfamiliar terrain, driven only by the hope of returning to Sokia. They travelled under the cover of darkness, and eventually found their way to Osman, who risked everything by hiding him and the other prisoner in the storeroom underneath his home.

It was there that he learned the truth. His stepfather was dead, Polyxeni too, and his mother, sister, and younger brother had fled to Smyrni. Osman did not waste words. He had told Dimitri that Nureddin Paşa had decreed all men of his age would now be classed as prisoners of war and were denied passage out of Turkey. If he were caught again, he would be sent to the interior. There would be no return from there.

He helped them make their way north to Kaisari (Çeşme). From that quiet coastal town, and under the cover of darkness, they crossed by boat to Lesvos. There they joined thousands of other desperate souls, seeking refuge and safety far from the chaos they had left behind.

What Dimitri found in Lesvos was much like what we had suffered in Chios—crowded, filthy camps filled with desperate families. Tents were packed tight, barely offering shelter from the harsh weather. Food and clean water were in short supply, and sickness was spreading quickly among the weak and weary. The air, he said, felt heavy with grief and exhaustion. Dimitri knew he wouldn't survive it. When word came that resettlement was possible, he accepted.

They sent him to Drama, one of the towns absorbing the flood of *Mikrá Asía* refugees. It was meant to be either temporary or permanent, a place to wait while the Red Cross traced the names he had given them of his family members who were missing. He shared a house with Thanasi, the other prisoner, and Vyronas, a man from the town of Aidíni whom they had met in the refugee camp in Lesvos, drawn together by chance, now bound by loss and the hope of receiving word that their loved ones were still alive. In the meantime, he worked in the tobacco fields, the region's lifeblood.

It seemed unbelievable to me. All that time he had been in Drama, a town not far from Kavala, while we were in Antiphillipi, barely a day's journey away by cart depending on weather and road conditions. He had been rebuilding a life across the plains. And we had not known. Now he was reunited with our mother and Stamatis, safe at last.

But not with me.

I was in Samos now. And once more, the bitterness came. I had been so close. Now I was once again so far away from him, from them.

*   *   *

Life moved forward, as life does, bringing with it both burdens and blessings.

In the summer of 1926, I received word that Dimitri was engaged to be married to a woman from the neighbouring town of Kipia. Her name was Georgia Zantali, and she had two brothers, Fotis and Manolis. I was overjoyed at the news. My brother deserved all the happiness that life could offer, and I hoped he would find it with the woman he had chosen to make his wife. It eased my heart to think, too, of what comfort this might bring to our mother. She would have a daughter-in-law by her side and eventually grandchildren, which would soften her loneliness and sorrow at losing her daughter to distance. Yet even as I rejoiced for them, there was a quiet ache within me, knowing I would not be there to witness such a blessed day.

My mother's letters spoke in careful words of daily life, yet between the lines I could sense the silent heartbreak she still bore and the regret that it was she who had set in motion the proxy marriage that had upended all our lives. It pained me to read her unspoken sorrow. Yet there was little point in ruminating on what might have been; the past could not be undone, no matter how deeply we mourned it.

I often thought back to the life I had once envisioned as a girl growing up in Sokia, the quiet certainty of belonging to a close knit family, where I would marry, raise a family, and live a life of comfort among the familiar fields and close family ties. That life had been stolen from me, not just from me, but from all of us. For everyone whose lives had been torn apart by the Greco-Turkish war; for those who had been slaughtered while fleeing to escape the retribution metered out by the Turks; for all those souls who had endured those terrible days and nights on the quay in Smyrni, with the flames at their backs and nowhere left to run. I thought of Persephone, of Konstantinos and his family, still missing, lost to us. In remembering them, I felt the grief of all we had lost. As for the memories, those were something that would never be erased.

CHAPTER NINE

Our son Emmanouil was born in 1927, and Ploutarhos followed in 1929. By then, I had grown accustomed to the rhythm of our days, waking before dawn to tend to the children, seeing to the needs of Georgios's grandparents, and managing the household. He too, rose before first light, making his way to the harbour to buy the freshest fish straight off the caiques. He had a keen eye and was well respected among the fishermen, who often reserved the choicest of their catch for him. His work was unpredictable, dependent on the sea's generosity, but he never faltered.

He worked tirelessly across the villages of Arvanites, Koumarathei, Mavratzei, and Pirgos, where he had built his reputation and established regular customers who trusted his judgment and the freshness of his catch. Rain or shine, calm or storm, he kept to his routine, guided by a quiet determination and the knowledge that families were relying on him. In the villages he visited, his presence was more than that of a fishmonger—he was a man whose dedication had earned respect and trust.

His work was varied, as it had to be. The land his grandparents owned provided us with some security. Trayana, the large block near the village, was a fertile stretch of earth where Georgios first planted watermelons. Later, he turned to Muscat grapes, their vines stretching over the land. The grapes, once ripe, were golden in colour and exuded their sweet perfume-like aroma. Higher up, beyond the village near the church of Agios Konstantinos, the family had another large plot. There, we grew crops and kept goats, pigs, and chickens in the shelter of a cave. Near the villages of Mavratzei and Milos, we had land where olives grew, which gave us the oil we needed and the surplus we sold. These plots of land had sustained his family for generations, and now they provided for ours. The work was relentless and back breaking. Yet, we were making a good living.

Slowly, steadily, we saved. The house we occupied was small. I had resigned myself to it, but in truth, I longed for a place that was ours, not just a space where we lived, but a home where I could breathe freely, where my children could grow.

Then came the bitter winter that changed everything. The wind cut through us with an unforgiving edge and howled through the narrow streets of the village. Georgios' grandmother had grown frail over the years. She fell ill. We did what we could, but age has its way of reclaiming its own. She passed in the heart of winter.

After her forty days had passed, Georgios's grandfather called us to him. His voice was soft, touched with age and sorrow, yet there was a warmth in it. "It is time for you to move into this house," he said, looking at Georgios. "It is already written that you will inherit it when I am gone. Why wait until then? You need the space. Your children will fill these rooms with life. It is only right."

Then he turned to me. "Eftihia *mou*, never doubt that we did not notice or appreciate all you did for us, how you cared for me and my late wife." He paused and then sighed softly. "Emorfia and Andreas have offered to care for me. It is too much for me alone, and I have decided it is time to go."

As I listened to him, a quiet warmth spread through me at his acknowledgment. I thought back to those early days, when my heart had carried resentment and bitterness, and our bond had been strained by circumstance. Yet, over time, that tension had softened. I had come to care for them, not from obligation, but from a deep, genuine affection that had quietly grown.

His offer had been entirely unexpected, but we accepted with gratitude. So we moved into the larger house. For the first time, we had space. It was not what I had known in Sokia, nothing ever would be, but it was a step forward. It was ours, and it was an improvement beyond what I had dared to hope for in those early years.

Not long after, the adjoining house, which had been vacant for years, was offered to us. We decided to buy it, expanding our home in a way we had never imagined possible. With careful planning, we built another bedroom adjoining the original one. Now, we had three large bedrooms upstairs, enough space for the children to have a proper place to sleep and grow.

The lower level housed a spacious kitchen, a sitting area where we could gather in the evenings, a laundry and bathing room with a fire grate where we could heat water for bathing, and a toilet. An outdoor staircase led to a large terrace that connected to the bedrooms.

Here was where I could sit in the quiet of the evenings, looking over the village below, and the plains which stretched to the sea beyond.

Our days continued, one folding into the next, life's steady rhythm carrying us forward.

*   *   *

Grief is a strange thing. It announces itself before it arrives, like a storm that is brewing on the horizon, its presence felt long before the first drop of rain falls. In the days leading up to Dimitri's letter, in the Summer of 1930, an unease had settled over me, a weight I carried without understanding why. I had no reason to feel such foreboding. Life was moving forward as it always had. My days were consumed with tending to the children, and the daily chores involved in keeping the house. Yet, in quiet moments, when my hands were still, a chill would creep up my spine. Something was coming, but I did not know what.

When the letter arrived, I knew. Before I even opened it, I knew. My fingers trembled as I broke the seal, my breath catching in my throat. I read the first line, and my world collapsed.

"Eftihia mou, my dear sister, it is with a heavy heart that I tell you that our Stamatis has passed away."

I stopped reading. The words blurred on the page as I gripped the letter tighter, as though doing so could somehow change what was written. 'No! No, this cannot be.' But the words remained, unchanging, indifferent to my disbelief.

My younger brother, my sweet, mischievous Stamatis, was gone. Dimitri's words explained how. A terrible accident, a mules kick, two days of suffering before death took him. But none of that mattered. What mattered was that he was gone. That I would never see him again. That I had not been there. That my mother, who had already suffered so much, had now lost her youngest child.

I could not breathe.

The weight of it pressed down on my chest, suffocating me. I sank onto the chair, my hands clutching the letter. My mind was reeling, unable to accept what I had read.

I was thousands of miles away. I could not be there to bury him, to hold my mother, to weep beside my older brother. I could not see his face one last time, could not whisper prayers over his grave. The ocean and land that stretched between us had never felt as vast, as cruel as they did in that moment.

A sob rose from my throat, but I swallowed it down. The children were watching me. Emmanuel, barely three, stood near the table, sensing my distress but too young to understand. Ploutarhos, just a year old, sat in the cradle, oblivious. My eldest, Angeliki, stood near me, her wide, blue eyes fixed on me. She was old enough to know that something was terribly wrong.

I had no words for them. How could I explain that their uncle—the uncle they had never met, the uncle I had spoken of with such warmth was now gone?

I needed air. I needed space to grieve, to weep without frightening my children. There was only one place I could go. I gathered them, pressing a kiss to each of their foreheads, and walked with them to the only people who could offer me solace—Gramato and Vangelia.

The path to their homes was familiar, but on that day, it felt unbearably long. My feet dragged, as though the weight of my sorrow slowed me with every step. The sun was high, beating down upon us, but I felt cold. I clutched the letter in my hand as if it were my last connection to my brother, as if it would dissolve the moment I let it go.

Gramato saw me first. She had been outside, shaking out a rug, but the moment our eyes met, she stilled. She knew. Even before I spoke, she knew.

"Eftihia *mou*," she said, stepping forward and taking me into her arms. I crumpled against her, my body shaking with the sobs I had held back. She said nothing, only held me as I wept.

Vangelia, who had been visiting appeared in the doorway, her expression shifting from confusion to understanding. She hurried forward, taking the children and ushering them inside, distracting them with food and gentle words.

Gramato led me inside, and we sat in her tiny kitchen. She sat beside me, her hand warm against my back. My tears fell freely now, my body wracked with grief. I tried to speak, to explain, but all I could manage were choked sobs.

"Stamatis. My beloved little brother. He was just a boy."

I closed my eyes and inhaled sharply, as if speaking his name could keep him near, as if remembering him could make him real again. He was always running, bursting with energy, always laughing. He chased the chickens in the yard, climbed the olive trees, and drove our mother to madness with his mischief. But he had a good heart—a kind heart. He was just a twelve-year-old boy.

She nodded, her eyes misted with tears. She didn't ask how. She didn't need to. Instead, she reached for my hands, pressing them between hers, grounding me in her steady presence. We sat in silence, the weight of loss heavy between us. In that moment, I was grateful for her—her quiet strength. She offered no empty words, only company in grief.

How much more? How much more suffering did our family have to bear? Hadn't we already lost so much?

My mind unravelled, unwinding through the years, through the cruelty of fate that had haunted us like a shadow that would not lift.

Stamatis had survived what so many others had not. He had lived through Smyrni—the fire, the screams, the crush of thousands fighting to escape. I remember that day on the quay, clutching his small hand as if my grip alone could keep him safe. Gunshots cracked, screams rose, and in an instant the chaos tore him from me, and Persephone from him.

He had only been five years old. Swept into that seething mass of humanity, swallowed by it, alone. Pushed onto a boat, carried away with no one to guide him. He could have landed on any of the islands taking in refugees, could have disappeared from us forever. Yet by some miracle, he came to Chios, where strangers cared for him until the day we were reunited.

And before that, Sokia. That black day when the soldiers had come to our home. The memory of it lived in my body, rising unbidden now as grief dragged me back into the past. My father's voice, rising in protest as the soldiers had escorted him away. The horror of what had befallen Polyxeni. My mother's screams. The disappearance of Dimitri. Stamatis had endured the journey from Sokia to Smyrni and the horrors we had witnessed as we had walked the streets, the bodies, how the Turks had slaughtered the people and then burned the city to ashes.

My little brother had been so young then. Just a boy. He should never have had to witness what he did. And yet, he had. He had carried all of that inside of him. And now, after everything, after surviving that horror, he was gone. God had taken him too.

The Divine had shown us no mercy.

The weight of my sorrow pressed into me, deep and relentless. I thought of him lying in the earth, of the coldness of it, of the finality.

I felt a sob rising in my throat. My mother must have wept until there were no more tears left in her. How much more could she or any of us endure?

I was so far away. Separated not just by land and sea, but by grief, by distance that could not be measured in miles alone. My mother mourning another child. Another piece of herself stripped away. And I could do nothing.

I could not hold her. I could not weep with her.

I could not see my little brother's face one last time.

All I was left with were memories. And memories were not enough.

That night, when the children were asleep, I sat by the oil lamp, Dimitri's letter spread before me. I read it again, though I knew every word by heart.

"Our mother is inconsolable."

How could she not be? I imagined her sitting in our home, or perhaps my brother was caring for her, her hands trembling, her face hollow with grief. She had already lost so much. Now, she had lost her youngest child.

What strength could remain in her after this?

I longed to be with her. To wrap my arms around her, to weep beside her, to mourn together as a family should. But that was not possible.

So, I did the only thing I could. I wrote to her.

"Mama *mou*, my heart breaks with yours. I cannot imagine the depth of your sorrow but know that I grieve with you. Our Stamatis. I cannot believe he is gone. If I could be with you, I would. But I am here, and you are there, and the world is cruel in its distances. I will pray for him, and I will pray for you. Please, hold on. Do not let this grief take you from us, from me, until I can come to your side and hold you once again."

I sealed the letter with trembling hands, knowing it was not enough. But it was all I had to give.

Then I left the house and made my way to the *platea*, to the church of Agia Paraskevi. No one stopped me. They must have seen the grief in my eyes, the purpose in my steps.

The church was quiet when I entered, the scent of beeswax and incense filling the air. I stepped forward to the candle stand, my fingers trembling as I picked up two of the thin beeswax candles. I lit one from the flame of another and placed it among them.

For my brother. For Stamatis.

I then did the same with the other, but this time it was for my mother — that the *Panayia* might grant her the strength to bear the weight of her loss.

I stood there, staring at the flickering flames. The tears came then, silent, and steady, running down my cheeks as I stood in the dim light of the church. I had not been there to bury him. I had not been there to say goodbye. But here, in this moment, I gave him my farewell.

"Anapáfsou en eiríni, adelfoúli mou. Tha eísai pánta stin kardiá mou. Rest in peace, my little brother. You will be in my heart always."

Then I made my way forward to the icon of the *Panayia* holding her child. For a long moment, I stood there looking into her eyes, wanting to break down and ask her why it had to be this way.

I clenched my hands together, pressing them against my chest as if I could hold my heart in place, to keep it from breaking any further.

"Why? "The word slipped from my lips. "Why did you not protect him?"

She held her son in her arms, serene and sorrowful. The mother of God, the mother of all who grieved, the one who had known the pain of losing a child.

Tears spilled down my face, unchecked, falling onto the cold marble floor beneath me.

"He was just a boy," I choked out.

My breath came in gasps, ragged and broken.

"Was it not enough?" I asked her. "Have we not suffered enough? Has my mother not suffered enough? Her two youngest children taken from her."

I searched her expression for an answer, for some divine reason that could make sense of this cruelty. But she only gazed back, offering no words. I reached out, my fingertips grazing the cold glass that protected her. A deep shudder passed through me.

"*Panayia mou*, give me the strength to bear this."

My knees felt weak. I bowed my head, pressing my forehead against the wooden frame of the icon, my body trembling as the sobs finally came, deep and raw.

"My mother, how will she go on?" My voice broke. "How do any of us go on?"

I stayed there, pouring my grief into the silence, until there was nothing left in me but exhaustion. Then, with a final, shuddering breath, I straightened.

I looked once more into the eyes of the *Panayia*. There was no answer there, only the same quiet sorrow that had been painted onto her face. My grief would not leave me, not today, never. But for now, I had surrendered it into her hands.

The days passed in a haze. I moved through my routines as though in a dream. The children still needed me. The household still needed me. Georgios, though sorrowful on my behalf, could not fully understand the depth of my loss.

Grief did not care about daily life. It did not care that bread needed to be baked, that clothes needed washing, that the sun still rose and set. It lived within me, an ever-present ache, dull and sharp all at once.

But I carried on. Because I had to.

On the fortieth day after Stamatis' passing, I did the only thing I could to honour him from afar. I held a *Mnimosyno*, a memorial service, in the church of Agia Paraskevi. They said the soul lingered during this time, wandering between this world and the next, before finding its place. Would he still be here? Would he see me standing in church, honouring him from across the sea?

I had not been there to lay him to rest, to see the earth cover him, to hear the prayers over his grave. I had not been there to take my mother's hand as she wept for her son, for the boy we had lost. But I could do this. I could pray for his soul. I could honour him as our people had done for generations, trusting that even in death, the bonds of family were never truly broken.

The church was quiet when I arrived, with the scent of beeswax and incense hanging in the air. The priest had prepared the table before the iconostasis, and in the centre sat the *kollyva*, a dish of boiled wheat mixed with nuts, raisins, and pomegranate seeds, sweetened with sugar, and perfumed with cinnamon. The wheat was a symbol of resurrection, a reminder that just as a seed is buried in the earth to grow again, so too would the soul find new life in eternity. Beside the *kollyva*, a small tray held the names of the departed, those for whom prayers would be said. And there, among them, was my brother's name.

Stamatis.

The priest began the service, his voice solemn as he chanted the *Trisagion* hymn. The mourners responded with the familiar words, their voices rising in unison. I closed my eyes, the prayers washing over me.

"Anápauson, Kýrie, tin psychín tou doúlou sou Stamáti. Grant rest, O Lord, to the soul of Your servant Stamatis."

When the prayers ended, the priest took the censer, swinging it gently so that the scent of burning incense filled the space. The smoke curled upward, carrying our prayers with it, and in that moment, I imagined it reaching my brother, wherever he was now.

At the end of the service, we shared the *kollyva*, each taking a spoonful in remembrance of him. A simple act, yet one steeped in faith and tradition. I held the sweetness on my tongue, knowing that even in grief, the bonds of family still held true.

Before I left, I went to the icon of the *Panayia* once more. I made the sign of the cross. This time, however, I did not ask why. I did not plead for answers that I knew would never come.

CHAPTER TEN

Three weeks had passed since the memorial service, and each day I waited for more news, a letter from my brother or even one from my mother. My thoughts constantly returned to her, longing for a letter that might bring me some news of her, some reassurance that she was managing as best she could in her overwhelming grief.

When the letter from Dimitri finally arrived one evening, I felt an odd mixture of anticipation and dread. I hesitated before opening it. I knew I could not bear to read it until the children were settled for the night and Georgios had come home from the fields. I would sit on the *terratza*, terrace, just like so many other evenings, and read Dimitri's words without distraction.

The house was still when I finally took my place on the bottom step. The air was cool, with a gentle breeze brushing against my skin, and I felt a measure of calm. The children were asleep, and Georgios, exhausted from his work, had retreated inside to our bedroom to rest. I held the letter in my hands, but as I unfolded it, the stains on the page—dark spots like tears—made my heart tighten. My brother had been crying while writing his letter to me.

As my eyes moved over the words of the first sentence, I felt a shudder run through me, a sense of foreboding. The words I read sounded like a bad omen.

"My beloved sister, Eftihia, I cannot begin to tell you the sorrow that has gripped me…"

I knew instantly that something was wrong.

"Our mother suffered a heart attack at the end of the memorial service held for our Stamatis."

I swallowed hard, trying to steady myself. I read on, and with each word, the weight in my chest grew heavier, until I reached the devastating line.

"It is with a broken heart, a broken spirit that I have to tell you that our mother passed away."

For a moment, nothing made sense. My mind refused to accept the truth of it. I had only recently lost my young brother, Stamatis, but this, this was the finality of it, the impossibility of ever seeing my mother again. It was too much. It was unbearable.

I let the letter slip from my fingers, the words spinning in front of me like a dizzying blur. I tried to breathe, but it was as if I had forgotten how. I couldn't take in what I had just read. My mother, gone. My mind screamed in denial, but my body refused to obey.

The scream tore from my throat before I even realised it. It was the kind of scream that comes from the deepest, rawest part of you, the kind that cannot be stifled, no matter how much you want it to stop. My body jerked with each breath, each sob. I felt my chest heaving, my heart breaking all over again as I rocked back and forth, unable to process the crushing truth.

Before I knew it, Georgios was beside me. His arms reached for me, his voice desperate, trying to comfort me, but I couldn't bear it. I shoved him away, pushing at his chest with every ounce of strength I had. The sight of him, the man who had promised my mother that he would never take me away from her, filled me with a sudden, overwhelming rage.

I stood up too quickly, the world tilting around me, but the dizziness was nothing compared to the anger surging through me. It erupted, years of resentment and sorrow colliding in a violent storm. In that moment, I let out my pain, unable to contain it any longer. It was he, I told him, who had broken his oath to my mother. It was him, his stubbornness, his selfishness, that had brought me here, forcing me to care for people I did not know because he had given them his oath. He had also given my mother his oath, and yet his family had taken precedence over mine.

His grandparents still had their daughter, her husband, and his other two brothers. They were not alone. But he had left my mother and younger brother on their own. He had turned his back on them, on my family, choosing obligation over the family that needed him most. They too had lost so much, just as I had. Yet he had taken me away from them, ripped me from the life I knew, and now she was gone. I would never see her again. The weight of that truth crushed me, and nothing else mattered.

Georgios took a step back, confusion flickering across his face, his eyes dark with sorrow. But I didn't care. I couldn't care. The pain I had buried for so long surged to the surface, unchecked. I wanted him to feel it, to understand the depth of what he had done.

When he reached for me again, I recoiled. The thought of his touch felt unbearable. I couldn't stand the sight of him, the man who had broken his word, who had torn me away from my family. Now, all that remained was emptiness. The sobs kept coming, mixed in with an anger that burned hot and sharp in my chest.

I felt Kyría Athena, our neighbour, stepping closer, her hands on my shoulders, trying to calm me. But I didn't want calming. I wanted my mother back. I wanted the life that had been taken from me. How could he have done this? How could he have promised and then gone against it? The rage boiled inside me, tangled up with my grief, leaving me breathless.

More of our neighbours came. It took the strength of some of the other women to pull me inside, to guide me away from Georgios. They tried to calm me, but I couldn't stop. They led me inside, pulling me into the bedroom, but I was too far gone. I collapsed onto the bed, my body wracked with sobs that wouldn't cease, my mind a whirl of grief and fury. He remained standing in the doorway of our bedroom, silent. I didn't care about him anymore. My world had fractured. My mother, was gone, and he was the cause of my pain.

A cool towel was placed on my forehead, and the women around me whispered words of comfort, but I couldn't hear them. It was as though I had retreated inside myself, a place where no one could reach me. I had lost my brother, Stamatis, just eight weeks before, and now my mother. The pain was overwhelming, stealing every bit of strength I had left. How could I face another day, knowing that they were both gone and that there was nothing I could do to bring them back?

I couldn't look at Georgios. I couldn't speak to him. How could I pretend nothing had changed? I couldn't. I didn't know how.

He had taken me away from my family. All I had left were raw, painful memories of a life I could never return to. There was only grief, loss, and the terrible ache in my heart. My mother was gone, and there was no one who could ever replace her.

*   *   *

The pain of loss did not pass. It settled in, like a heavy stone pressing against my chest. Days turned into weeks, each one indistinguishable from the last. I moved through them in a haze, functioning only because the children needed me to. I fed them, bathed them, helped Angeliki settle into school. But I was no longer truly present.

How does a woman come to terms with losing her mother?

She doesn't.

Not at first, and maybe never completely.

My mother had been my guide, my unwavering strength. I had admired her all my life for her quiet courage, for her kindness that never wavered. She had suffered, endured, carried more than her share, and even so, she rose each day to face what life would give her. And that strength had made me believe she would always be there. Even in my resentment, in the months and years when I lived away from her, when letters had bridged the distance between us, I believed she would wait for me. That I would see her again. That I would have time. I thought if anyone could defy death by sheer will alone, it would have been her.

But even she had her limits.

I told myself she was at peace now. That she was with my father, with Polyxeni, with Stamatis, with the others we had lost. It gave me some comfort, a small flicker of light in the darkness that threatened to consume me. The separation was absolute. Death had taken her from me, and no words, no prayers, could close the chasm it had left behind.

I felt as if the foundation of my life had shifted. The ground beneath me, once certain, was gone, leaving me unsteady, unsure where to place my feet or how to move forward. Memories of her haunted me with cruel clarity. Her voice, her hands, which had soothed away my distress, the way she had been a quiet strength in my life, all now was beyond reach. Even in sleep, I could not escape it. In dreams, I would reach for her, only to find that the distance between us was insurmountable.

Even imagining her at peace could not soften the ache of her absence. Death had made our parting final, irrevocable, and I was left to carry the weight of longing alone, feeling the emptiness of a world forever altered by her loss.

I barely spoke to my husband. The few words we did exchange were clipped, functional, discussions about the children, household needs, things that required coordination but no warmth. I didn't trust myself to speak freely to him. I feared what would come out. Because beneath my grief was a fury, I couldn't extinguish.

I wrote to Dimitri. I poured myself into that letter as if my brother could carry some of this burden for me, as if he could make sense of the chaos inside of me. I confessed everything, the resentment that had been festering for years, the bitterness that boiled over when our mother died. I told him how the sorrow pressed in on me from all sides, how I felt betrayed, not just by fate, not just by death, but by the man I had married. I told him how hollow I felt, how much I hated Georgios for what he had done—for dragging me away from our mother, for putting his grandparents' needs above ours.

I told him I had reached a point where I no longer knew if I could stay with Georgios. I wanted to take the children and go. Go back to Antiphillipi, where I had last known peace.

I knew what Dimitri would say. I wrote it plainly in the letter. Do not bother replying with lectures on duty, on the sanctity of marriage, on my role as a wife and mother. I did not want to hear it. I had consented to marry Georgios, yes. But it was he who had broken his oath, not I. He had promised my mother he would not take me from her. He had stood before her, looked her in the eyes, and made that vow. And then he broke it.

Wasn't that enough? Wasn't that betrayal enough reason to leave?

When I folded the letter and sealed it, I sat with it in my lap for a long time. I didn't know whether to send it. But something inside me needed to be heard. That afternoon, I handed it to the postman.

*　　*　　*

The village of Chora moved at its own rhythm, unbothered by the heaviness that had wedged itself into my heart. From the kitchen window, I watched the daily procession of women carrying baskets of laundry to the communal washhouse, old men in flat caps walking to the *kafeneion*, children chasing chickens down the alleyways. Life went on here, whether you were ready for it or not.

There were days when I nearly turned my thoughts into action, to book a passage back to the north. But then I would look at my children. Chora was the only home they had known. Angeliki, my eldest, was now at school. Their Greek was now tinted with the Samiot accent. It would be difficult to uproot them, to take them away from their father, despite the distance that still stood between us. Georgios, for all his faults, loved them. He worked tirelessly to support his family. I knew he would be broken by their absence. And I knew I would be judged for it. A woman who left her husband? Not a widow, not abandoned, but one who walked away willingly? They would say I was weak. That I had failed in my duty as a wife, that my grief had turned me selfish.

What would Dimitri say, or the neighbours in Antiphillipi, where my mother and brother's graves now lay. They would not see it as courage. They would see it as a betrayal of my husband.

And yet, I was still torn. Some nights, after the children were asleep, I would sit alone in the kitchen. I wondered if my mother watched me from wherever she was. If she could see how weighed down I had become with sorrow. How I still longed for her.

The silence between Georgios and me grew more pronounced. He knew letters had arrived from Dimitri, but he didn't ask me what he had written or if I had replied. Perhaps he didn't care. Or perhaps, he didn't know how to reach across the chasm that had opened between us.

I took to walking the narrow path up to the church of Agios Athanasios in the early mornings before the heat settled in and the day took shape. The little chapel offered a kind of refuge where I could simply sit and let myself remember her not just as my mother, but as a woman who had been resilient and brave. She had endured so much and still showed kindness. I asked myself if I was capable of that.

Dimitri wrote back. His response was not what I had expected. He didn't scold me. There was no reminder of duty or role. He didn't tell me what to do.

He didn't tell me to leave, nor did he tell me to stay. Just the quiet presence of a brother who had known the same mother, who too had lost as much as I had and who now grieved her in his own way.

"I understand the weight of the pain you carry, my beloved sister," he began. "And I would never judge you for the anger and resentment you feel towards your husband's betrayal of the oath he made to our mother and to you. No one can walk through such loss untouched by the emotions you feel. You have lost so much, more than most could bear."

But it was the last line of his letter that stayed with me, lingering long after I had folded the letter and set it aside:

"She would not want you to break from the pain of losing her."

One evening, Georgios stood in the kitchen doorway, holding his hat in both hands, looking uncertain. There was weariness in his shoulders that I hadn't seen before. I looked up from the table where I was folding the washing I had done earlier in the day. For a long moment, neither of us spoke. I thought he had come for water or to ask something about the next day. Then he said my name, and something in the way he spoke it made me stop mid-fold, my hands still clutching the linen.

Then he said he was wrong, that he should never have brought me here. He had broken his oath, not just to me but to her. He stepped closer, not waiting for a response, and confessed that he had promised to care for us all, to never separate us. But he had done exactly that.

He believed, back then that he was doing the right thing, repaying a debt he felt he owed his grandparents. But now he saw it, the harm he had caused, the pain he had inflicted. His voice cracked, and in that crack, I heard all the sorrow he carried.

He apologised. Quietly. Said it should have come sooner. Maybe I would not have wanted to hear it, but he believed I still deserved to hear it now.

I didn't respond. Not immediately. The weight of his words left me stunned. Then he admitted it all, that I had given up everything for him. My family, my home, the only world I had ever known. And he had been too stubborn to listen.

He reminded me I had lost them, my brother, my mother, and I could not be there to bury them, to grieve beside my family. That was a sacrifice he never meant to impose, he said. And now he must live with that shame.

I remained silent. The pain was too full in my chest to let anything out. So he kept going.

He spoke of the hardships I had been forced to endure in those early days, the house we lived in that was never meant to be a home, the burdens I had carried from the day we arrived. He said he should have protected me. That he should have spoken up, that he should have kept his word to my mother and to me. He saw it all now. Too late, yes—but he saw it and acknowledged the hurt he had caused.

I looked at him then. I saw what he carried though it was different from my own grief, but nonetheless it was heavy in its own way.

He didn't wait for forgiveness. He simply turned and left me there. Where he went, I do not know. Off to the fields, or the village *kafeneion*, or wherever men go to escape the weight of their own guilt.

I sat in the stillness long after he had gone. His apology did not change the past. But as the days passed, something inside of me shifted. Not forgiveness —not yet. But a slow, steady understanding. Maybe life did not need everything to be made right. Maybe it only asked that we endure.

The next morning, the children rushed into the kitchen. They needed breakfast. They needed their mother. So I stayed. For them. For Georgios. For the life we had built in this village. And perhaps, in time, for myself.

*   *   *

On the fortieth day after my mother's passing, I found myself once again in the church of Agia Paraskevi. Another *Mnimosyno* Another name spoken aloud. Another soul released. I had stood here weeks ago for Stamatis, and now I stood here again, this time for the woman who had given us both life.

The church smelled the same—beeswax, incense, and the warm scent of candles. Familiar hymns rose and fell from the *psalti*, the chanter who leads the congregation in liturgical hymns and psalms, his voice resonating with a solemn cadence that seemed to carry the prayers of generations. The table had been carefully prepared, just as it always was. In the centre sat the *kollyva*, for all the departed souls being honoured that day. Wheat and sugar, symbols of memory and faith. I walked closer, my chest tightening with a mixture of reverence and grief.

And there it was. Her name.

Maria.

For a long moment, I simply stood there, letting the scents, sounds, and sacred quiet surround me. The sweetness of the sugar was a reminder of life, of continuity, even as her absence pressed heavily on my heart. I had not been there when she left this world. I had not held her hand or whispered the words a daughter ought to whisper at the end. I had not laid her to rest beside my brother. The weight of that absence sat heavy in my chest. But I could do this. I could light the candle. I could speak her name. I could honour her as our people always had, trusting that she, too, would feel it from wherever her soul now lingered.

As the incense rose, curling towards the vaulted ceiling, I closed my eyes.

"Anápauson, Kýrie, tin psychín tis doúlis sou Marías. Grant rest, O Lord, to the soul of Your servant Maria."

The priest chanted the familiar prayers. The mourners responded softly. And among them, I noticed faces I had not expected. Women who had once turned their backs on me, who had looked through me when I first arrived in Chora. Now they stood in quiet reverence.

One touched my arm and said gently, *'Na ti thymásai me kamári* May you remember her with pride."

Another added, *"I Sokiáni státhike ópos éprepe.* The woman from Sokia stood as she should."

I Sokiáni. Once a dismissal, now it was something else. A nickname, something which stayed with me throughout my life.

At the end of the service, we shared the *kollyva.* I let the sweetness settle on my tongue, though it turned bitter the moment it touched me. What comfort could there be in a spoonful of boiled wheat, when my mother's whole life had been nothing but suffering? She endured as no woman should have endured. Every humiliation, every loss, every heavy burden forced upon her, until her body and spirit gave way.

I could already hear the words whispered to me in condolences.

"Ítan thélema Theoú". It was God's will.

As if that explained anything. As if that sanctified her pain. What kind of God wills such misery? What kind of God stands by and watches a woman like her break under the weight of a life she never deserved? My mother gave everything—her strength, her very soul—and was rewarded with pain, grief, and a bitter end. To say this was 'God's will' felt like an insult to her memory. If this was God's will, then God's will was cruelty itself.

The thought stayed with me long after the incense faded, shaping my grief into fury. No prayers could soften it. No priestly words could explain it away. I would not allow her suffering to be swept under the silence of that phrase, dismissed as divine intention. I would remember her not as some meek servant of God, but as a woman wronged by life, who endured because she had no other choice.

Earlier in my grief after my brother's death, I had been filled with questions. Why did this happen? Why wasn't I there? Why did he have to suffer? But now, in the aftermath of losing my mother too, I had moved past asking questions. There we no answers to be found. The truth was clear enough. The world is cruel. It stole her life, and God did not intervene. That was all.

That silence burned inside me, leaving me angry, raw, unwilling to forgive. Long after the incense faded, the question gnawed away at me, shaping my grief into fury, sharp-edged, restless, unyielding. I carried that anger with me and vowed to remember her, not in quiet sorrow, but in defiance. Against the silence of God, against the injustice that broke her, and against those who dared to dismiss it all with '*Ítan thélema Theoú*'.

Before I left, I stood before the *Panayia* again. I crossed myself, though my hand trembled. I whispered, "Forgive me."

It was not a prayer to her. It was to my mother. Forgive me for not being there. Forgive me for this helpless rage that faith cannot calm. Forgive me for not believing that God ever cared. And though I had not been there at the end, I would carry her memory with me and the love that endures beyond her absence.

*   *   *

Life in Chora was never easy, but it was steady. The land provided enough, and through hard work, we did more than survive, we began to prosper. The children, all three of them, were growing, playing in the streets of the village, their tongues fluent in the Samiot dialect. When they went to school, I worked the earth beside Georgios.

There were the olive harvests in autumn, the grape in late summer, the pruning of vines in February, and we also planted tobacco. Tobacco had sustained my family in Sokia, then again in Antiphillipi, and now here too it gave us a steady return. The state controlled everything. The *Regie* dictated the seed, the weight, the sale, but if you followed their rules and knew your craft, the profit came. We were fortunate. Our tobacco was good, and we were known for it. Our tobacco was clean, well-sorted, and in demand.

Still, the work never ended. I laboured in the fields throughout the day and returned to a house full of needs. There were mouths to feed, clothes to wash, and household chores to be done. The children brought me strength. They were different, each of them. Angeliki, the eldest, was my helper, steady and dependable, always by my side without fuss or noise. Emmanuel had a sharper tongue, always questioning, pushing, insisting on his way. He reminded me of my brother as a boy, both restless and bold. And Ploutarhos loved to be amongst us in the fields. He took to the soil naturally. I knew he would be the one to continue what his father had built.

Gramato and Vangelia were growing old. Their hair had gone white, their steps had slowed, but they still smiled and welcomed me and the children when we knocked at their doors. I visited whenever I could, always with something in hand, fresh bread, eggs, sweets I had made, or a small plate of food. We sat together and spoke of the past, of the people we had loved and lost.

There was no ease in those years, but there was pride. We had rebuilt our lives with our hands, and though I often fell into bed aching, I slept knowing the children were fed, we were prospering and tomorrow would come. We thought those steady years might continue. But there were rumours now, carried in letters, of conversations in the *kafeneion*. Italy, Germany. War. It felt distant at first, as if it was something unfolding far beyond our island. But I had learned to listen closely where such rumours were concerned.

In the spring of 1938, I learned I was pregnant again. I was carrying twins.

There had been no doctor to confirm it, only the midwife and the signs my body knew, the way it swelled too fast, how tired I felt so early, the strength of their kicks. Georgios had seemed surprised at first, then pleased.

But it was not to be.

One morning in the heat of August, I slipped on the stone steps of our house. I don't know what caused it, perhaps the weight of my body or the weight of my exhaustion. I fell hard. I remember the sickening sound of it, the sharp burst of pain, the sudden wetness spreading between my legs.

Labour began almost at once. There was no time to prepare, no way to stop it. Waves of pain tore through me, each one sharper than the last, leaving me doubled over and gasping. There was no rest between them, only waves of agony that dragged me under. In the midst of my pain, I cried out for my mother, though she was not there, only my neighbours and the midwife rushing to my side. I remember clutching the bedframe and biting my lip to stop myself from screaming too loudly, but still the cries came. Each contraction became sharper than the last, my body convulsing with effort as I fought to bring them into the world.

They were born hours later. Tiny. Fragile. I held them against me, but their chests rose and fell with terrible effort, the sound of life already slipping away.

We named them Alexandros and Stelios. We wrapped them in soft cloths, held them for as long as we could, and then buried them near the chapel of Agios Athanasios, the little whitewashed church nestled in the cypress pines in the hills above our home. Georgios dug the grave himself. I stood with him, together with the priest who performed the burial service. We placed two small wooden crosses, which had been carved by a carpenter from the village, at their graves.

That place became special to me. It held our children, taken too soon, and quietly carried the weight of my guilt. I felt responsible for their deaths. I should have been more careful. I had often scolded the children for rushing down those stairs, yet in the end, it was my carelessness that cost their lives. That truth never left me.

CHAPTER ELEVEN

When the second world war began, I had four children. I knew life would be hard, but I could never have imagined the hunger, the fear, the long nights spent wondering if we would make it to the morning. At first, here in Chora, the war felt like something happening elsewhere. The Italian invasion, the call for men to report for duty, the early victories in the north. Greece was pulled into the war in October 1940. Our son Eleftherios had only just been born a month earlier, a quiet boy with a furrowed brow, as if he had already sensed the state of the world he had been born into.

The day Georgios left with the other men who had been called up to fight in the war, was one of the longest of my life. They were loaded onto a truck to take them to Vathy. From there they would board a ship for the journey to Athens, away from us, towards a war we barely understood.

However, two weeks later, much to my astonishment, he returned. I had spent each day expecting the worst, forcing myself to continue on as if life had not changed. When I saw him step through the front door, I thought I was imagining it. The authorities had asked him how many children he had, and when he replied he had four, they sent him back. Four children needed a father to provide for them, and the authorities decided it was enough to spare him.

The world was at war, and Greece had fallen under the brutal control of the Axis powers—Nazi Germany, Fascist Italy, and Imperial Japan. Samos, like so many of the islands, was occupied in 1941 by the Italian army, soldiers of the Cuneo Division. They marched in, setting up their posts in the major towns and taking control of everything. Some were only boys. Others were older, exhausted from fighting. There was no violence at first, no overt cruelty but make no mistake, they were occupiers. We kept our distance. We nodded when we had to. We fed them when they came through the village asking for what little food we had. What choice did we have?

To weaken the Axis hold on occupied territories, the Allied powers, including Britain, the United States, and the Soviet Union, imposed a naval blockade. This meant that ships could not deliver food, medicine, or other essential supplies to Greece. The blockade was intended to disrupt the Axis supply lines. However, the Allies had not considered the devastating consequences it would have on us civilians. With local production already strained under the occupation and much of our island's produce requisitioned by the Italians, the blockade only worsened an already dire situation. We were cut off, left to survive on our own.

That blockade, along with the occupation, brought famine. Real famine. Even so, we endured. We had no choice. We survived because we had to, for our children and for each other. We did what we could. Families had to survive on whatever they could grow or forage. The Italians offered food, a little flour, or beans, rice, but it was never enough. In our village, we relied on hidden stores of grain and oil, whatever the land could yield, and the strength of the community coming together to survive those darkest years. The black market became our lifeline. Money was useless, but trade kept us alive. We bartered whatever we could behind closed doors, hoping the Italians would not notice.

We had been careful and had prepared ourselves before the war, storing our supplies of grain, legumes, rice, olives in brine, dried fruit and nuts and our oil, together with fodder for our animals, in the large store room built beneath the house. It was this hidden supply which kept us alive. We also turned to the land, planting whatever we could.

One of our plots lay high in the hills, offering sweeping views over the sea. To reach it, we had to walk through dense shrubs, tall trees, and thick undergrowth where snakes and scorpions sometimes hid, however, its remoteness kept it well concealed. Georgios usually made the trip by horse, though when it wasn't safe, he went on foot. We called the land Agios Konstantinos, after the nearby church. Alongside the small crops we planted, there were fruit trees of many varieties — figs, pear, apples, apricots, and peaches, that helped sustain us. Georgios also tended to the goats and chickens we kept hidden in a cave. This was our protection against starvation but for how long?

Even with the land, even with the hidden food, it would not be enough. I would walk the hillside with the children, teaching them how to identify edible plants. We learned to make do with what the land offered. Dandelion leaves, nettles, horta and purslane, anything that could fill our stomachs without poisoning us. At first, the children resisted, longing for the comfort of the food they had once known. But hunger is a teacher, and soon they learned to eat whatever I placed before them.

Food did not just become scarce. Hunger gnawed at us. I had known hunger before in the refugee camp, but not like that. Not the kind that made your hands shake when you held a spoon. The famine took more lives than the bombs did.

Late one evening, after dusk had settled, I made my way to the chapel of Agios Athanasios. There, among the cypress trees, I found them, three Italian soldiers, gaunt and weary, their faces etched with exhaustion. They raised their hands in surrender, their eyes filled with fear. Though I was a woman in my forties, and they were the occupiers, it was clear they feared me more than I feared them.

They had deserted their posts and were well aware of the severe consequences if they were caught. I, too, understood the risks of offering them shelter. Communication was limited; their Greek extended only to *efcharisto*, and I knew no Italian. I gestured for them to stay where they were, and I would return with some food. Georgios had not yet returned, and an hour later, when darkness had fallen, I told Angeliki that I was going to visit Gramato and that I would not be long. Instead, I went back up to the church, where the Italians were still waiting with whatever I could spare, some bread, some walnuts, and some fresh figs. They ate slowly, their hands trembling. When they had finished, under the cover of night, I led them down the hill and hid them in the shelter beneath the house.

When Georgios arrived home, I had no choice but to tell him what I had done. He was furious at first.

"If the Italians find out we are hiding these deserters, they will kill them," he warned. "And then they will turn on us, including the children."

I did not fear the Italians as much. I did, however, remind him of the consequences if one were caught by the Turks. I had not forgotten Smyrni, nor the death marches, nor the fate of the women dragged away and never seen again. I told him how they showed no mercy, how capture meant not only death but degradation, humiliation, a slow unravelling of one's humanity. With the Turks there was no appeal, no reprieve, no hope of pity.

Their kind of cruelty, was the kind that clung to families for generations. I had seen it and lived through it.

He said nothing more. He knew I spoke the truth.

The following night, two men arrived, bringing clothes for the soldiers to change into. One of them spoke Italian. They came with a plan. Georgios would help them. Together, they would take the Italians to Vlamari, where a caique would wait to take them to Kuşadası. From there, they would make their way to Egypt and then back to Italy. By the morning, the Italians were gone and so was the trace of what we had done.

Such escapes were perilous but not uncommon. Word would spread quietly through the village that the British were moving again. There were no men in uniforms. What came were small boats, caiques, that looked no different from our own. But they were manned by British sailors and Greeks who had fled earlier in the war. They slipped between the islands under the cover of darkness. These British sailors, worked alongside Greek volunteers, and brought in badly needed food for the locals, ammunition for the Allied soldiers and the resistance fighters. They also smuggled out deserters and Allied agents heading back to Cairo.

They called them the Levant Schooner Flotilla. We knew these men risked everything to reach us. Ordinary villagers like us were not part of the resistance, but we knew better than to speak about what we had heard or seen. Germans and Italians searched for them constantly, but Samos was full of hidden inlets and brave locals.

*   *   *

In September 1943, we heard the news. Italy had surrendered. I was also six months pregnant with my fifth child. The surrender of the Italians came suddenly, though we had sensed something had been shifting for weeks. Word travelled fast and even faster in times of war. Rumours reached us that Italy had capitulated. Mussolini was finished.

At first, there was a strange sense of hope among the villagers—maybe the war was nearing its end. Maybe the island would breathe again. The Italians, who had occupied the island since 1941, were caught in a state of confusion. Some wanted to lay down their arms. Others feared what the Germans would do next. We watched as the tension thickened, not knowing who was friend and who was the enemy anymore.

The Italians, now unsure of their orders, began retreating. Many of them did not want to fight for the Germans. They had families waiting for their return. They were tired. Some fled into the hills, deserting their posts, and hid either in the hills or in abandoned houses. We, together with other sympathetic villagers, and with the help of local resistance fighters, did what we had previously done. We smuggled them off the island disguised as locals, under the cover of darkness and sent them to Kuşadasi by caique, where they eventually made their way to the Allied forces in Egypt.

The bishop of Samos, Eirenaios, tried to hold the island together in those brief days between the Italian collapse and the German occupation. A temporary local administration was formed with Greek, Italian, and resistance members working together. Samos was, for a brief moment in history, the first part of Greece to taste liberation.

But it did not last.

In November 1943, the Germans arrived. They didn't arrive quietly. German aircrafts filled the skies over Samos. We heard the bombers before we saw them. The capital was hit first. It was bombed relentlessly, with planes coming in waves of ten to fifteen at a time. It felt endless. Twenty percent of the town's buildings were destroyed. Soldiers and civilians alike were killed or wounded. One hundred and forty civilians were killed in a single afternoon. We had no anti-aircraft weapons, but somehow, our defenders hit one of the bombers, bringing it down. Buildings had collapsed. People streamed into the streets, clutching their children, while others dug through rubble with their bare hands to find missing neighbours or relatives.

Tigani (Pythagoreio) was also ruined.

We took shelter in the storeroom, shielding our children as the ground shook and buildings collapsed. If we had once feared the Italians, we soon came to realise the Germans would be far worse. And we soon came to understand what it would take to survive them.

By the end of 1943, the Germans had taken full control of Samos. Their presence was harsher, colder. There was no pretence of tolerance now. Things turned darker. The Italians, for all their faults, had seemed human. Some of them even grew fond of the island and its people. Some had stayed and married local girls.

The Germans, however, treated us like animals. We asked for flour to bake our bread to feed our families. They brought us bags of cement.

Reprisals were swift and merciless. Entire families were taken from their homes, accused of helping partisans. We heard the gunshots from the hills and knew what they meant. The Germans requisitioned what little food remained to feed their garrisons. Fishermen were shot for sailing without permission. Curfews were enforced with bullets. Anyone seen in the street after dark could be shot without warning.

We heard of one man from the village who was caught fishing illegally at night. They beat him in front of his wife and children to within an inch of his life. Someone had betrayed him, and so we stopped speaking freely, even amongst ourselves. A single careless word could end a life.

Georgios would go up to Agios Konstantinos less often now, even though the Germans rarely reached that high. We relied on that land like never before. The hunger worsened. We rationed every grain of wheat, every drop of oil. The one goat that remained in Agios Konstantinos now gave less milk. The others, including the hens and the pigs, had been killed off slowly to sustain our family.

In January 1944, I gave birth to another daughter. By then, Samos had suffered too much, and we had no strength left to celebrate new life. It had been dulled by hunger, fear, and exhaustion. Food was scarcer than ever, and we lived with the whine of air raid sirens overhead and the dull thunder of bombers crossing the sky. Still, in the heart of winter, with the island gripped by hunger and fear, she came into the world, and we realised that life would continue, even amid the ruin and the misery.

We named her Emorfia, meaning beautiful. Because she was. And because I needed to believe beauty could still exist in such a world. It was also to honour her paternal grandmother.

She was a quiet baby, with dark hair and dark eyes that searched our faces as though she already understood the gravity of the world she had been brought into. Her skin was pale, her fingers tiny, but she latched on to life with a quiet determination. We wrapped her in layers for warmth, and I held her close to my chest and wept not just from the pain, but from the miracle of her presence.

Holding her for the first time, I couldn't help but wonder what kind of world we had brought her into. But she was here now. I felt the warmth of hope stirring within me, but it was also tangled up with worry. The war still raged around us, and I feared my children might grow up knowing only fear and hunger. I longed for a world where they could live in peace, not merely survive it.

One day, we were sheltering in the storeroom beneath the house. The Germans had been conducting air raids on the island again, and we knew the sounds too well by then, the low rumble of the planes, the whine of bombs dropping, the staccato burst of gunfire. We heard the planes approaching and knew an attack was coming. The baby had begun to cry, her small voice echoing in the cramped space. I thought she was thirsty, so I left the safety of the shelter, hurrying down the stairs to fetch water from the house.

Just as I was about to return, I heard a roar overhead. I looked up and saw the German plane sweeping low and dropped to the ground. A volley of gunfire erupted from the aircraft above. Instantly, I crouched down, pressing myself against the high wall of the stairs, my heart pounding in my ears. The shots ripped through the air, striking the walls of our house. Dust and debris exploded around me.

For a moment, I did not move. I did not even breathe. Then, slowly, I realised it was only the stone wall where I had sheltered, that had saved me. If I had taken another step, if I had moved just a second later, I would have been killed.

The wall had taken the force of the gunfire. My body trembled as I forced myself to move back into the shelter where Emorfia still cried. I knelt beside her, offering her the water with hands that trembled. Her cries quietened as she drank, and I took her from Angeliki and cradled her against my chest, trying to steady my breath.

The children and I sat in silence after that, listening to the distant thunder of bombs falling further up the valley. I kept thinking how close I had come to dying, how easily my children could have been orphaned in an instant. Later, I found myself shaking—not from fear, but from rage. Rage that a mother retrieving water for her baby could be gunned down like an animal.

That evening, after the raids had ended, Georgios returned from Agios Konstantinos. He had heard the planes and had remained in the shelter of the cave. When he saw the bullet holes in the stone and the gouges in the steps, he said nothing. He held me tightly while I cried for the first time in months.

By the autumn of 1944, the Germans began to retreat. We had heard rumours passed from village to village that they were pulling back across the Aegean. None of us dared to believe it. Too many false hopes had already cost us too dearly.

Then, one morning in late September, things felt different. No patrols passed through Chora. There was no shouting in the streets, no orders barked in a language that had ruled us with fear. We waited, tense, until it became clear that they had gone. No fanfare, no final destruction, only an eerie silence where oppression had lived for three long years.

The British arrived without warning at first light. We watched from our terrace as their ships made their way to the harbours of Vathy and glided into the harbour at Tigani, grey silhouettes against the sharp blue of the morning. Some villagers cheered. Others stood quietly, arms folded, as if unwilling to trust that freedom had truly returned.

Soldiers in unfamiliar uniforms arrived by trucks into the village. They didn't come with grand speeches or celebration. The schoolhouse became a distribution point where the soldiers worked methodically, dispensing the supplies with quiet efficiency. No one pushed or shouted. Hunger had taught us patience.

The soldiers worked methodically, setting aside parcels for families with young children, ensuring the milk went to where it was needed the most. Mothers were given tins and told how to dilute the powder, how much to feed their children. For some, it was the first proper nourishment their children had received in over a year.

They brought sacks of flour and rice, dried legumes, powdered milk, condensed milk in small tins and powdered eggs. There were tins of sardines and meat, canned goods, boxes of biscuits, sugar, and salt and soft crackers that could be soaked for babies. There were cartons of soap, disinfectant, bandages, and iodine to tend to long-neglected wounds, and bottles of cod liver oil. We were told to give the children a spoonful each day. It was thick, bitter, and hard to swallow, but vital. During the war, cod liver oil had been used widely across Europe to prevent rickets and other diseases caused by vitamin deficiencies. It helped keep children's bones strong when fresh food was scarce, and now it would do the same for ours.

And amid all the necessities, small luxuries appeared—bars of chocolate, wrapped toffees, and fruit drops. These simple treats brought immense joy to the children. One soldier, barely older than my Angeliki, handed her a bar of chocolate. With a kind smile and a gesture, he let her know it was for her and that she should share it with her brothers. She stared at it in disbelief, as if it might vanish if she blinked. The children had forgotten what such things tasted like.

The British soldiers had arrived without fanfare, but their presence also signalled not just the arrival of food and medicine, but the return of compassion and proof that we had not been entirely abandoned. For the first time in years, we walked through the village square without fear and revelled in the sound of children's laughter slowly returning to the streets.

*　　*　　*

After the Germans withdrew in 1944, Samos, like the rest of Greece, fell into a brief, uneasy calm. We thought we might finally breathe again. But peace, it seemed, was only an illusion, something just out of reach for a country so worn down by war and grief. It wasn't long before our island, like the rest of Greece, would be torn apart by its own people.

There were families who welcomed the return of the monarchy, who trusted the government in exile and who supported the British. And then there were those who had fought from the mountains, who believed in a different Greece, one shaped by the people, not the crown.

The civil war that followed would tear the country in two. It began in earnest in 1946, but its roots were planted years earlier, during the resistance. The Democratic Army of Greece (DSE) the military arm of the Communist Party of Greece (KKE) had grown powerful during the occupation, and when the British-backed government tried to reassert control, fighting broke out in Athens.

The rebels, men who had once fought bravely against the Nazis, now called themselves the Democratic Army and battled the National Army, which was now armed with support from the British at first and then the Americans, who feared communism would spread through Greece. The fighters of the Democratic Army of Greece, were the partisans who had once stood shoulder to shoulder with us against the Italians and the Germans. Now they were hunted like animals, branded enemies of the very country they had once fought to liberate.

Samos, isolated as we were in the Aegean, was not spared. The DSE had a strong presence here. They knew the terrain and found refuge in the mountains, especially Mt. Kerkis. Clashes broke out across the island, and we lived once again with gunfire in the distance, checkpoints, fear of informers, and the knowledge that anyone could disappear.

Every family knew someone who had gone off to fight, or someone who had died. And every time I went to the small chapel on the hill to sit near the graves of Alexandros and Stelios, I wondered how many more mothers were sitting beside the graves of their sons and asking why.

Georgios did what he could to keep us safe. The children were growing. My three eldest were old enough by then to understand that things were not right, that people were afraid, that food was still scarce and that men could suddenly disappear. Eleftherios and Emorfia were still young, too young to understand what war meant.

It was the end of 1945, when men from the village began disappearing. Some were arrested, accused of having helped the resistance. Others left quietly at night to join the growing numbers in the hills.

We did not sleep soundly. There were nights when shots echoed through the valley, and in the morning, word would spread of someone being found dead—no trial, no explanation. Just gone. Even priests were cautious. No one dared speak openly. Government patrols came through the village regularly, asking questions. There was no safety in neutrality. If you said nothing, they suspected you of sympathy with the other side. If you gave bread to a hungry boy in the hills, you risked arrest or worse. If your son served in the army, you were loyalists. If he had joined the resistance during the war, they called you communists.

I remember one visit too clearly. Two soldiers stood at our doorstep, holding rifles, and asking where my sons were. My heart thudded inside my chest, but I had faced much worse than these young soldiers. I told them they were at the fields. They asked me what they were doing there.

"Growing food," I replied tersely. "What else would they be doing?" They looked at me for a long moment and my gaze never wavered before they smirked then turned and walked away.

The fighting on the mainland grew worse. Our village escaped the worst of the violence, but even here, the tension seeped into daily life. Prices rose, food once again became scarce, and families left in the night without explanation. Some said they fled for fear of persecution, others because they could no longer endure the fear.

I remember the day the tobacco factory in Karlovasi went up in flames. November 1948. The DSE was blamed. It was a final blow to our already struggling island economy. Tobacco had been one of our greatest sources of income. Now it was just another loss and by the time the war ended, tobacco production had fallen, and it was no longer viable for us to grow and cultivate it as we once had done with care and pride.

In 1949, word came that the war was finally over. The communists had been driven out or had fled across the northern borders. The Americans had poured weapons and money into the National Army, and the end came quickly. But it didn't feel like a victory. The cost had been unbearable. Tens of thousands were dead. Villages destroyed. Families broken.

When it ended—when they finally declared the war over—it didn't feel like peace. Nearly two hundred Samiot fighters of the DSE were killed. Others were arrested, exiled, or executed. The country was shattered. The island was fractured. Families mourned the dead, and those who had survived carried scars too deep to show. Some neighbours never spoke again. Some families were left without fathers, brothers, sons.

There was no celebration. Only silence. The island had been drained of life. Some families never found their sons. My heart ached for Greece. We had endured the horrors of occupation, the fear, the hunger, the foreign soldiers who had marched through our villages and taken what they pleased. We had believed that once the invaders were gone, we might rebuild, heal, find some measure of peace. And yet, now, we devoured ourselves. This time, it was not foreign hands that brought suffering, not distant soldiers who cared nothing for our lives—but our own. Greek hands had done the wounding. Greek voices had shouted accusations, Greek eyes had turned on neighbours, friends, even family.

My sorrow ran deep. How does one live with the knowledge that the cruelty came from our own people, a nation turned against itself, consumed by its own divisions?

And yet, even in those dark years, life continued. During this time, my three eldest children married. Those stories, though—the weddings, the joys and the sorrows tied to them—I will tell later. For now, it is enough to say that even as the world seemed to fall apart, our family kept moving forward, one step at a time.

CHAPTER TWELVE

The late summer of 1948 was heavy with heat and tension. Our eldest, Angeliki, had blossomed into a young woman. She had always been Georgios' favourite. From the moment she was born, he held her with a reverence I had not seen in him before. Perhaps because she was our first, or because she reminded him of his own mother.

Angeliki had fallen in love with a local boy, Michael, a kind-hearted young man who worked as a tailor. He worked hard, cared for his widowed mother, and carried himself with dignity despite the little he had. He had approached Georgios for her hand in marriage, but he would not hear of it.

Then one day, Georgios came home and announced he had been approached by a man from our village who had asked him for Angeliki's hand in marriage. Aristides was his name, a man ten years her senior who came from a well-respected family, made good money as a first engineer on merchant ships, and owned a home in Chora. He had two sisters who were well established. Elizabeth, the eldest, was a spinster who kept house for the local doctor, and Vasiliki, was married to a wealthy man in Vathy.

In Georgios' eyes, Aristides was everything a father could want for his daughter — stability, wealth, social standing. Love, for him, had no place in the decision.

"A man like him does not come along often," Georgios had told her.

I knew Aristides. Everyone in the village did. He had only recently broken off his engagement to a girl from Chora named Pipina. She had a reputation and was considered the kind of woman men used but never married. And now he had set his sights on my daughter.

Angeliki went pale. She wanted nothing to do with him. She wanted Michael. She told her father no.

I tried to step between them, tried to calm Georgios down, but his pride and stubbornness were like a wall. He didn't take it well. I will never forget the sound of shouting echoing through the house that evening. He called her ungrateful, foolish, disobedient. And then, in a rage, he took the whip to her.

I can still hear her screams. I can still feel the way her body trembled as I held her afterwards. I was forty-five then and heavy with another child. My arms could not shield her. My voice could not save her. All I could do was sit at the edge of her bed and stroke her hair as she wept, whispering the only thing I had left to give her, my love.

I confronted him that night, my voice trembling with rage and grief. I threw the truth at him, how his stubbornness had shaped our marriage from the beginning and cost me so much in those early days on Samos. I spoke of the years of hardship, but most of all, of the loss of my family, the grief I had carried in silence. Then I asked what guarantee he could give me that Aristides would bring our daughter happiness. What life was worth living if it began in violence and forced submission?

But my words fell on deaf ears. He remained unmoved.

"A father knows what is best," he said. "It is done. She will thank me one day."

I said nothing. I only held his gaze, letting the silence speak for me. She would never thank him, not for the life he was forcing upon her. The day would come when he would see what he had done. And when it did, the weight of his regret would be his alone to bear.

When Michael heard that Georgios had accepted Aristides' proposal to marry Angeliki, he was livid. His outrage was not quiet nor contained. Word spread that he had stormed into the *kafeneion* at the *synántisi*, the common meeting place where the men gathered as they did most days, sipping coffee, talking politics and the weather. In Chora, it was also the junction at the start of the village where the road forked, one way to Pythagoreio and Mytilini, the other towards Pirgos.

The altercation between them turned quickly. Harsh words became threats. Michael's voice rang loud in that quiet place, and he didn't mince his words. He called the decision a betrayal, said Georgios was sentencing his daughter to an unhappy life, that he was giving her to a man who would crush her spirit. Voices rose, tempers flared, and the other men had to step in and pull them apart before fists were thrown or worse. Michael made threats. If he had a gun, he would shoot Georgios. They parted with bitterness and the threat of violence still hanging in the air.

I watched Angeliki retreat into herself over the following weeks. People in the village whispered. Some pitied her. Others said she should obey her father, that it was the way things were. I did what I could to protect her, to soothe her wounds, physical and otherwise, but I could not undo the damage her father had already caused her.

Aristides, to his credit, was generous in the lead-up to the wedding. He sent gifts and arranged for new furnishings for their house. His sister, Vasiliki, and her husband, Theodore, welcomed her warmly. Their kindness offered a small measure of comfort. Elizabeth, however, remained reserved. She watched from a distance, her smile thin and practised. Whether it was disapproval or indifference, I could not tell.

Then, just days before the wedding, Angeliki came home looking pale and unsettled. She told me she had been stopped in the street by Pipina, Aristides's former fiancée. Everyone remembered how their engagement had ended quietly, without explanation. Pipina had congratulated her with a tight smile, but her words lingered.

"He is generous, yes," she said. "But you should know that he does not like to share what he thinks is his. Be careful with your smile. Be careful with your friends."

Jealousy, perhaps? Or something darker. I could not be sure. Were they a bitter woman's parting words or a genuine warning? I saw the doubt it planted in my daughter's eyes. However, there was no room left to harbour either fear or caution. The wedding was upon us.

So she went forward, dressed in white, and the entire village watched as she took her vows. I stood beside her, steadying her with my hand. She looked beautiful but not joyous. There was something else in her eyes. Fear. As if she were already preparing herself. And though the music played, and the people danced, I could feel it, a heaviness beneath the celebration.

*   *   *

It was during a visit to Vathy that Pipina's warning proved to be the truth and not the bitterness of a woman scorned, but a clear glimpse into the man Angeliki had married.

They had gone to dine with his sister Vasiliki and her husband, Theodore. They were gracious hosts, and despite his privileged background, Theodore had a warmth about him that set people at ease. He was a kind-hearted man, attentive and perceptive. He was protective of Angeliki and was someone who had long understood the darker nature of his brother-in-law.

That evening, they sat at a taverna, the four of them enjoying a meal under the soft glow of lanterns strung above the tables. Another group of diners sat nearby. They were young men, who were laughing and talking loudly amongst themselves but not causing any particular disturbance. But Aristides, as always, was watching. One man happened to glance in Angeliki's direction. It was nothing more than a casual look. Yet Aristides saw it, and in it, he found insult.

The accusations began the moment he brought her home. He demanded to know who that man was and why he had been looking at her. Did she do something to catch his eye? Angeliki remained silent while his voice rose and fell, each question sharpened by suspicion. What could she say? She knew from experience that denial only fed the fire. So she waited, quiet and still, until it burned itself out.

When Theodore and his wife next visited, he found a quiet moment to speak with Angeliki alone. His tone was gentle but firm. He told her he had seen everything that night at the taverna, the glance from the stranger, the darkening cloud that passed over Aristides' face, and the tension that followed. He asked her directly whether Aristides had berated her when they had returned home. Angeliki said nothing, her gaze fixed on the floor, her silence saying more than words ever could.

It was then that Theodore gently placed a hand on her arm and told her what she needed to hear. He had already confronted Aristides, he said. He had made it clear that if he ever discovered that she was being mistreated, he would step in without hesitation.

"You are not to keep quiet," he told her. "You are not to protect him with your silence." He made her promise that if anything happened, any cruelty, any unkindness, she would come to him. "Jealousy is a curse," he said quietly, "and unfortunately, Aristides is burdened with it."

*   *   *

Aristides worked as a first engineer on maritime vessels, which meant long absences—weeks, sometimes months at sea. These were the stretches when Angeliki could finally breathe, when she could reclaim a quiet sense of self, free from his watchful eye and simmering suspicions. Yet even in his absence, she remained cautious. One careless word, one perceived misstep, or a whisper from someone eager to stir trouble could unravel everything. She learned to live with a careful grace, balancing her presence in the village so as not to attract attention, nor either admiration or envy.

When he returned, his trunks were laden with gifts such as fine linens, silk stockings, delicate lingerie, and items for their home. He showered her with tokens of affection, each item a marker of his pride in her. These offerings were genuine, acts of love in his own way, but they could not mask the darkness that lurked beneath.

Psychologically, Aristides was a contradiction. He was kind and outwardly generous, proud of his wife and eager to please her materially. But his love was laced with a possessiveness that turned cruel when threatened. Jealousy, once ignited, transformed him. It warped his judgment and stripped away reason, replacing it with interrogation and mistrust.

Theodore once tried to help Angeliki understand Aristides. He sat her down one day, his tone gentle but firm. Aristides had been the youngest of seven children. When he was just eight years old, tragedy had struck. One of his sisters had foraged mushrooms and cooked them for herself and three other siblings. They ate together, unaware that the mushrooms were poisonous.

All four died within hours. Within a year, their mother and father, both crushed by unbearable grief, had passed away as well. Aristides was left orphaned and was raised by his two surviving sisters.

Theodore believed that this early trauma had carved something deep within Aristides. He had lost everyone he loved in the space of a year—his siblings, his parents, his childhood. From that moment on, a fear had taken root in him, the fear of loss, of abandonment, of being left behind. That fear grew into a warped need to hold on tightly to what he loved, even if it meant hurting it in the process.

His jealousy, Theodore believed, was not born from cruelty but from fear, that his marriage, his home might vanish as suddenly as his family once had. He feared losing Angeliki not because she had given him reason to doubt her, but because somewhere inside, he feared that anything good he loved was destined to be taken away. And so, in his desperate effort to keep her, he tried to control her.

Angeliki had listened, her heart heavy with the weight of understanding. It didn't excuse his behaviour. But it explained it. And sometimes, that was the only comfort she had.

*　　*　　*

In March 1949, I gave birth to my youngest, a daughter we named Maria Eugenia. I was older by then, and wearier, but the child brought a small light into my life during a time of great strain. My joy was real, but the responsibilities did not end there. A few months earlier, Angeliki had discovered she too was with child. Mother and daughter carrying babies at the same time became the quiet talk of our *geitoniá*, neighbourhood. Some women smiled at the coincidence. Others wondered how I would manage—my own infant on the way while guiding my daughter through her first pregnancy.

Life offered no pause. I cared for my children, managed the house, helped Georgios whenever I could and watched Angeliki grow heavier and more anxious as the months passed. By early October, her time had come. She went into labour in the middle of the night, and the pains took hold quickly. The birth was long and difficult. I stayed at her side with the midwife, wiping her face, steadying her hands, speaking whatever comfort I could find.

The Greeks had always turned to herbs, infusions of chamomile to soothe, sage to calm the womb, compresses of arnica and yarrow to ease pain. That knowledge had been passed down through generations. But there were limits to what even the wisest of women could do. Complications during childbirth were a different kind of danger, sudden and too often fatal for both mother and child.

When the baby was finally born, he was blue, silent, motionless. In that awful moment, we feared the worst.

The midwife acted quickly. She rubbed his back, flicked the soles of his feet, cleared his nose and mouth of mucus, and wrapped him to keep him warm. I remember her lips on his tiny mouth, giving him breath when he could not find his own. And then, by some miracle, as if the *Panayia* herself had intervened, he gasped and let out a wail.

In that moment, I understood how thin the veil was between life and death. And in that moment, all the grievances and resentments I carried seemed weightless compared to hearing the sudden cry from this little miracle who had just been born.

Angeliki was too weak to even hold him. She had lost so much blood, and the labour had left her exhausted. She could barely lift her head. Nursing her newborn son was out of the question. This tiny little infant needed to be fed. I could not let him go hungry, not after we had come so close to losing him. Not while Angeliki lay in bed too weak to move. And so, I did what had to be done.

I was still nursing her youngest sister then, not yet weaned. I took my grandson in my arms, and I put him to my breast. He latched on without hesitation, as if he had always belonged there. For over a fortnight I fed them both, my daughter's child and my own. One was born from my body; the other from hers. It was difficult. My body ached from the demands of nourishing two little ones, and I prayed every night that I would not run dry.

And slowly, day by day, my daughter's strength returned. When she could finally put him to her breast and feed him herself, I stepped back. I watched as she cradled her newborn son and saw the tears in her eyes. But I will never forget the weight of my young grandson in my arms, or the quiet strength it took for me to feed them both.

*　　*　　*

In late summer of 1952, whispers reached me about my son Manolis and a girl from the village—Maritsa Mitsinis. They had been seen laughing and flirting together at the *vrisi*, under the old *platanos*, where the villagers gathered for water and gossip. At first, Manolis denied anything serious, but when I pressed him, he admitted he had considered asking for her hand in marriage.

The news shocked and unsettled me.

Since Angeliki's marriage, he had grown increasingly resentful and antagonist towards us. I knew he had not forgiven us, especially Georgios, for giving his sister a piece of land as part of her dowry, land he had long believed would one day be his. Now, clinging to this girl from a family we had never approved of, felt as if this was his way of punishing us.

Maritsa's people were not ones I would have chosen to align our family with. Her mother had been openly cruel and vicious in her treatment of me when I had first arrived on Samos, when I was still trying to find my place. They looked down on those of us who worked the fields, as if honest labour were something to sneer at. Her father drove a truck for a living, hauling stone and lime across the island, and yet they acted as though they were above us. I had even heard they left the old grandfather to sleep on a rug on the floor, as if he were an animal.

And now, my own son had chosen to align himself with them. It felt like a betrayal, a bitter reminder that family loyalty could be so easily bent by pride and by spite. I could not help but feel anger, sorrow, and disbelief all at once. How could he not see what they truly were, and what he was becoming by following them?

Still, Manolis would not be swayed. He was apprenticing as an electrician, a trade with promise. He could have had his pick of better matches, but he clung to Maritsa, if only, I suspect, to defy us.

And so, I said nothing more, no matter how misguided I believed his choice to be. But the wound festered quietly between us. A mother knows when her son's choices are not born of love, but of resentment.

Despite my misgivings, Manolis went ahead and married Maritsa. The ceremony was small, without joy on our side. From the beginning, there was tension. He drew closer to her people, took his meals at their table, listened more to her father than to his own. The divide between us grew, not with shouting but with silence. Manolis had made his choice. We simply had to learn to live with it.

*   *   *

By the early 1950s, the war had ended, but hardship had not. Greece was battered and scarred not just by bombs and bullets, but by hunger, suspicion, and division. The village, though quieter now, still carried the tension of everything we had endured. Our people began to drift, to Athens, to Thessaloniki, and farther still, across oceans to Australia, America, Canada.

It began with letters. A cousin writing from Melbourne, speaking of steady work, of wages in pounds sterling, of sending back enough to build a newer, bigger, more modern house. Some invested in property and in later years built hotels for tourists. Then a neighbour's son boarded a ship out of Piraeus. Then another. Each departure left a small vacancy in the village.

I still remember the first time electricity came to Chora. It must have been the early 1940s. Until then, our nights were lit by oil lamps. We knew Vathy had electricity as early as 1927. They even had lights strung along the coastal road, or so people said. Karlovasi followed a few years later with its own power station, and by the 1930s, both towns had street lighting and homes with switches that turned darkness into light.

But for us, it took time. We waited through the war years, through scarcity and fear, and when the electricity finally reached our village, it felt like a kind of quiet triumph. I had five children by then, and every day was a rhythm of work, and then tending to the household duties, washing clothes by hand, lighting the fire to cook. As soon as the sun dipped below the hill, everything slowed down. The younger children did their homework by lamplight, squinting over their notebooks.

I will never forget the night the electric current came to our village. The children squealed when the single bulb in our kitchen glowed to life, a soft, steady light unlike anything they had ever seen. For the first time, we could sit together in the evening without rushing to finish before dark. It was just one light in that area, but it changed everything. It made the house feel warmer, the nights less heavy, the future and all the possibilities it could bring us, just a little closer.

My eldest son, Manolis, was working as an electrician for the *Ilektriki Etaireía Sámou* (The Electric Company of Samos) or the *Electriki*, as we all called it then. It was a respected job, and I was proud of him. He had done his apprenticeship and was now helping to wire homes and streets, bringing electric light to people's lives.

On one particular day, I had taken my youngest, Maria, who was three at the time, to Vathy. I had errands to run, official papers to lodge and a visit to the *Ethniki Trapeza* (Greek National Bank). Maria had become tired of walking about and wanted to go and see her brother. It was a simple request, and since we were already in town, I agreed. We asked around and were directed to where he worked that day.

When he stepped out to meet us, I saw his wife was with him. She had come to visit too, though it was clear from the moment her eyes landed on us that our presence was unwelcome. The look on her face — I will never forget it. Disdain, like something foul, had crossed her path. She said nothing at first, but when Maria rushed forward to hug her brother, his wife stepped between them.

"Take your daughter and go home," she said to me coldly, as if we were strangers, or worse, something beneath her. I looked to Manolis, expecting him to speak, to ask her to show some respect for his mother and sister. But he stood silent. Just for a moment, but it was long enough. And then came the words that felt like a slap.

"Mother, go home."

That was all. No explanation. No warmth. Just those three words.

I turned and walked away, holding Maria's hand as tightly as I could, swallowing the lump in my throat. I never forgot that day. Not because it hurt, though it did, but because it told me something I had already suspected. There was a force in that marriage, and it was not my son.

In February 1953, both Angeliki and my daughter-in-law learnt they were expecting. Their pregnancies progressed well. My eldest son waited eagerly for his first child while Angeliki awaited her second. Aristides, her husband was away at that time.

On the 15th of November, my daughter-in-law, Maritsa, gave birth to a boy, Diogenis. They named the child after Maritsa's father. We heard the news from a neighbour long before Manolis came to tell us himself, and even longer before we were allowed to see the baby. Each day that passed it was hard not to feel disappointment, even anger, at how his wife and her family controlled every moment, deciding when—or if—we could share in the first glimpses of our grandson. Georgios said nothing, yet I felt his quiet disappointment, one I shared. Tradition dictated that the first-born son be named after his paternal grandfather — not only custom, but respect and continuity. That Manolis chose otherwise, and without a single word to his father, felt like a deliberate slight.

Georgios did not argue. He only nodded at the name and went about his day, carrying that stillness he always held when something cut deeply. People say it is only a name, yet to us Greeks it is more than that. It is a way of saying: 'I honour you. I carry you forward.' To break from that, with no conversation, felt like a dismissal — of him, of us, of the traditions we had instilled. It was as though our place in his life, and in his child's life, had been quietly pushed aside. Not just by Manolis, but by the influence of his wife and her family. We saw clearly where the decisions came from, and if they found an opportunity to strike at us, they took it. What saddened us most was that our son allowed it. Whether through choice or weakness, he was complicit. In time, Georgios did let it go. He had lived long enough to know where the real blame lay, though the wound remained.

The very next day, on the 16th of November, Angeliki went into labour. Her second delivery was much easier than her first and she gave birth to a little girl, who was named Paraskevoula Alexandra, after her paternal grandmother. And a little angel she was, with her mother's features, blue eyes, and light hair. Aristides was overjoyed when his ship finally docked and he received the news that Angeliki had given him the daughter he had hoped for. His face lit up in a way I had seldom seen. The strain of months at sea slipped from him the moment he held her.

For us, her arrival felt like a blessing after the disappointment of the day before. A small reminder that life had its own way of restoring balance. She filled the room with something pure, untouched by family disputes or old wounds. She was also a small blessing, her tiny presence softening the heaviness that had lingered in Georgios' eyes. He took her in his arms, kissed her tiny cheek and with tears in his eyes said, *"Na mas zísei i mikroúla mas,"* and the blessing settled over the room. May she live for us, may she thrive — the simple, instinctive prayer every Greek family offers a newborn.

*　　　*　　　*

In the middle of November 1954, Manolis came to see me. He told me that he and his family were leaving Samos. They had been accepted as migrants and would be departing for Australia on the first of December. I was taken aback. He had never mentioned applying to emigrate, never even hinted at it, and now here he was, telling me they were moving to the other side of the world.

He held a respected position with the *Electriki*, one many young men would have given anything for. But I knew there was no use in questioning him. His decision had already been made and not by him. I gave him my blessing, though it sat heavy on my heart. I knew my words would carry no weight. His life was being lived in someone else's hands.

Two days before my son was due to leave for Australia, his grandmother, Emorfia, Georgios' mother, passed away suddenly in Mavratzei. The funeral fell on the very day they were meant to board the ship in Vathy. My son and his wife did not attend—her influence over him had long shaped the distance between us.

He waited until we returned from the funeral to say goodbye. Manolis brought our grandson with him, barely a year old, the little boy clutching his hand, unaware of the weight of the moment. His wife did not come. She had stayed behind seemingly too busy, she claimed, to pay her respects, to offer a final farewell.

The grief of losing my mother-in-law was still raw, and now my son was taking himself—and his family—so far from us. Maria, his youngest sister, was only five and could not understand the journey he was making. When it was time for him to go, she burst into tears, clinging to him. "Are you coming back next week?" she asked.

There were tears, yes, how could there not be? To see my eldest son leaving, taking his family so far away, not knowing when or if I would see him again. But beneath the sorrow was something sharper. Bitterness. It clung to the edges of my heart, not because he was leaving, but because of the silence, the distance, the way she had made herself absent even at the end. And he let her.

I held my grandson tight that day. I wanted him to remember the warmth of my arms, the feel of his Yiayia's embrace, something solid and familiar in a world about to change around him. I whispered a blessing into his hair, brushing it back from his forehead the way I used to when he was smaller. He smiled, and looked up at me with those wide, trusting eyes, too young to understand the finality of the moment, and that only made it harder.

I gave Manolis a parting blessing, even as my heart clenched. He kissed my hand, respectfully, but there was a distance in him, one I could no longer reach across. I watched them walk away, the boy glancing back, waving, and then they were gone.

Georgios and I stayed home. We couldn't bear going to the port. We had already said our goodbyes. What more was there to say? Our relationship with our eldest son had shifted, and it would never return to what it had been previously.

*   *   *

In the spring of the following year, news came that Aristides had made a decision. They were leaving for Australia. He saw the opportunity in the promise of a new life one that would not require him spending months away from his family as he currently did with his work as a first engineer on maritime ships. Angeliki spoke little about it. She carried on as though everything was fine, but I knew her too well. Behind her composed silence was my daughter, who felt trapped in a marriage she could not escape.

She and Aristides now had two young children. Her son, Emmanouil Konstantinos, who resembled his father with his dark hair and brown eyes, a bright and spirited boy, and my sweet Paraskevoula Alexandra, still a toddler with soft golden curls and wide, curious blue eyes inherited from her grandfather and mother.

What a little rascal my grandson was. His mother used to sew the overalls he wore, and on this day he had been so lost in play that, when nature called, he had wet himself. I was outside watering my garden, when I saw him appear, his overalls hoisted onto a large stick like a flag. Having rushed up the steep streets from their home to mine high in the village, he was breathless, his cheeks flushed with exertion.

"*Ti sto kaló káneis, petháki mou?* What on earth are you doing, my child?" I asked, curiously.

"*Katourithika, kai prospathó na ta stegnóso, yiayiá.* I've wet myself and I'm trying to dry them off, Yiayia," he gasped, trying to catch his breath. "*Yiati i mamá mou tha me sakatépsei sto xýlo!* Because my mother will beat me!"

I laughed softly, shaking my head at his ingenuity.

I watched Angeliki prepare for a life she hadn't chosen. She never said she was afraid, but I sensed it. She was leaving behind her village, her family, the security of those around her, and she was doing it because her husband had decided for them all and she had no say in the matter.

A strange, unsettling sense of déjà vu washed over me. I remembered that same feeling, so many years ago, when Georgios had made a choice for me. And now, history seemed to echo itself. Just as I had been taken from the embrace of my own family, so too was my daughter being led into a life shaped by another's will. The memory stirred a bittersweet ache. It was a painful reminder that some cycles repeat, that the lives of the women in our family, despite their strength, were still being shaped by the choices of the men around them.

Aristides told us it would only be for five years, time enough for them to save money for them to return and invest in property or to buy his own caique. He spoke with a smile as though to reassure us. But I heard the certainty in his voice. It wasn't a plan; it was a command. I could see it for what it was, another way to separate her, to tighten his hold. Away from her family, her roots, he could mould the life he wanted, and she would have no choice but to follow.

That night after they left, I lay awake in the dark. My heart ached for her. I thought of all she had endured, how much she had buried inside of herself. And now she was sailing across the world with two small children and a man who wanted to control her for fear of losing her. I couldn't sleep for thinking about seeing her off at the port, of watching the ship take them away, growing smaller and smaller until it was just a blur on the horizon.

I remember the day they were getting ready to leave. I had risen early and gone to help Angeliki prepare for the long journey they were about to embark on. She had bathed young Alexandra, dressed her, and sternly instructed her not to wander out of the house. With final preparations underway, no one noticed that Alexandra was missing until the crucial moment of departure. Panic swept through the household; missing the boat to Piraeus would throw their entire travel plan into disarray.

As time slipped away, I hurried back to my house, sensing Alexandra might have gone there. It was her morning routine; she often came to eat *rizogalo*, the rice pudding I prepared, and to watch me milk Kabakyio, the goat tethered in the enclosure at the side of our home. Opening the front door, I called out,

"Alexandra mou, pou eisai?" Almost immediately came the sweet reply, *"Etho ime Yiayia."* There she was, with that cherubic little face and those innocent blue eyes looking up at me. My heart broke. I wished desperately to tell her to stay where she was and that I would go back to inform my daughter and her husband that I couldn't find her, anything to delay them.

I scooped her up into my arms and held her tightly, her warm little body pressing into mine as if she too sensed the pull of what was to come. She smelt of soap but also of that unique scent that was my beloved granddaughter, and as she nestled her head on my shoulder, I felt the tears escape.

"Yiayia, giati klais? Grandmother, why are you crying?" she asked, stroking my cheek with her tiny hand.

I didn't know what to say. How could I explain that this was the last time I would hold her like this, under this roof, where her first steps were taken, and her first words spoken? The house suddenly felt hollow, like it too knew it was about to lose something precious.

I walked her back myself, each step heavier than the last. Angeliki spotted us first and rushed forward, relief washing over her face, then dissolving quickly into urgency.

There was no time for long goodbyes. The ship would not wait, and neither would the life they had set in motion far across the sea. But as they left, I stood rooted to the spot, my hand raised in farewell though they couldn't see it.

What I didn't know then was that I had also said goodbye to something in myself that day. The house grew quieter. Kabakyio eventually stopped bleating for her. And every morning, I still made the *rizogalo*, just in case. And perhaps, in her young heart, Alexandra *did* know. Children often do. They sense what we refuse to see. And maybe that's why she went to our house that morning, one last time, to anchor herself before the tides of fate carried her away.

Years later, when the pain surfaced in her stories, in the questions she asked and in the silences she kept, I would understand. She had always known. That day, my Alexandra had had a premonition of how her and her mother's lives would unfold in Australia.

The emptiness left behind by Angeliki's departure lingered. I tried to hide my sorrow for the sake of the others, but it was as if a limb had been torn from me. The laughter of her children, the way little Alexandra would call out Yiayia as she stood at the entrance to the kitchen where she would often find me, had vanished. Only silence remained.

I kept busy. There was always work to be done, but I felt the weight of her absence. It pressed down hard on me. I worried about her constantly. I worried about Emmanouil, how he would fare in a land so far, so foreign. I worried about my sweet Alexandra, only a toddler, growing up without her grandparents around her. I wondered if she would forget us, forget our village, forget the sound of our voices.

Georgios sat beside me, but he remained silent. I think he felt it too, the weight of his choices, the sting of watching his daughter move away from him. He wouldn't speak of it, too proud to admit regret, too fixed in the righteousness of his decision. And I carried that weight with me, too, the quiet knowing that what had come to pass might have been different, if only he had listened.

But years later, when the silence between us had softened and age had humbled him, he would admit what I had always known — that he had failed her. In forcing her into that marriage, by letting his pride dictate her future, he had robbed her of something precious.

She deserved more than duty; she deserved the right to choose. A daughter should be allowed to marry with the prospect of a lifetime spent with a man she loved, not one that had been wrapped in fear and a beating metered out by her father. He saw security, reputation, standing. I saw a lifetime of control, of jealousy, of threats. A lifetime of pretending that all was well, of hiding behind a facade, lest people realised the truth.

Even now, I wonder what her life might have been like if love had been allowed to lead her instead of expectation. I prayed her children might bring her solace, that she would find small moments of joy. But I feared that what had been taken from her, that spark of choice, of freedom would never return.

And she blamed her father for the unhappiness in her marriage. She remained bitter until her final years, whenever she spoke of the way he had beaten her into submission. There was no forgiveness, only the ache of what might have been had she been allowed to marry the man she was in love with and he with her.

And in his quiet confession, long after it was too late, Georgios voiced his deep regret. *"Ékapsa to pio kaló mou paidi,* I destroyed my best child,"he told me with tears in his eyes.

CHAPTER THIRTEEN

Life in Chora continued. Eleftherios, our third child, was now working as an apprentice motor mechanic. Emorfia, born in the cold of January '44, was now a curious girl with a quiet strength. She resembled my mother in her stubbornness, a trait I feared and cherished in equal measure, and Maria, my youngest, missed her young cousins the most.

Letters arrived from Angeliki, not often, but when they did, her words were careful, but I could read what was unwritten. She missed us. She felt alone. Aristides, as I suspected, had no intention of returning after five years. That was just a promise made to keep us quiet.

I wrote back, sending news of her siblings and the village. Sometimes, I would take her letters and the photographs she would send and walk up to Agios Athanasios, where Alexandros and Stelios rested. I found comfort in that chapel. It was the one place where my grief could breathe.

More departures began from the village. Others were looking to Australia, to Germany, to America, anywhere with work, with a future. Samos, like much of Greece, was still reeling from the war and the civil conflict that had followed. The scars were deep, and for many, staying meant continuing to endure hardship without hope of change.

I feared what more we might lose. How many more of our children would leave? How much more silence could our home bear?

A few months had passed since Angeliki and her family departed, and after receiving another heartfelt letter from my brother Dimitri, I made a firm decision. I sat Georgios down and told him I was taking our youngest, Maria, to travel to Kavala and then onwards to Antiphillipi to visit my brother. It had been too long since I had seen him, and the ache of not being there to bury my younger brother and mother gnawed away at me. I could not bear the thought of something happening to my elder brother without seeing him once more. Eleftherios, was now in Athens working as a mechanic's apprentice, and Emorfia, at eleven years of age, was old enough to support her father with the help of Ploutarhos and his wife, Eftihoula.

My brother had married during my absence and now had six children, and for me this meant that I had three nephews and three nieces. Giasemina, Tassoula, Stamatis, Christos, Mariegoúla and Yiannis. They had built a new home on the land where we once grew tobacco but had still retained the old home I knew. Boarding the ship in Vathy, I felt a mixture of trepidation and excitement. Finally, I would reunite with what remained of my family.

I had not seen Dimitri since the day he had rushed out of our home in Sokia to find a doctor for our Polyxeni, only to never return. During the entire time he had been missing, there wasn't a single day I didn't think of him, wondering if he had survived, if he was safe, if he remembered us. The not knowing was its own kind of grief.

Memories flooded back from our time as refugees, sailing towards Antiphillipi for a new beginning. I couldn't help but wonder how different life might have been for us if my mother had decided instead to remain in Samos rather than to move us away to what awaited us in Antiphillipi. But we do not live life hypothetically.

The journey to Kavala was long but filled with anticipation. I sat still most of the way, holding my thoughts close, afraid to hope too much. Maria, too young to fully grasp the significance, kept my spirits buoyed with her innocent curiosity, pointing out every little thing with wide eyes. Her chatter grounded me in the present, but my heart remained tethered to the past.

When we finally arrived at the port of Kavala, weary yet hopeful, the ship docked. From the deck I saw him—my brother—waiting there with his wife Georgia and their two eldest boys. I simply stood there, taking him in. His once-dark hair had turned silver, his frame was broader, his face tanned from the sun, fine lines fanning out from his eyes, carved by years of toiling under it and smiling through life's trials. Yet it was unmistakably him. My brother. My Dimitri. The last thread of my childhood, standing before me, real and within reach.

No words came at first, just the kind of silence only siblings can share, thick with everything that had been lost and all that had somehow been found again. When we embraced, the years collapsed between us. His arms wrapped tightly around me, and we both wept, openly and without restraint. I felt the sobs rise from deep within him, decades of sorrow and longing finally given a voice.

And just like that, we were two souls who had been torn apart by war and fate, now trying to piece together what little we could of what had been stolen from us. For the first time in a long while, something that had been broken inside of me felt the first stirrings of being whole again.

Those around us grew still. Georgia wiped at her eyes. Even the boys stood quietly, misty-eyed. It was as if the weight of all those missing years pressed gently on everyone present.

"And this must be Maria," he said at last, emotion thick in his throat as he turned to my daughter. He bent down to her level, brushing her hair softly from her face and kissed her. He pulled her into an embrace, and just like that, she was his too. Maria, wide-eyed, went without hesitation, as though something in her already knew that this man was part of her.

They settled us and our two bags comfortably into their horse-drawn cart, and we set off toward Antiphillipi. The landscape felt familiar, and although it had been altered by time, in its own way it brought both comfort and nostalgia. There were more cultivated fields, which stretched out along the plains, and the roads were now wider and smoother. Dimitri spoke about his children, some now grown, his youngest, Yiannis, just twelve years of age, still full of energy and curiosity. He spoke of the challenges of raising his large family in a town that had transformed around them. He had opened a *kafenio,* but also took on agricultural work, dividing his days between tending the land and managing the café which had grown into a small but thriving hub of local life, with the help of his wife and children.

As we entered the town, I was struck by how much it had grown and prospered since I had last seen it thirty years ago. Houses had been rebuilt or newly constructed, their stone and brick walls standing firm, roofs neatly tiled, and gardens blooming with flowers and vegetables. The air carried the mingled scents of freshly baked bread from the bakery, and coffee being roasted. Streets that once seemed narrow now stretched wider and were now lined with an array of shops. The air was filled with the sound of children's laughter, while neighbours greeted one another warmly, some pausing to wave as we passed. The *kafenio* Dimitri had spoken of stood at the corner of the square, its windows bright with light and life. Everywhere I looked, life pulsed with energy and resilience, and although I felt a pang of longing for the Antiphillipi I had left behind, it was accompanied by a deeper, almost painful awareness of the hardships I had endured in the years since.

Dimitri had built a new double-storey home on the block adjacent to the house where we had once lived and cultivated tobacco. Yet my eyes were inevitably drawn to that old home I had shared with my mother and brother, still standing quietly among the others. The town welcomed me, and joy stirred within me at the familiar sights and sounds.

Once we were settled, neighbours began dropping in, their familiar faces now lined with years and softened by time. Reunions unfolded with those I had left behind, many now married with children and even grandchildren of their own. They arrived bearing small gifts for me and for my daughter Maria, handmade sweets, a brightly embroidered tablecloth, a little doll for Maria, and we spent the afternoon exchanging news, laughter, and stories of the lives they had lived in my absence, and I told them of my family and life on Samos. Their voices, warm and welcoming, carried the rhythm of a community that had prospered and grown, and I felt the quiet joy of being remembered, even after so many years.

The evening was spent with a large family gathering. The eldest Giasemi, Tassoula and Stamatis, were now married and arrived with their young children. The house was filled with laughter, the clatter of dishes, and the kind of warmth that only comes when family gathers under one roof. Maria sat wide-eyed beside me, taking in the faces and voices she had only heard about from the letters my brother wrote to me.

Amidst the joy, there was a quiet undercurrent of sorrow. It was felt most keenly in the pauses between stories and in the glances shared among the older ones. We all carried the weight of those we had lost. I knew that in the coming days, I would have to pay my respects at the place where they now rested. It was a duty, but also a longing, to stand beside them again, if only in silence.

Still, that night, we allowed ourselves the quiet comfort of our reunion. My brother and I sat side by side, hands clasped, marvelling at how at last we had found one another again, after years of fear, separation, and uncertainty. Distance had kept us apart, and I thought of all that my children and I had lost, all the moments we might have shared with him, and his family, had Georgios not uprooted me. Yet the warmth of our clasped hands, the steady cadence of his voice soon eased my thoughts.

The table groaned under the abundance of food that had been prepared, stirring memories of Sokia, where my brother, I, and the rest of our family had once gathered around the dining table for celebratory dinners. There, we had shared conversation, laughter, and the warmth of family in a way that now felt achingly familiar. The smell and sight of the meal brought it all rushing back. We ate together, remembered, and rejoiced in the simple pleasures of family and abundance. Before parting for sleep, we held one another a little longer. It was not merely a return to a place I had once called home; it was a tentative reclaiming of what had been lost to time, distance, and circumstance.

The next morning, I awoke early. The sounds of children playing in the yard drifted in through the window, but my thoughts were elsewhere. Dimitri seemed to sense it. He didn't say much, just brought me a small coffee and told me he would take me whenever I was ready.

We walked to the cemetery just outside the village. The road was quiet, and the morning air was still cool. Maria held my hand tightly, not fully understanding, but knowing this was something important. When we arrived, I stood before their graves, the white marble headstones bearing the names of my mother and younger brother.

There were no words spoken at first, only a silence that pressed heavy against my chest. I knelt and touched the smooth white marble slab, cool beneath my palm. At its centre stood a white marble box with a glass front that held the *kandili*. In our custom, the light of the *kandili* is never just a flame. It is the soul's light, a prayer that does not end, a way of keeping the bond alive between the living and the dead.

It felt strange to be saying goodbye so late, to be grieving again when the tears had already been shed years before, in absence and guilt. But then the tears did come, sudden and unstoppable, spilling freely as I knelt beside her grave, my fingers caressing her name, which had been inscribed into the white marble headstone.

Dimitri stood a little distance back, giving me space. I could feel his presence, steady and patient. After a while, he joined me, and together we lit their *kandili*. Maria placed a small bunch of flowers we had picked from Dimitri's garden on each grave, quiet and solemn.

I spoke a few words to them both, words I had carried inside of me for too long. Regrets. Love. And the promise that, though I had not been here with them at the end, they had never been forgotten.

We walked away slowly, but each step I took felt like another goodbye. I had finally come home to my family, but the two precious members I had left behind had not been here to welcome me back. It was nothing like the reunion I had imagined, the trip I would make when my children had grown, and I had the opportunity to travel back to Antiphillipi to be reunited with them. This was not what I had wanted, to return and find them both lying in the earth.

And in that moment, the wretchedness I thought I had buried deep inside came rushing back, raw, and unforgiving.

*   *   *

In the early months of 1956, my son Manolis began writing regularly to his younger brother Eleftherios, encouraging him to make the journey to Australia and join the rest of the family. He promised him opportunity and support. The fare would be three hundred English pounds, he wrote, an amount Manolis said he would cover. He wouldn't make the journey alone, he reassured him; his brother-in-law George would accompany him.

Our relationship with our *sympetheri* (my son's in-laws) had always been strained. When Eleftherios came to us, letter in hand, asking what we thought, I hesitated. Something inside me held back. But I also knew there was little left for him in Greece, no prospects, no stability and so, despite my reservations, we gave him our blessing.

Manolis had assured him there would be plenty of work, that he had already secured employment with a government organisation. It sounded respectable. Promising. And so, in June 1956, I watched another one of my children depart.

But when Eleftherios arrived in Australia, the reality was far from what had been promised. Yes, Manolis met them at the dock and welcomed his brother-in-law into his home. But Eleftherios was sent to live with Angeliki and her family. That alone was painful to hear. More painful still was what came next. He was told by Manolis that he would have to repay the three hundred pounds for his passage. Only later did we learn that no such demand had been made of his brother-in-law.

And the job? The mechanic's work he had been led to expect? Manolis had arranged a position for him. Labouring. Just like Aristides before him. Digging trenches for water pipes in the government's engineering and water supply department. Gruelling work under the hot summer sun and the bitter cold of winter, nothing like what had been promised to them.

We also learnt that his brother-in-law George had secured a position as a heavy machinery operator. It hurt to know that one son had treated another so unequally.

What hurt most was how he had treated his brother and his brother-in-law, Aristides. Neither of them complained, but I knew they had felt humiliated. Aristides had been working for a big steel company in Newcastle, earning a decent wage, hoping to build a new life for his family. But Manolis, with all his talk and empty assurances, convinced him to leave it behind. He promised a better job, stability, and that he and his family could stay with them while they became settled and searched for a place of their own. That never proved to be the case. Manolis uprooted the family and then abandoned them. Aristides found himself in a foreign place with no support. And the job that had been promised to him? That had never materialised. He had been left with the shame of having trusted a man who he had once called brother.

One day, Eleftherios approached a supervisor and mentioned that he had once worked as a mechanic and had experience in driving heavy machinery. The man was surprised. He had not been told any of this. He said that if he had known, he would have placed him elsewhere from the beginning. Manolis had deliberately downplayed his brother's and brother-in-law's skills, telling the supervisor that labouring work would be 'more than adequate' for them both.

Those revelations were a quiet wound, and the bitterness of my son's betrayal towards his siblings and brother-in-law, cut deep. I never spoke to Manolis about it. What would be the point? He had made his choice. He had elected to remain loyal to his wife and her family. But in my heart, I mourned the closeness that might have been between my son and his siblings.

As the years went by, I found it harder and harder to understand Manolis. His behaviour towards our family grew colder, more antagonistic, especially towards Angeliki. He avoided family gatherings, and when he did appear, it was alone, never with his wife Maritsa.

At times, I wondered whether he was still resentful of the land we had given to her. But surely he could not still be harbouring such resentment after all these years, nor justify taking it out on his siblings. It pained me to think my son's heart had grown so cold and unfeeling towards his family.

*　　*　　*

A few weeks before the 26th of October 1956, the feast day of Saint Dimitrios, I had sent a card and letter to my brother to wish him *'Chrónia pollá, kai to chróno na eísai kalá, me ygeía kai eftychía.* Many years ahead with health, happiness and next year may he be well.' I wrote him a brief note, telling him what little news I had to share, how we had opened a shop in the *plateia* selling fresh fruit and vegetables from the farms in Vlamari, grapes and watermelons and olive oil produced from our own crops. It was well patronised by the local residents. I had even enclosed a photograph of Maria and me standing beside the crates of oranges, smiling. Just a small token to let him feel a little closer to us.

On the 27th of October, a day after the name day of my brother, Angelo from the post office, which was in the *plateia*, came rushing up to the shop.

"Eftihia, come quickly. You have a telephone call from Antiphillipi."

With that, I dropped what I was doing and ran after him, my heart pounding, my apron still tied around my waist. My thoughts immediately went to my brother. Of course, it was Dimitri, calling to thank me for the card and photograph and my good wishes. I imagined hearing his warm voice, his laughter, him telling me briefly his own news about Georgia and the children and grandchildren.

Angelo handed me the receiver. It was not my brother's voice I heard but that of my brother's eldest daughter, Giasemi. Instantly, I felt the knot of dread tighten in my gut.

'Éla, petháki mou,' I managed, slightly breathless. *'Na chairómaste ton babá sou* Let us celebrate your father.'

But the only answer I heard was her sobbing. The tears on the other end told me all I needed to know. I closed my eyes, trying to still the tremor that rose through me. My knees went weak, my hand gripped the receiver as if it were the only thing keeping me standing.

"Theá mou... péthane o babás. Aunty, father has passed away."

The words struck like a stone to my chest. I stumbled and fell back, still holding the receiver. Everything around me blurred. The room tilted. I could see mouths moving, Angelo, the women who had been in the office at the time, but I heard nothing except Giasemi's urgent voice over the telephone line.

"Theá mou? Eísai kalá? Aunty, are you alright?"

But I was gone. I stared into the distance, frozen. In my mind, I saw Dimitri standing at the port again, tears in his eyes, arms outstretched wide. The way he had looked at me as though he was trying to catch up on the years he had lost. The way we had clung to one another sobbing. It felt impossible that he could be taken away from me—again.

Angelo gently pried the receiver from my hand and spoke to Giasemi. I sat there on the floor of the post office, surrounded by people. I heard them talking, someone fetching me water, trying to help me to my feet to sit me in a chair, but none of it registered.

Later, Angelo told me what had happened. My brother had gone to a *panigyri,* a religious feast day celebration in the town of Eleftheres, on the eve of *Agios Dimitrios,* his name day. He had begun to feel unwell, complaining of a tightness in his chest. Georgia and two of the boys had insisted on taking him home and calling the doctor immediately. But it was too late.

He died of a heart attack before they reached home.

And here I was, cloaked once more in blackness. Grief wrapped itself around me again like a shroud. Dimitri, my last remaining sibling, my tether to our childhood, to Sokia, to all that had come before, was gone. We had spoken of so much during our time in Kavala. Of visits to come, of making up for lost years.

But now, all that remained were those plans that would remain unfulfilled. The memories we had only just rebuilt had been swept away, leaving in their place the hollow ache of silence, the kind that follows a last goodbye. And the weight of grief, that heavy, familiar mantle I had worn too many times before. Because now, I was the last one left.

Once more, I found myself in the church of *Agia Paraskevi,* the scent of beeswax and incense hanging thick in the air, the echo of prayers and chanting rising and falling. Another *Mnimosyno.* Another farewell. This time for Dimitri. I had stood here before — first for my younger brother, then for my mother — and now, for the last of them. I moved through the motions as though guided by memory rather than will. I lit candles for them, crossed myself and bowed low as I kissed the sacred icons, and recited prayers I no longer believed could reach beyond the dome of the church.

After the service, I stood again before the icon of the *Panagia*. The Blessed Mother looked down upon me, her sorrow unchanging, her painted eyes holding that same stillness I had once turned to for comfort. I had no more questions to ask her. There had been no answers when my younger brother and then my mother were taken, no consolation in faith since. Dimitri and I had been torn apart that day in Sokia — the day everything changed. When he had been lost to me once before, I had prayed for his safety and heard only silence. And though we had been reunited at last, it was only for a fleeting moment in a lifetime of loss. Barely a year, and now he too was gone, leaving behind a wife, and his children, the youngest, Yianni, merely thirteen years of age, who would now grow up without his father.

I could not bring myself to say it was God's will. Yet, that was what they all said — again — with the same gentle resignation that had followed every other loss I had endured. It was intended to soothe, to offer meaning where none existed. But I could not find solace in it. Why had I been the one left behind? Why had I been spared only to stand here again, surrounded by shadows of all those I have loved and lost?

The candles flickered before the icon, their flames bending with the faintest breath of air. I closed my eyes, not in prayer, but in surrender — to the silence, to the bitter ache of absence, to the truth that faith had long since ceased to mend what grief had broken.

CHAPTER FOURTEEN

Of all my children, only Ploutarhos remained. While the others boarded ships to Australia, one after the other, chasing the dream of prosperity and stability far from this island, he stayed. There was a steadiness in him, a quiet loyalty, and perhaps a sense of duty that rooted him to this land, the way his father had once been.

My two younger daughters also left for Australia, Emorfia in 1967, and my youngest, Maria, in 1969. The house that had at one time been filled with laughter, quarrels, and conversation now lay still, heavy with absence. Having raised six children only to watch them scatter to faraway lands left a quiet ache within me — pride that they were forging better lives for themselves and their children, yet sorrow that I could not be with them to share in their joys, their triumphs, or watch my grandchildren grow. Though Ploutarhos remained, his presence could not fill the space left by so many who had gone. I sat in the stillness of our home, feeling the years of devotion and love pressed into memory, yet confronted by the emptiness that life's changes inevitably left behind.

Georgios had grown older, slower, the years etched into the lines around his eyes and mouth. Much of the weight of tending the fields, the olive trees and the vines, fell on Ploutarhos. And though his back was straight and his hands strong, it was a hard life, the kind of life we had both hoped our children would never have to endure. Yet here he was.

I worried about him often. The world had changed. Greece had changed. The wars, the occupation, the civil conflict had left scars on the land and on the people. Farming was no longer enough. Prices fell, debts grew, and the young no longer dreamed of toiling in the soil. They dreamed of Australia, America, Canada, of places where Greek could still be spoken, but the prospects were far greater than what Samos could offer.

But Ploutarhos had not gone. He married a local girl, Eftihoula, one of the few who hadn't left or been matched to someone abroad. They made a life for themselves in the old way — modest, dignified, rooted in the island's soil. They also kept animals in the cave high above in *Agios Konstantinos*, just as we had done in earlier years, not only for their own consumption but also to sell the milk, eggs, and meat. Fresh vegetables were also grown on the land there, and those too found their way into the shop. Each morning, Eftihoula made the climb to tend to the animals, feeding and watering them and returned again to do so in the evening.

They had children of their own to raise, and I often looked into their eyes and saw something of the old strength that had once carried our family across war, famine, and sorrow. Still, there was no escaping the hardship. The land gave, but only when tended to with relentless effort. And as the years passed, the cost of staying became clear. Machinery was expensive. Hands and bodies grew tired.

My heart often ached for them both, for what they had inherited, for what they bore without complaint. Sometimes I asked myself if I had failed Ploutarhos by not insisting he leave as the others had. But he was his father's son, proud, steadfast, and unwilling to abandon what he saw as his place in this world.

Georgios, in his later years, took some comfort in that.

In the quiet of the house though, when it was just me and my thoughts, I missed the laughter of my daughters. Letters came, and photographs too, sometimes packages with surprises from the other side of the world.

But it was Ploutarhos who came through the door each evening who smelled of fish and earth. It was his children who ran up to hug me, their voices echoing through the pathways that led to our home. It was a difficult life for him and his wife, but with their hard work they prospered. And perhaps that was enough.

*   *   *

It was late one afternoon, and I was at home with my youngest daughter, Maria, or Maritsa, as we called her. She was sixteen then, bent over her sewing, her long hair falling forward across her cheek. A knock sounded at the door, firm and unexpected. We looked at each other in surprise.

There in the open doorway stood a soldier, a wide smile on his face.

"Kalispéra, Theá Eftychía. Good evening, Aunt Eftihia," he said warmly.

For a moment I simply stared at him, unable to place who he was. He read my confusion and then added, *"Then me thymásai?* You don't remember me?"

I stepped closer, searching his features. *"Poios eísai, pethakáki mou?* Who are you, my boy?"

"Eímai o Giánnis, o anipsiós sou apó tin Antiphilipi, I am Yiannis, your nephew from Antiphillipi," he replied with a broad smile.

Yiannis—my brother's youngest son. Tears clouded his eyes as he stepped forward, and suddenly mine were falling freely as I let out a choked sob. I pulled him into my arms and clung to him, with all the strength I had, sobbing. My brother had been only twenty-two when the Turks had taken him. It had taken thirty-four years before we had been reunited again, a single year before his death. Now, before me, stood his child, no longer the boy of thirteen who had buried his father, but a grown man in uniform.

Maritsa rose quickly from her chair and, with tears in her eyes, wrapped her arms around him too.

"How is this possible?" I asked when we had drawn him inside and sat him down.

"They were going to send me elsewhere for my national service," he explained, "but I asked if I could be stationed on Samos. And they agreed. So here I am."

I could scarcely breathe. To have him here, in Chora, felt like having my brother returned to me. When I looked at him, I saw the same set of shoulders, the same dark eyes, the familiar smile. It was as if a piece of my brother had walked back into my life after all these years of absence. It filled me with warmth and sorrow in equal measure. His presence was a comfort, but also a reminder of all that I had lost.

For the next two years, Yiannis became part of our household. Off duty, he ate at our table, helped Georgios and I whenever he could. He was like a brother to Maritsa, steady and protective, and to me, he was both my nephew and a living memory of my brother. Those years shone brighter because of his presence. When I watched him smile, I could almost see my brother standing there again, as if time had folded in on itself and brought him home to me.

*   *   *

My beloved granddaughter Alexandra first returned to Samos when she was twenty. I will never forget the moment I saw her step off the plane at the airport in Samos. She had grown into such a beautiful young woman, tall, graceful, with that mane of blonde hair, and yet, as she rushed into my arms, she wept like a child whose world had come undone. Her whole body trembled against mine as if she had been holding everything in for far too long.

I held her tightly in my embrace and kissed her as she wept.

That afternoon, we gathered on the terrace for lunch to celebrate her return to the island of her birth. The table was full of delicious food that had been prepared, and we all gathered together to share a meal and welcome her.

Later that evening, we sat together on the steps outside her room, with the cicadas humming in the distance, the moon rising slowly over the plain. Her head rested in my lap, and I stroked her hair the way I used to when she was little. We sat in silence for a while, looking out towards the sea and the airport beyond. Then, quietly at first, she began to talk. And when she did, it came like a flood.

So much pain was being held inside my granddaughter. So much disappointment, frustration, and anger. She told me about the life she had tried to build, about the dreams that had been crushed by her parents, mostly by her mother. Her parents had clung so tightly to the old ways where their daughter was concerned, never allowing her to truly assimilate into the new world she was growing up in, never being allowed to express her individuality. What had once been a village mindset in Chora had followed them across the world, binding them even in a place as far away as Australia.

Then she told me about him, her first love. A German. She said his name, and then looked up at me, almost bracing herself for judgment. But I said nothing. I just kept stroking her hair and listening. She told me how her mother had berated her, how her father had beaten her.

She was so wounded by it all, by how her love had been turned into something shameful. I told her she was safe now, that she didn't have to be anything other than herself in my house. All I asked was that she behave in a manner that did not set the tongues of the local gossips wagging in the village, that was all.

And over the six weeks that she stayed with me, I watched her slowly blossom again. She smiled and laughed more. She revelled in the freedom she was given and dutifully respected it. The seeds of her awakening were planted here, on this island, in that summer. With me.

When Elias appeared unexpectedly on the island, that was when I saw something truly shift in her. There was something magnetic between them right from the start. I could see it in their eyes when they looked at one another, something unspoken, intense. But the complication that existed between them was that Elias was married, not happily, but it was still a complication. My granddaughter was so unsure of herself, so afraid to trust what she felt. She came to me, again and again, full of questions and turmoil, and we spoke at length about it all.

I knew then, just as I know now, that this was a connection meant for her. But fate doesn't always bend to the heart's desires. The timing was wrong. Elias disappeared, and with him, the light in her eyes dimmed once more.

She returned to Australia broken-hearted and confused, and soon after, she married a man not for love, not for joy but simply to escape the suffocating tension at home. A house where tradition had become a weapon, where fear of shame held more power than the happiness of one's own child.

And I, I could see the cycle for what it was. My husband had thrown our daughter, her mother, into the fire. He had bound her to the old ways with anger and punishment, and when she finally broke under the weight of it, she turned around and did the same to her own daughter.

Angeliki may have believed she was protecting her child, preserving our values, but in truth, she was stifling her. She smothered Alexandra's spirit in the name of honour, dragged her dreams into the dirt to uphold appearances. And in doing so, she threw her own daughter into the very same fire she herself had once been burnt by.

*   *   *

Over the years, my children came back to me, one by one. The first was Emmanouil, in 1966 followed by Eleftherios in 1969. Both made the journey alone, yet their presence filled the house with a warmth I had longed for. Later, Eleftherios returned with his wife, Keti. Together they went north to Kavala to visit their cousins, holding on to the threads of family that distance created. I remember watching my sons go, as both pride and sorrow mingled, knowing how far away their lives were from mine, and how quickly our days together had passed.

My Maria and her husband Manolis came too, bringing their children, little Eftihia, and Dimitri and then on another visit, their youngest, Nancy. They carried with them cameras unlike any I had seen before. These did not just take photographs—they captured us moving, alive. To see myself and those I loved on a screen, laughing, speaking, existing, it was like holding on to life itself. A living memory, a treasure no time could erase.

Angeliki also returned, bringing Aristides with her. The years had not been kind to him. A series of strokes had left him diminished, his body frail, his movements slow. It pained me to see him so, and it was harder still for my daughter, who bore the weight of his care. For her, it was no holiday. Yet for me, her presence was a gift. From morning until night, I had her company, her voice in the house, her quiet strength close by.

Each visit reminded me of what distance had taken from us. Our children were scattered across the world, their lives unfolding far from Samos. Their return brought joy, but it also tore at me, for I knew that soon enough they would leave again. And when the time came, I stood at the doorway watching them depart, holding on to the memory of their embrace, the echo of their voices, my heart already aching with the silence that would follow.

*   *   *

In May 1976, news came that Ploutarhos' son, George, who had been working on a cargo ship, had deserted his vessel while docked in Australia. He was not alone. Two other sailors had left with him, and the three had gone into hiding. It was a serious matter. Ploutarhos and Eftihoula arrived at my door visibly shaken, worried that his son would be found by the authorities, detained, and deported back to Greece.

Not long after, word reached us by telephone that George had contacted one of his uncles, sharing their whereabouts. Without hesitation, my son Eleftherios and my two sons-in-law were on their way to retrieve their nephew. Though we were relieved to know where he was, there remained an undercurrent of anxiety. What consequences might still follow? And what risk was involved in helping him?

George and his friends were brought back safely. At first, he stayed at my daughter Maria's home, and soon after, with the family's help, he found work. It wasn't long before plans were in motion for a proxy marriage to a girl from a Rhodian family. Her name was Sevasti. The engagement took place in November that year, followed by a wedding in January.

George had hoped his parents would attend, but only his mother, Eftihoula, could go. My son was unable to travel. His heart condition and newly fitted pacemaker made the journey impossible.

When Eftihoula returned, she was glowing with praise for what she had seen. Australia, she said, was a land of opportunity in every sense. All the children had their own homes, big spacious ones which were comfortable, most with large backyards where lemon trees and fig trees grew, and vegetable gardens which grew all manner of vegetables. Every one of them was working, some in trades, some in factories, others in small businesses of their own and all were prospering.

She spoke admiringly of how clean the streets were, how orderly everything seemed. She told me how the schools were good, how the children spoke both English and Greek with ease. There were Greek churches, community halls, bakeries, and continental food shops that sold all manner of things Greek. She spoke of festivals where the community came together to celebrate, to eat and dance to Greek music under strings of lights and the open sky.

Eftihoula was moved by the closeness of the Greek community there. She spoke of how at a name day celebration she had attended, strangers embraced her as if she were family. There were youth groups, associations for the elderly, and Saturday schools where children learned the language of their parents and grandparents. Even in that distant land, the parents were teaching their children to nurture their Greek roots.

She marvelled at how the community had preserved its customs so far from home yet had adapted and flourished. The pride they took in being both Greek and Australian left a deep impression on her. And yet, what struck her most was the feeling of possibility—of being able to work, to build, to hope for something better.

Eftihoula brought out the photographs, spreading them across the table, and I leaned closer to study them. "Look at him," she said softly, her voice full of pride as she pointed to my grandson. He looked so handsome in his suit, standing beside his bride. Eight bridesmaids and groomsmen surrounded them, laughing, holding bouquets, caught in the joy of the moment.

And then she showed me the one of herself standing with her son and his bride. I studied my daughter-in-law carefully. She looked radiant, dressed in a long chiffon gown, her hair styled, a trace of make-up highlighting her features. I had never seen her look more beautiful. It was a world away from the life she knew here in Chora, from the never ending routines and the grind of daily life. There was no rest. Each day began before dawn and ended long after nightfall. It was a hard life for my daughter-in-law, one that tested both her body and her spirit. Yet she endured it all in silence, her strength measured not in words but in the quiet persistence with which she met each day.

As she showed me each photograph, Eftihoula spoke with admiration, yet I could hear the faintest trace of regret in her voice. There was a quiet bitterness there, too, as she admitted how disappointed she felt that my son had not chosen to follow his siblings, to seek a better life abroad for their family. There was also the realisation that with his marriage in Australia, her son had put down roots. She would only see him when he and his family returned to Samos, and communication would only be by telephone. His children, her grandchildren, would be absent from her life also, glimpsed only in photographs like these.

That longing for Australia never left her.

*   *   *

The years were passing by, and I could see them etched into Georgios, each one deep into the lines of his face, the curve of his back, and the sound of his breath. He had been a heavy smoker and drinker for most of his adult life. I had warned him, pleaded with him even, to temper his habits. But men like Georgios didn't take kindly to such suggestions.

"Leave me be," he would say, waving me off with that same hand that held the glass or the cigarette. And so, he carried on, until his own body turned on him.

At first, it was the coughing. A dry, rattling sound that gradually became wet and thick. I noticed the way he would pause after climbing even a few steps, his hand pressed against his chest. Then the blood came, staining his handkerchief and scaring us both, though he wouldn't admit it. He slept more during the day, complaining of a tightness in his chest and shortness of breath.

Eventually, I insisted he see a doctor. He was taken to the hospital in Vathy, where he was examined. They listened to his chest and ordered tests. The look on the doctor's face told me more than any words could. It wasn't good.

Even so, Georgios refused to rest. He still dragged himself down to the *kafeneio*, stubbornly clinging to his routines. But the return journey up the steep incline to our home left him pale and gasping, wheezing so loudly I could hear him before I even saw him. I would stand at the top of the last incline, watching him struggle, too proud to ask for help, too worn to deny that the years, and his choices, had finally caught up with him.

There is a quiet grief in watching the man you've shared a life with deteriorate slowly in front of your eyes. I didn't say, "I told you so." What good would that have done? I just did what I had always done. I carried us both the best I could.

As the months passed, Georgios's condition worsened. The doctor in Vathy confirmed what I had already suspected. *Pnevmonikó emfýsima*—emphysema. A sickness of the lungs brought on by years of smoking, drinking, and a stubborn refusal to listen. There was no cure, only tablets to ease the tightness in his chest and a syrup to calm the cough that racked his body day and night. I boiled thyme and sage leaves for tea, had him breathe in steam with eucalyptus oil, rubbed his chest with warm olive oil the way my mother used to, but none of it changed the slow, steady unravelling.

The climb from the *kafeneio* to our house became impossible. He would return home bent over, one hand pressed to his chest, his breathing ragged and loud enough to alert me that he was struggling to get home. His handkerchief, once used for wiping his brow, now came away streaked with blood and phlegm. He stopped going out altogether not long after.

He stayed mostly in bed by then, propped up with pillows to help him breathe, resting between fits of coughing that left him too exhausted to speak. The lines on his face had deepened; his frame had hollowed. I did not need a doctor to tell me what was coming.

Only Ploutarhos and his wife, Eftihoula, were here now. All the others were far away in Australia, building lives of their own. But he was lucky, in a way; he had his son, his daughter-in-law and their two remaining children, Evangelia and Eleftherios. On the final day, they came early in the evening and sat with him quietly.

As the sun began to set and the coughs had quietened into a shallow, rattling breath, I saw the weariness in their eyes. I told them to go home to rest.

If anything changed, I would send one of the neighbours to alert them. Eftihoula hesitated, but I insisted.

Soon afterwards, the wheezing became worse than usual. I had just placed a warm compress on his chest when he looked at me and whispered, "Eftihia, I am tired." And I knew. I sat with him through the night, holding his hand, praying quietly. By morning, he was gone. No drama. No final words. Just a long, ragged breath and then silence. It was the morning of the 27th of April 1978.

I buried my husband with the dignity he deserved. Whatever our struggles, whatever his stubbornness, he was the father of my children, the man I had shared a lifetime with. He lived hard, and he paid for it. But in those final months, he let me care for him, and that, I suppose, was his way of saying thank you.

And so, I carried on. Because that is what women like me were taught to do.

After Georgios had passed, the house felt too quiet. The stillness pressed in around me, heavy with memories. It wasn't long before the letters started coming, one after the other, my children writing from Australia, urging me to come. They said it was time, that I shouldn't be alone anymore.

I was seventy-five years old. I scoffed at the idea. What business did an old woman have crossing the world? I told them I was too old, too set in my ways. My home was here in Chora. And yet, my heart longed for them. For the children I had raised and let go of one by one. For the grandchildren whose faces I only knew through photographs.

But even though I resisted, I could feel that the rhythms of life in Chora had changed. The quiet simplicity we had fought to preserve through war and famine was slowly being swallowed up by something shinier, louder, foreign. Foreigners arrived. At first, it was just a few, wide-eyed tourists from Sweden or Germany, curious and polite. But they kept coming. They bought the old stone homes at prices the villagers could not refuse.

The village began to serve them. Taverns once filled with neighbours now catered to sunburned travellers asking for Americano coffee and omelettes. I saw the older women, always dressed in black, walking the streets slower than they used to, unsure of the voices around them.

And the men. Some of them couldn't resist. Marriages collapsed quietly. Some younger men left their wives for northern women with blonde hair and blue eyes and money in the bank. Others stayed but wandered. There was gossip of husbands seen slipping away at night, of scandal and shame no one had the energy to confront anymore.

It pained me to watch the essence of village life fray this way. There had been so much loss already. And now, a different kind of loss was upon us, the kind that doesn't come suddenly, but in slow, quiet erosion. The church was still there, but the soul of the village felt like it was slipping away.

Although I was far from my children, the news that came from Australia warmed my heart. My son Manolis, ever industrious, had opened a Continental Food Store in the Central Market in the heart of the city they lived in. He had also purchased acres of olive groves to produce his own olive oil and sell it. I was proud of his efforts and the life he had carved out. He now had four children, two boys and two girls, but despite the passing of time, the relationship between myself and his wife remained cold. Nothing had softened my feelings towards her, or her family, and it was reciprocated. My son had even sponsored his in-laws to Australia but had not extended the same offer to us.

Eleftherios was the only one of my children to marry a foreigner, a Dutch girl named Keti. But their road had not been easy. One baby girl was stillborn, and later, they lost their little boy George in a terrible accident when he was only eighteen months old. The grief was unimaginable, and even from afar, I mourned with them. They had two daughters, Eftihia and Constantina, and later they were blessed with another son, George, and a daughter, Sophia. Both Keti and Eleftherios were enterprising. Together, they opened two fish and chip shops. He also ran a motor repair workshop and eventually bought several taxis.

My daughters, Emorfia and Maria, also married well. Emorfia's husband, Georgios, was a decent man from the Peloponnese. He drove taxis and provided a good life for his family. They had two children, Panayiotis and Tassoula. Maria, our Maritsa, married a Rhodian man named Manolis, and together they had three children, Eftihia, Dimitri, and Nancy. I took comfort in knowing that my daughters had secured a good life for themselves and their children.

Angeliki and her husband Aristides worked hard and were financially secure. Their children never lacked for anything. Aristides was a good provider; he never forbade her anything in material possessions. Every pay week, he would take a small amount for his tobacco, and the rest went to my daughter. But I knew Angeliki. I knew the private cost of that security. Aristides could be consumed by jealousy, accusing her of things she had never done. She bore it all with the stoicism expected of a Greek wife, but it left bruises on her heart.

When he died, Angeliki was just fifty-six years old. One might have thought she could finally be free, that she could breathe in the life she had been denied. But instead, she wrapped herself in the black veil of grief, just as tradition demanded. Another woman her age might have shaken it off, but she wore it like a shroud, as though she had spent the last thirty four years waiting for that moment—and when it came, she didn't know how to live outside it. Every gesture, every habit of her long marriage seemed to haunt her still. I couldn't help but feel a deep sorrow for my daughter, seeing in her the life she might have had, the love she had never been allowed to follow, and the years she had silently spent paying the price for it.

As the years passed, I found solace in the successes of my children, even as I navigated the complexities of our familial dynamics. The thread of tradition and familial bonds bound us together, despite the distance that separated us physically and emotionally.

*   *   *

One day, I received the news that Manolis was divorcing his wife. He called me, his voice heavy with resentment, and poured out his grievances, how she had manipulated him, how their life together had become unbearable, how she had driven a wedge between him and his siblings. He spoke as though he were the only one wronged, but I knew better. The anger he carried had long been turned outward, mostly at those who loved him most.

I remembered too well the terrible argument he had provoked between Angeliki and her husband. Aristides, never a man to mince words, had thrown Manolis out of his house and told him never to return. It was a moment that fractured something in our family. At times, it seemed as if Manolis could not bear to see his siblings prosper. Yet when it suited him, he had no shame in using them for his own benefit.

The divorce, when it finally went through, was bitter. I felt no joy in its outcome, only sadness that so much damage had been done. Then, not long after, a telephone call came from Australia. It was Manolis calling to share his news. He had become engaged. He wanted my blessing.

His fiancée was a woman from Chora, also named Maritsa, the sister of our village mayor. I knew Maritsa and her family well and had always held them in the highest regard. I remembered her as a striking woman, tall and dark-haired, who carried herself with both dignity and warmth. She was always kind and patient, kept a good home, and possessed everything my son needed in a partner. I thought, quietly to myself, that she was too good for him. Still, I hoped—truly hoped—that she might bring him some peace.

But peace was not in my son's nature. One evening, after a quarrel, he abandoned her and left her to find her own way home. I wasn't surprised when she ended the engagement. I was only sorry for her. My son was the one who had lost the most. It would have been a good union. Maritsa would have looked after him, stood by him, and honoured our family, unlike his previous wife, who brought only turmoil and division. With Maritsa, there could have been stability, even happiness. But it was stupidity on his part that let her slip away.

Years passed, and my son Manolis married again, this time to a Filipino woman named Alexandra. She gave him two more children, Michael, and Eugenia. She embraced our Greek ways, cared for him dutifully, and even he admitted she looked after him better than he deserved. But his temper, always simmering beneath the surface, undid that marriage too.

In the end, it would not be rage or pride, but silence that claimed him. Dementia took hold, and he spent his final years in a nursing home, a man diminished by time and memory. I grieved not just for his passing, but for the life he might have lived, had peace ever found a place in his heart.

*   *   *

By my seventy-eighth year, I rarely left the house without a purpose. Most days I spent in the garden, tending my flowers or talking with my neighbours. There was Kyría Athena, her daughter Vasso, and her husband Costa and her only son, Dimitri. And then there was my other neighbour, Eleftheria. I called her *i Zampounína*, at times, using the surname of her husband Manolis Zabounis, as was common in Greece. She still called me *i Sokianí*, the woman from Sokia.

I had become one of the old women I used to glance at in my youth, still watchful and still kept things close to my chest. My children spoke to me often in their phone calls, urging me to come to Australia, to be with them, to live out my last years surrounded by family.

I still resisted. This land held too much of my past. My mother, my siblings. The earth by the chapel of Agios Athanasios still held my sons. How could I leave? My husband's remains were now lying in the chapel at the Monastery of Zoodochos Pigi built on the slopes of Mount Ambelos, also known as Karvounis, near the town of Vourliotes. It was surrounded by pine forests and the monastery was well known for its beautiful frescoes, traditional monastic architecture, and the spring *'Zoodochos Pigi'* or 'Life-Giving Spring' that was said to have healing properties.

Still, they insisted. They said I had earned a rest. That I had given enough. That it was time for them to care for me now. And so, one spring morning, I saw her standing at the entrance to my home. My granddaughter Alexandra. Not a girl anymore, but a tall, warm-hearted young woman with my daughter

Angeliki's blue eyes and my fire and spirit. She had come to take me to a new life on the other side of the world.

She had taken leave from her work, left her husband and son behind, temporarily, she said, with my daughter Angeliki moving into her home to care for them both in her absence. I watched her move through the house, her eyes shining with happiness, but underneath it all, I could sense her pain. I wanted to cry, but I didn't. In the quiet of the afternoon when the village slept, we sat together as we had done so on numerous times during her first visit to Chora.

She told me about her unhappiness in her marriage, the façade she wore. Although she spoke of her desperation to leave the family home following her return after her first holiday on Samos, she had learned the hard way the consequences of her actions. The trauma of losing her first child to miscarriage had marked her deeply, a sorrow she carried in silence. But then came the son, a beautiful boy, both healthy, and full of life, who gave her purpose again. She said he was her redemption, the one thing that steadied her when everything else felt so uncertain. Her voice never rose in anger as she spoke. Only weariness and quiet acceptance. What could she do, she told me. There were expectations of a Greek girl in Australia, and her mother, my daughter, lived her life strictly by them. She had survived much, she said, but survival came at a price.

My intuition told me there was a darker side to this union, but I remained silent. I stroked her hair as she spoke and thought about the happiness I had seen in her eyes during the period she had come to me, when Elias had been a part of her world. I wondered whether their story might find an ending, whether it was possible for two people who had been drawn so intrinsically to one another to find their way back. There had been such light in her then, something that only love can bring. I held on to hope, even if she could not. Sometimes love does not vanish. It simply waits, buried beneath the layers of grief and time, waiting for the moment when fate deems it right to surface again.

Alexandra asked me to give her my stories. I told her about her great grandparents, of Sokia, our journey to Smyrni and the horrors we had seen and lived through. I told her about our struggles in Chios, our eventual journey to Antiphillipi, and about my mother's strength amidst the devastating grief she carried. I told her my story because I wanted her to carry all of it, to understand what we had gone through, so that our family and what we had endured would never be forgotten.

On the morning of the day we were to leave, I walked slowly through the house. I walked up to the chapel, sat by the graves of Alexandros and Stelios, and whispered a goodbye. Australia awaited. I didn't know what life there would hold for me, but I knew this: I had survived the destruction of my family and home, had lived through trauma, fire, and hunger, through betrayal, loss, and the hard work of forgiveness. And through it all, I had emerged with my dignity and spirit intact. Now, I would begin again, not because I wanted to, but because life had called me to move forward. And I had learned, over a lifetime, to move forward when it called.

*   *   *

We boarded the small plane from Samos to Athens, just the two of us. I clutched Alexandra's hand as we lifted into the sky, and the sensation of rising above the island that had been my world for so long was both thrilling and terrifying. That night, we would stay in Athens before continuing to Australia the following day.

The moment I stepped out of the aircraft after it had landed at the airport in Glyfada, the heat wrapped around me. The metal stairs radiated warmth beneath my feet, and I paused, gripping the rail, blinking into the harsh glare of the sun. A gust of wind carried the smell of aircraft fuel straight into my face. I pulled out my handkerchief and held it over my nose and mouth. It barely helped. The smell was everywhere.

Alexandra helped me to slowly descend the stairs, her hair lifting slightly in the hot wind, her expression calm. She was used to it all, but I had to force my feet to move, one step at a time. Buses waited on the tarmac, their doors open, and we were herded towards them, and I could feel the heat rising off the ground. This was Athens. My first impression: noise, heat, and smoke. We hadn't even reached the city, and already I felt overwhelmed.

Alexandra had organised everything. A taxi was waiting to take us to Syntagma. As we drove from Glyfada towards the city centre, we drove past rows of apartment blocks, their balconies crowded with laundry and television antennas. The noise was constant. The traffic didn't move so much as shuffle forward, horns blaring in frustration, people shouting across lanes as if the traffic were a marketplace. I had never seen such chaos, cars weaving in and out, scooters darting through impossible gaps, pedestrians bold and indifferent, as if daring death with each crossing.

As we passed Syntagma Square, I caught sight of the Parliament building, standing pale and still above the mess of buses and taxis and people. The taxi came to a stop outside the hotel. Two young men in uniform rushed forward. One opened my door with a smile, the other began unloading our suitcases. I sat there, frozen for a moment, unsure what to do.

"*Éla, Yiayiá.* Come, Yiayia," he said gently, offering me his hand, as if coaxing a child.

I stepped out slowly, blinking up at the towering building before me. A brass plaque gleamed by the entrance: *NJV Athens Plaza.* The name meant nothing to me, but the feeling it gave me did. This was a place for important people, not women like me, who had spent their whole adult life in a village called Chora, and until motor vehicles arrived in the village, had used a horse and cart as her means of transport.

Inside, it was another world. Cool, quiet, and polished. Marble floors spread out in every direction, and chandeliers hung above like crystal flowers. The air was scented, clean, floral, nothing like the smell of petrol and pollution outside.

Alexandra walked confidently to the front desk while I had been comfortably settled into a wide velvet chair in the foyer area. I watched as the porter brought in our bags and wheeled them away towards the lift without a word.

Never in my life had I imagined that I would stay in a place like this. I had left everything behind — my home, my garden, my neighbours — and now here I was, sitting comfortably in a palace of glass and marble, with strangers calling me *madame* and rushing to carry my things. I was seventy-eight years old, and somehow it felt as if life was just beginning again.

Our room was large and luxurious, with soft carpets and beautiful furniture and beds that would fit two people, with mattresses that felt as if you were sleeping on air and linen that was so white and crisp. I looked around, half afraid to touch anything. That evening, as night fell, Alexandra asked me what I would like to eat. I told her I wanted some grilled fish. She was looking through a small book, and I assumed we would leave the hotel to dine somewhere locally.

About half an hour later, there was a knock at the door. Alexandra opened it and greeted whoever stood on the other side as if they were old friends. Then two young men entered, one holding what appeared to be a fold-up table, the other pushing a silver trolley covered in dishes.

"*Kalispéra, Yiayiá.* Good evening, Yiayia," they both said warmly as they stepped in. The one with the trolley looked at me and asked, "*Yiayia, eísai étoimi yia to apogevmatinó?* Are you ready for your evening meal?"

I stared at him, confused. "*Edó tha fáme?* Are we eating here?" I asked.

He grinned. "*Nai, Yiayia. Den théloume na vgíte éxó, mi Theós sas klépsei kanénas Alvanós.* Yes. We don't want you venturing out and being stolen by some Albanian."

I burst out laughing. *"Eíde palopítha!* You cheeky boys!" I replied, shaking my head.

They gently helped me to settle into the chair they had set up at the table, and I watched in amazement as they laid out each dish Alexandra had chosen. The aroma was heavenly, grilled fish, roasted potatoes, salad and warm bread and spanakopita, which when I tasted it was even better than the one I used to make at home.

Once they were done and had wished us *"Kalí sas órexi.* Enjoy your meal," Alexandra poured two glasses of water and handed me one. She lifted hers gently and looked at me with that soft, knowing smile of hers.

"Kaló mas taxídi, yiayia mou. A good trip to us both."

I raised my glass, tears prickling in my eyes. "I will never forget this," I told her, my voice trembling. "What you have done for your Yiayia, I will carry it in my heart forever."

The next morning, a taxi arrived right on time to take us to the airport. Alexandra had organised everything once more. She moved with the ease of someone who knew exactly what she was doing, calm, confident. She told me she now worked for an airline company, and that her role often involved liaising with staff in the cities where the airline flew. It explained everything. I watched her speak to the man at the check-in desk and then to another, who greeted her with a delighted smile, and then kissed her on both cheeks. The way they greeted me and asked me whether I was ready for the long trip to Australia.

Once we made our way through the formalities and sat in the departure area, she leaned in and pointed through the large window to the plane waiting on the tarmac.

"That is our plane over there, Yiayia," she told me.

I looked at it, that enormous metal bird and shook my head in disbelief.

"Kai pós eínai dynatón aftó to práma na sikothí apó ti gi? And how is it possible for this thing to be lifted off the ground?"

She just smiled.

We finally boarded and settled into our seats. Two young hostesses came down the aisle, smiling graciously as they greeted each passenger, offering us a drink before we departed. My eyes widened with delight. They were graceful, with delicate features and a calm elegance. Their uniforms were richly coloured and patterned, with long fitted skirts and snug bodices. Traditional, yes, but elegant.

"Koukles íste, koukles!" I told them, clasping her hand in mine. *"San vasilopúles féneste!"*

Alexandra laughed gently. "She says you're like princesses," she translated with a smile.

The stewardess gave me a wide smile and then bowed her head slightly. "Thank you, *madame*," she told me, her accent soft but clear. I could tell she meant it. Such poise in someone so young. I watched them as they moved down the aisle. Everything was so orderly, so calm. The scent of jasmine drifted faintly in the air, or maybe I imagined it.

When it was time for us to finally depart Athens, I tried to still the nerves fluttering in my chest. Could this huge machine, filled with so many people and our bags, truly take to the skies? But it did. With a gentle rumble along the runway and then a sudden lightness, we rose above Athens. I gripped Alexandra's hand tightly, watching the earth fall away beneath us as I held my handkerchief to my mouth, smelling the 4711 *Eau de Cologne* I had dabbed onto it.

The journey was long and tiring, but it carried joy too. At one point, Alexandra took me for a walk along the aisle to stretch my legs. The plane was mostly filled with Greeks, many of them families or young men and women travelling alone, who were going to Australia to begin a new life or were returning from a holiday. They looked at me with curiosity, this old woman, walking arm in arm with her granddaughter, dressed in her simple black clothes and stockings.

"Where are you going, Yiayia?" one of them asked with a grin.

"I'm going to Australia to be with my children," I replied proudly.

And just like that, I became the centre of attention. Hearing the warmth of their voices, the comfort of familiar words and for a little while, I forgot where I was. They gathered around me, leaning in with eager curiosity, asking questions and delighting in what I shared with them. I told them I was born in Sokia, Turkey and that my family and neighbours in Samos called me *i Sokiani*. I spoke of the Great Fire in Smyrni, how we became refugees, and how later, I had married and moved to Samos.

Some smiled knowingly, saying they had visited Samos themselves and loved its greenery, its pine forests and *azure* blue sea. I told them my granddaughter was taking me to Australia, about the hotel, a place so grand that I could only describe it as a palace. I watched their eyes widen in delight, their laughter spilling over as I recounted my experiences.

Then Alexandra appeared beside me again, telling me that we had to return to our seats. *"Yiayia,"* she whispered, *"Se lígo tha mas servíroun fagitó.* In a little while, they will serve our meal."

I excused myself, and as she led me back to our seats, I couldn't help but smile. I was flying to the other side of the world, but I was surrounded by the voices of home.

The flight seemed endless, stretching across oceans and skies I had only ever imagined. Alexandra stayed by my side through it all, helping me with my shoes, bringing me water, making sure I was comfortable. I don't know how I would have managed without her.

When we arrived in Singapore, I pressed my face to the window. It was night, and the city sparkled below us like a jewelled carpet. The plane shuddered as it touched the tarmac, and Alexandra held my hand through it. Once inside the terminal, it was alive with people from everywhere—men and women, children and travellers, voices in languages I did not understand, the bustle of aircraft arriving and departing. Alexandra guided me slowly around, our small bags balanced in a tiny trolley, my arm through hers, letting me rest and stretch my legs. We wandered past the shops, their bright displays and curious scents making me pause and marvel, my little home in Chora feeling impossibly far away. Amidst the noise and hurry, I felt a mixture of awe and disorientation, holding tightly to Alexandra's arm, grateful for her steady presence in this strange, overwhelming, and yet wonderful new world.

CHAPTER FIFTEEN

The moment the plane touched down in Australia, I felt both relief and nervousness settle over me. From the air, the city had seemed impossibly vast, stretching in every direction, so unlike the quiet, clustered homes of Chora. The sun shone with a harsh, unfamiliar brightness, and the airport hummed with movement and strange sounds. And yet, beneath the unfamiliarity, a single thought steadied me: my children were waiting.

We made our way through customs and into the arrivals hall, and then I saw them, all standing there in a large group, waving, calling out my name. My heart lurched inside my chest.

Eleftherios was there with his wife Keti, tears already in his eyes. Beside him stood my daughters, Emorfia, Maria, Angeliki, all of them older now, but still with the same faces I remembered. And their husbands, and my grandchildren, so many of them.

When they rushed forward to greet me, I felt their arms around me warm, holding me tight. I kissed their faces one by one, overwhelmed. We cried, all of us, because there was too much time between us, too many years lost to distance and duty. And yet, in that moment, we were together again.

Bouquets of flowers were pressed into my hands. Before I knew it I was being guided out of the airport. I was no longer just a memory or a voice on the telephone. I was there, in this new country, being held in the arms of my family. And in that instant, I knew I had done the right thing.

Everything in Australia felt vast, the roads, the houses, even the sky. The air was different too, dry, and crisp, but in the gardens of my children, the air carried with it the scents of home. I was so proud of them all. They had all done well for themselves. They owned beautiful homes, had secure jobs and business which were prospering, and their families were close knit.

The first few days were filled with visitors. Family, friends, neighbours, all eager to meet the old Yiayia from Greece. They brought flowers, sweets, and warm embraces. I tried to remember names and faces, but there were too many. What stayed with me were the voices, the mixture of Greek and English coming out of mouths, especially from the grandchildren.

Still, there were moments of deep silence within me. The nights were the hardest. I would lie awake in this new bed, in a new house, listening to strange noises in the dark. I missed the stillness of my home in Chora, the familiar creak of my bed, the smell of smoke from the neighbour's woodfired oven.

But then I would wake to the sound of my name being called, and my grandchildren tiptoeing into my room, kissing my cheek, and asking me if I wanted a coffee or if I needed anything. I would watch them move about the kitchen, talking and laughing with their parents as they went about their daily routines.

"You don't have to do anything now, Yiayia. Just be with us. That's enough."

And maybe it was. Maybe, after all the loss and struggle, simply being together with my children and grandchildren was the greatest gift of all.

* * *

Those years in Australia were quiet, filled with the comfort of routine and the warmth of family. I did not need much, and my children made sure I never went without. My time was divided amongst them, but most often I stayed with Maria. She and her husband Manolis had built me a little space of my own, a room with its own bathroom and a small sitting area. But I didn't like to sit alone for too long. I preferred to sit in the heart of the house, watching the comings and goings, listening to the grandchildren and the television murmuring in the background.

When they went off to work or school, I would retreat to my room. In the late afternoon, the grandchildren would rush in to greet me, still wearing their school uniform, throwing their arms around me, and kissing my cheek, before coming to sit beside me, eager to tell me their news. I found comfort in their presence, in the way their Greek mingled with English.

And every so often, I would go and stay with one of my other children, sometimes for a week, sometimes longer, to give Maria and her husband a rest from looking after me. Each household had its own rhythm, its own familiar chaos. I never felt like a burden. They made sure of that.

There were times, especially in the quiet afternoons, when I would sit near the window and my thoughts would drift. I would see Polyxeni's face, hear her laugher echo in the kitchen of our childhood home. Persephone's hands would be guiding mine as we rolled out the dough or stuffed vine leaves. Polyxeni and I would sit there wide-eyed as Persephone explained how a spotless home and good food made a house feel like a home. We had listened carefully then, wide-eyed, and eager, trying to learn all she knew. And now, all these years later, my daughters carried those same lessons forward.

My daughters made me proud. They kept their homes spotless, their children well-dressed and polite, their husbands well-fed. They were true *nikoukiries*, just as Persephone used to teach us in the kitchen all those years ago.

They cooked the dishes which brought with them memories of Samos. I would sit at the table, watching as they prepared lamb shoulder, stuffing it with sauteed diced liver, onions, rice, pine nuts and spices of cinnamon and cloves, just as I had taught them. It would then bake slowly in the oven, or in the woodfired oven, until the meat was so tender that it fell of the bone, in juicy, succulent strands. They made *revithokeftedes*, those crisp chickpea patties, *moussaka*, *spanakopita*. And oh, how the children devoured the *tiyanites*, especially when they were still warm and glistening with honey.

I was proud. Not just because they had become excellent housewives, but because from where my life began, in Sokia, in a time of loss and heartbreak, where I had crossed oceans, endured wars, I had carried something precious with me. What Persephone once taught us in our kitchen, what my mother showed me in quiet moments of care, had not been lost. My daughters now carried that forward in this far and distant land. And it would live on in their daughters.

For my 80th birthday, they organised a surprise birthday celebration at Maria and Manolis' home. The whole family was in attendance, together with my grandchildren, and great-grandchildren. I remember sitting in the armchair, quietly watching them all, my heart full. There were endless platters of food, and in the backyard, a lamb was roasting over charcoal on the spit. It was Manolis and Georgios who took charge of it and, the whisky bottle as well. They kept a careful eye on the coals, while brushing the lamb occasionally with a bunch of oregano dipped in a lemon and olive oil marinade, while taking sips of whisky in between, singing and dancing to the Greek music that was playing.

Ah, those two *palopitha*. Practical jokers both of them, and when they teamed up, chaos and laughter were inevitable. Their teasing, their silly antics, especially when one of them would dress as a woman and they danced together as a couple, left everyone in stitches. I could barely keep a straight face around them.

Georgios loved to tease my daughter Angeliki. Sitting there in her black, he would declare that he was going to arrange a proxy marriage for her and that he had just the right man in mind. Out of the corner of my eye, I could see Alexandra smiling and nodding her head in approval. She would chime in, saying how she often told her mother that she needed another man in her life, and maybe we should find out if Michael—yes, that Michael, the man she had been in love with before her proxy marriage, perhaps he too was a widower now.

Angeliki would wave them off, scolding them with a mock seriousness. '*Eiste treloi!* You are both insane!"

I would sit back quietly, watching the back-and-forth, the warmth that existed between them all despite everything. My eyes would fall to Alexandra's little one, that sweet baby boy who carried the name of his grandfather. He was a joy, that child, full of life. But her husband. I had my reservations. He was polite, always welcoming, always smiling, but there was something too smooth about him. Too sure of himself. I sensed something underneath, a darkness. But I kept quiet. For my granddaughter's sake. She found happiness in her darling son. That was enough, I told myself. It had to be, although my mind couldn't help but wander to those heady days she had spent with Elias.

Then came something that truly surprised me. They brought out a birthday *torta* on a tray, candles flickering on top. Can you imagine? In Sokia, we always celebrated our name days, not our birthdays. But here in Australia, things were done differently. Birthdays mattered and reaching the age of eighty was a milestone to be celebrated. They lit the candles—thankfully, there were not eighty of them—and then the young ones began to sing, their voices ringing together:

> *Na zisis yiayia mas kai chronia polla,*
> *Megali na ginis me aspra malia,*
> *Pantou na skorpiseis tis gnosis to fos,*
> *Kai oloi na lene na mia sofos.*
> May you live, our grandmother, many years,
> May you grow old with white hair,
> May you spread the light of knowledge everywhere,
> And may everyone say, 'What a wise one!'

I cut the cake as they cheered, and tears misted my eyes from a happiness so full, it spilled over. There were speeches in Greek, my children telling me how much I was loved, how I had sacrificed so much for them and how happy they were that I was now here in Australia with them. They all wished me a long and happy life.

And then as the music began to play. Those two *palopítha* Manolis and Georgios, came to stand either side of my armchair. At first, I thought they were just being playful, trying to drag me into their nonsense for a laugh. I even waved them off, telling them to leave me be. But before I could protest, their hands were under my arms, and with a grin and a wink, they brought me up onto my feet.

And then suddenly, there I was, eighty years of age, dancing the *Mbaló*, the traditional dance of Samos.

I saw the faces around me, my children, my grandchildren, all clapping, and cheering, some with tears in their eyes.

Then the room seemed to fall away, and in that instant I was no longer an old woman with aching bones, carrying the weight of years and distance. I was once again Eftihia from Sokia, young, light on my feet, alive with joy, on Christmas Day, my beloved father's name day. The music he loved filled the air, his eyes shining with pride as we danced together. There was laughter, glasses raised in celebration, the house alive with warmth.

As I grew older, one of my father's young friends would sometimes take my hand for the *karsilamás*. We would stand facing one another, our steps small and measured, the rhythm drawing us closer and then apart again. His eyes carried a playful challenge, and mine answered in kind, while all around us the circle clapped and cheered. It was a dance of mirrors, of teasing grace, a dance that made me feel radiant and free. Even now, in this land so far from Sokia, my body worn with age, I felt that same lightness, that same love of the family I had lost, the love that had bound us together, surrounding me. It was a moment. A beautiful, precious moment.

When the song ended and I returned to my seat, breathless and red-faced, Alexandra handed me a glass of water, kissed my cheek softly, and said, "Bravo, *Yiayiaka mou.*"

I smiled and kissed her back and told her, "Don't ever think the fire in our soul goes out because life brings us challenges. No matter what life does to you, or how heavy your heart feels, never let them put out that fire, that spirit inside of you. Promise me you will remember that."

*   *   *

Ploutarhos, my son who had remained in Samos, called often. He didn't say it outright at first, but I heard it in his voice. He wanted me home.

"Mother, when your time comes you should be laid to rest beside Father. This is where you belong."

And it was true. The monastery of Zoodochos Pigi was where Georgios lay now, his bones resting in the crypt with those of the other departed souls. It was a quiet place on the mountain, away from the villages, where the pines kept the air cool even in summer. I had not seen it in years, not since I left Samos, yet I could picture it clearly.

I had always thought of it as a place set apart from the world, a refuge which had held steady through wars, occupations, and the shifting fortunes of the island. Its church, built more than a century before any of us were born, held the silver-covered icon of the *Panagia Zoodochos Pigi*, as the Life Giving Spring. It was venerated by the people of the island and pilgrims alike, in whose heart it carried the hope of divine mercy. I could still picture the dome, and the four marble columns that supported it — said to have come all the way from Miletus, carried there centuries ago as if by some miracle. From its courtyard, the Mycale Strait stretched toward the mountains of Turkey. Once, I might have looked upon that view as a kind of bridge, something that tied me to the land I loved, a thread across the water leading back to home. Now it was nothing but a wound—sharp, unhealed—marking the place I had been forced to leave and could never return to.

I had put down deep roots in the soil of Samos, having spent most of my adult life there. But my life was also now here, in this strange, wide country, surrounded by people who had become my whole world.

Australia brought with it a gentler rhythm. My children, all five of them, were gathered around me. My grandchildren would visit often, sometimes bringing their own children. It was a comfort I hadn't known in decades to be cared for, truly cared for, without expectation or burden. The Australian government had granted me permanent residency, and with it, a sense of freedom. I no longer needed to leave unless I voluntarily wished to do so.

I delayed the decision for as long as I could. But as the years passed, and I felt my body tiring more quickly, I finally gave in to his request. I was 89 years old when I returned to Chora. My granddaughter came with me once again, just as she had when she brought me to Australia. Her strength was a comfort. Alexandra had tried to convince me to change my mind throughout our journey back to my son's home. She didn't say outright that I would come to regret it, but I knew that was what she had intuited. She sensed what I had refused to admit—that my return was less a choice than a surrender to what I felt was expected of me.

She stayed for a few days before returning to Australia. When the time came for her departure, she wept openly, as though it would be the last time she would see me. Her tears stayed with me long after she was gone. It was only several weeks later, when I stood in the stillness of my son's house, that I realised she had been right. I had made a mistake in coming back. Still, I told myself I would endure it, as I always had—steadfast and unyielding. Yet in my heart, I knew I had to carry on, because it was the only way to keep sorrow from consuming me.

No. It was not the return I had imagined.

My son's home was located on the main road that ran through Chora, right opposite a small mini-market. A modest verandah jutted out from the front, but the ceaseless noise and fumes of motorcycles and cars which parked outside the house to shop at the mini-market, made me long for the quiet stillness of my own home high above the village. The house had been closed up before I left for Australia.

There were tensions, subtle but persistent. Not open fights, but enough sharp words that lingered too long in the air, and silences that stretched into uncomfortable hours, making the walls seem narrower, closer than they were. I came to understand that love—even the deep, unspoken kind between parent and child—was not always enough to carry one through the long hours of the day.

Ploutarhos and Eftihoula worked tirelessly, and their intentions were kind, even generous. Yet I found myself alone for most of the hours, wandering from room to room, listening to the muffled sounds of life outside, feeling like a visitor in a house that should have felt like home.

In the end, my stubbornness got the better of me. I returned to my own house. It did not offer the comforts I had known in Australia, nor those of my son's home. But it was quiet, familiar. Loneliness, however, became a constant companion. My thoughts drifted back to Australia, to the warmth of being surrounded by those I loved. How often I silently regretted returning—never more so than what awaited me in the months ahead. My decision placed a heavy burden on my son and daughter in law too. They had to find time in their long, tiring days to bring me food. Though they said nothing, I could feel the subtle undercurrent of their resentment.

I was ninety one when the pain began. At first I ignored it. What was one more ache in an old woman's body? But it worsened. The doctor said I needed an operation to remove my gallbladder. My youngest daughter, Maria, flew over from Australia to be with me. I remember seeing her at the hospital door and feeling both relief and shame. Relief that I would not be alone. Shame that my decision had caused her to cross the world to care for me.

The surgery went ahead. But my body was too tired to heal. An infection set in.

I drifted in and out in those final days. At times, I thought I was still in Australia, hearing the voices of my children. At other times, I was back in Sokia, then in Antiphillipi calling for my mother. And then, in the quiet hours, I saw them—my family on the other side with Georgios, standing beside them. They weren't speaking. They were simply waiting.

That was when I knew.

It was not the return I had hoped for, but perhaps it was always meant to end this way. In the village where I had raised my children. In the land where I had buried the people I loved most. Where I had fought, suffered, endured, and lived.

My story began in Sokia but in the end, it was here in Samos where I would be laid to rest.

So I closed my eyes for the last time and allowed myself to move into the light to be reunited with the ones I had loved and lost.

Thank you for reading *A Stolen Life*. I hope you enjoyed this first book in the series, as it carries the voices of my great-grandmother and grandmother. After everything they endured, they deserved for their story to finally be told—not lost to silence, not buried in history, but spoken aloud.

Yet Eftihia's story does not end here. She entrusted her memories to her granddaughter, who in turn tells her own story, a continuation of survival, loss, and hope across another generation. In the next book, you will step into her world, where her voice carries forward the legacy she inherited.

As always, please consider leaving a review as these are always greatly appreciated.

If you would like to keep up to date with my latest releases, follow me on **Amazon, Good Reads** or on my **Facebook Page.**

Until next time,

Voula

Other books by Voula Antoine
Fire From The Ashes
Love And Betrayal
Reunion In Tuscany

Look out for Book 2 which will bring you Alexandra's story.
Happy reading!

OPA! A MODERN GREEK TRAGEDY

In this intense and at times heartbreaking story, Alexandra vividly recalls her family's migration from the Greek island of Samos to Australia. A happy childhood gives way to rebellious, angry adolescent years, as she chafes against the strict traditions imposed upon her and yearns to express her own individuality.

By twenty, she has avoided an arranged marriage, much to the lament of her parents and extended family and returns to Samos for a three month stay. There, amidst the island's beauty, she reconnects with her beloved grandmother and falls hopelessly in love with a married man—only for him to disappear without explanation.

Back in Australia, heartbroken and emotionally fragile, she accepts a proposal from a Greek man who promises stability but delivers cruelty. Her married life is one marred by abuse, lies and betrayal. When she asks for a divorce, threats and intimidation follow. Her husband's arrest and the seizure of their assets ignite a relentless fight against the justice system and its treatment of victims of crime. It is a battle that tests her strength and her sanity yet she finds the courage to fight for herself and her son.

On a return visit to Greece, Alexandra is unexpectedly reunited with her former lover. They marry, build a tight-knit family, and finally find happiness until he succumbs to a premature death. Tragedy strikes again just three years later, plunging her into a darkness that almost claims her life.

On her way home from a healing therapy session, a chance encounter is the pivot that changes her life's direction and provides the catalyst for a madcap series of events in which history repeats itself.

Passionate, funny, and unflinchingly honest, this story is a powerful testament to resilience—a woman's journey overcoming cultural taboos and personal devastation and finding the power to rise when life itself conspires to break you.

Content note: This book contains themes of domestic abuse, trauma, suicide and mental illness.

PROLOGUE

LIFE DOESN'T ALWAYS BRING ROSES

Rebellious of nature from an early age, I often acted on impulse without giving too much thought to the consequences of my actions. As I made the transition from child to womanhood, my head filled with dreams and aspirations for my future, I soon came to realise that harsh penalties could be imposed on Greek women who tried to be different from the norm. My parents and our extended circle of family and friends expected me to conform to the puritanical aspects of my culture, which effectively brainwashed us into believing that a woman's freedom, her right to self-expression and her desire to claim her unique individuality were both sinful and shameful. My family adhered to cultural guidelines and strictly applied their rules and in the process did their very best to crush my dreams and my spirit.

As humans we are all fallible. Inevitably, life can be both highly intoxicating and deeply regrettable. One cannot have wisdom without living life. The challenge to each and every one of us is to glean the valuable lessons inherent in our mistakes and failures. As babies and children we need nourishment and the gentle touch of love to feed our souls, to help us grow into our own uniqueness. Our cultural backgrounds can either nurture that individuality or destroy it with painful or limiting attitudes. True to my nature, I rebelled against the restrictions imposed on me and found myself continually at odds with all aspects of my Greek heritage.

Sometimes we may not understand why life deals us the cards we are given. As I navigated my own journey through life and wrestled with the events and circumstances that were presented to me, I often found myself bewildered by the hand that fate had dealt me. At times, I seemed to have absolutely no control over my life and that realisation and the events that unfolded threatened to send me into a downward spiral of confusion and despair. Many a time I would ask myself the question why? Why me for God's sake?

Predictably, it was a struggle to find an explanation. All too often in those periods of retrospection, the only logical explanation I could offer myself when I felt so overwhelmed by my life's events, was that a greater power was intervening. Ultimately, if I could hold onto my sanity and survive, then surely it would be for my own higher good. I've always tried to remain positive, to rise above life's challenges, but it wasn't always easy.

Experience had taught me that my path would cross with individuals only too eager to gloat at my misfortune as they watched you rapidly decline into a deep dark God forsaken pit of despair and misery. Often when my life seemed to be spiralling out of control, I was tempted to bury my head in the sand. Unfortunately, it's only possible to hide for so long before we are forced to face our demons, acknowledge our failures, take ownership of them and do something constructive about them. My grandmother once said to me, "We can either accept our fate and lie down and let life crush us in the midst of a crisis, or we can rise above it and challenge it, learn from it and endeavour to make ourselves into better and wiser people."

Wise words indeed.

CHAPTER ONE

I was born on the Greek island of Samos, and, as was the custom, I was named after my paternal grandmother. My birthplace, Chora, was once the capital of the island, a village of whitewashed houses and terracotta roofs that rose gradually from the plain at its base to the heights of the hill above, where the houses commanded magnificent views of the vineyards below and the sparkling blue of the Aegean in the distance.

Along the winding streets that climbed through the village, one was greeted by a profusion of bougainvillea in a riot of colour, mingled with honeysuckle and jasmine that assailed the senses. There was a deep sense of unity and belonging then: women gathered at the 'vrisi', the communal washing place just off the 'plateia', the village's central square, to wash their clothes with water carried down from the mountains and to exchange the latest gossip.

In the early 1950s, Greece struggled to rebuild its economy in the aftermath of the war, and employment was scarce. Although my father held a prestigious and well-paid position as a First Engineer on a merchant shipping vessel, many in our community found it difficult to secure regular work and, as a result, to provide adequately for their families.

During this period, Australia launched a recruitment drive to encourage Greek migration. We were told it was the land of opportunity, and assisted passage was offered to those willing to take the chance. Many families therefore chose to leave the land of their birth in the hope of building a better life in a foreign country.

When I was two years old, my father made the momentous decision to uproot our family and migrate to Australia. News of our departure shocked many in the village. By local standards, we were comfortable. We owned our home, there was always food on the table, and my father often returned from his voyages around the Aegean laden with gifts for the whole family.

The Greek island of Kastellorizo, lying in the eastern Mediterranean, was undoubtedly one of my father's favourite ports of call. He returned with beautiful carpets, damask linen, silverware, and crystal glasses, and always something that had caught his eye for my mother. For her, there were silk stockings, lingerie, exquisite shoes, and matching handbags. We were also the first family in our village to own a radio, a distinction that made us the envy of our neighbours.

My father's work meant he was often away from home. He married relatively late in life and began a family almost immediately, and my mother found his frequent absences difficult. He missed the birth of both my brother and me. We were born at home, delivered by a midwife, as was customary at the time. It was unheard of for women in the village to give birth in hospital, and it was not unusual for labour to begin while women were working in the fields, particularly during the olive or grape harvest.

At first, the plan was to emigrate to Australia for five years, to work hard, save enough money to return to our homeland, and invest in property. My father even dreamed of buying his own fishing schooner. Many migrants who undertook that long journey did so with exactly the same intention.

According to my grandmother, on the day we were to leave Samos, my mother bathed and dressed me and forbade me from going outside, as we would soon be leaving to board the ship bound for Piraeus. I promptly disappeared, making my way to my grandmother's house, where I hid. I shared a strong bond with her, and it was not long before she returned home to look for me. All it took was for her to open the front door and call out, "Alexandra, where are you?" for my young mind and mouth to answer automatically, "I'm here, Yiayia."

And so our possessions were packed into a large trunk and four suitcases, and our journey began. It took a month to reach Australia via the Suez Canal, with stops at Port Said in Egypt, Aden in Yemen, and Colombo along the way. My only memory of that voyage is being allowed to accompany my father ashore in Colombo to buy bananas. Even at that early age, I had a spirit of adventure and loved talking to people. How could they resist a blue-eyed, blonde-haired little girl? The locals were entranced. Women stroked my hair and spoke to me in words I could not understand; some pressed sweets into my hands, tied ribbons in my hair, or gave me a bracelet of brightly coloured beads. I do not know whether they understood my attempts to thank them in Greek. I was captivated by the colour of their skin, the vivid clothes they wore, the music that filled the air, the scent of food cooking outdoors, and the constant bustle of life at the port.

My father held my hand firmly, wary that I might slip away at the first opportunity. Had he possessed even the faintest inkling of the rebellious daughter I would later become, he might well have exchanged me for two branches of bananas.

I remember little of our arrival in Australia, other than being held in my father's arms as we stood at the ship's railing while it docked in Sydney Harbour. Below us, the wharf was crowded with people, and beyond them stood the galvanised iron customs sheds. I have often wondered what must have passed through my parents' minds as they looked out upon what would have seemed a flat, featureless land, so unlike the picturesque Greek village we had left behind.

My first memories of Australia were of Villawood. The migrant hostel was little more than a collection of grey, corrugated iron Nissen huts scattered across the sprawling grounds. The huts were functional but harsh, their interiors sparsely furnished with little more than metal beds, thin mattresses, and a shared table. Privacy was a luxury and the noise of other families, crying babies, muffled arguments, bled through the thin walls, reminding us that we were not alone, even when we wished to be.

There were no private kitchens, no bathrooms of our own. We queued for communal meals that too often were inedible. Mothers despaired, forbidden to cook for their children, forced instead to feed them food that was bland, poor in quality, sometimes unfit for little ones. For many of us, this was not the Australia they had been promised.

My father, Aristides, had served as a First Engineer on a merchant vessel in Greece and was respected for his skill and experience. In Australia, however, none of his qualifications were recognised, despite clear assurances given by immigration officials before we left Greece. Overnight, his years of training and responsibility were rendered meaningless. Like many newly arrived migrants now classified as unskilled, his only options were manual labour and English language classes held at night. He was approaching forty years of age, having married later in life, and the prospect of sitting in a classroom held little appeal. He had a wife and two young children to support, and if manual labour provided a wage, then so be it.

At Villawood, he was reduced to a number, just another hopeful immigrant waiting for a work assignment. When word finally came that he had been allocated a position at the Newcastle steelworks, relief swept through our family. We gathered our belongings, packed what little we had, and left Villawood behind, travelling north to Mayfield West with other families.

At Mayfield West, the huts were still simple, but they were newer, with fibro walls and wooden floors, giving families a little more space to breathe. The communal dining hall was still in use, yet the kitchens seemed less harsh, and the food a little more nourishing. A recreation hut offered a place for the men to play cards, smoke, and read newspapers passed from hand to hand. For the children, open paddocks provided space to run and play games of soccer, a sense of freedom unknown at Villawood's crowded grounds.

On Sundays, families gathered together. The men debated politics or discussed the future, while the women clustered together, sharing news, gossip, and laughter, leaning on one another for comfort when tears came. The air was filled with voices and sometimes music—a bouzouki or harmonica drifting across the camp. Even in hardship, those moments offered strength. Surrounded by our own people, we began to feel less like strangers in this new land.

Most of the men worked at BHP. Each morning, my father would rise before dawn, washed quickly in the shared bathroom blocks, the clatter of the communal kitchen already in full swing as he and the other men prepared for the bus ride to the steelworks.

Not everyone welcomed the influx of migrant workers. The Ironworkers' Union initially opposed their placement at BHP, seeing them as outsiders taking jobs. After tense negotiations between the union, the government, and BHP management, the migrants were allowed to work, but the resistance lingered. My father entered the steelworks fully aware he was not universally accepted, and that knowledge deepened his frustration and sense of displacement.

The steelworks were a harsh, unforgiving place. His days were filled with the roar of machinery, the acrid scent of smoke and molten metal, and the relentless physicality of the work. His frustration simmered with each passing day, compounded by the language barrier that left him feeling voiceless. When he returned to Mayfield at night, exhausted and defeated, weariness was etched in his eyes. My father never spoke much about it, only that the work was hot, hard, and dangerous Still, he bore it without complaint. He would sit with my mother and his shoulders bore the invisible weight of a man trying to hold his family together in a foreign land. However, it was a daily reminder of the distance between his past life and this new one.

Twelve months later, my parents made the decision to move interstate. My mother's brother and his family had migrated from Samos six months earlier. We were hopeful, envisioning a reunion that would ease our move interstate and offer a fresh start. However, hope quickly gave way to disappointment. The uncle who had encouraged us to leave Newcastle now turned us away. His wife refused to let us stay. Disheartened, we found a room to rent with an Italian family. Their warmth and hospitality stood in stark contrast to the cold rejection we received from my uncle and his wife, and though the space was cramped, it became a temporary refuge.

For my father, the betrayal cut deep. Anger simmered beneath his calm exterior, a bitter sense of estrangement from a brother-in-law he had once trusted. He had left behind the stability of his position at the steelworks, trading it for uncertainty. Yet, as he sought new opportunities, his resolve to build a better life for us never wavered. Those months spent in the rented room were challenging, especially for my mother. We looked forward to the day when we could afford to buy a home of our own.

He found work as a manual labourer with the Engineering and Water Supply Department and worked tirelessly, taking as much overtime as he could. His tasks were physically demanding—digging trenches for pipelines, repairing burst water mains, moving heavy materials, and assisting skilled tradesmen on construction sites. The work was back-breaking and carried out in all weather conditions, a far cry from the life he had known in Greece. Yet, amid the gruelling days, he forged friendships with other Greek and Italian migrants.

Eventually, we purchased a three-bedroom bungalow with an inside toilet and a bathroom complete with a shower and hot running water—a luxury by Greek village standards, where bathing meant boiling water over an open fire. The house had an expansive backyard, carefully cultivated by the previous Australian owners, with manicured lawns and native trees.

That was before us Greeks moved in. Within weeks, the lawn and trees had vanished, replaced by a sprawling vegetable garden and trees more familiar to a Greek backyard: lemon, orange, olive, fig, pomegranate, nectarine, and apricot. We also planted grapevines—cabernet sauvignon and muscat—which, as they climbed their supports, eventually created a shaded loggia at the rear of the house. There, we enjoyed meals on balmy summer evenings and entertained friends and family. That garden became my father's passion. When I was young, we spent hours tending it together, and his care ensured a steady supply of fresh, home-grown vegetables and fruit.

He also grew tobacco from seeds sent by my grandfather in Samos. The plants grew tall with pink blossoms, and when harvest time came, he taught me how to pick the leaves, thread them onto string with a large darning needle, and hang them on bamboo rods to dry in the sun. Every day we checked their progress, and when my father finally declared the crop ready, I watched as he shaved the tobacco finely with a sharp knife and rolled his first cigarette. Fascinated, I watched him draw in deeply and exhale, then he passed it to me, saying that since I had helped cultivate it, I should sample the fruits of our labour.

It was the first—and last—time I ever held a cigarette. If that was his way of ensuring I never smoked, he succeeded. Still, we proudly boasted about our tobacco crop. Perhaps it was illegal to grow it at home, like cultivating marijuana today, but to me, it was an unforgettable experience, a mixture of wonder, learning, and father-daughter bonding.

Australia changed our lives forever. Many blamed migrants for everything —taking their jobs, the unseasonal weather, even the food we ate. Grilled octopus and squid were delicacies to us, but to them, they were nothing more than fish bait. Along with the racial slurs came shouts of, "Get on the bloody boat and fuck off back to where you came from." They made it clear that, given the chance, they would have happily sent us back to our homeland.

They called us WOGS.